The Joy of Medical Practice

Forty Years of Interesting Patients

To Jean

I hope you enjoy these stories

John C. Rutter

The Joy of Medical Practice

Forty Years of Interesting Patients

John C. Barber M.D.

iUniverse, Inc.
New York   Bloomington

iUniverse books may be ordered through booksellers or by contacting:

iUniverse
1663 Liberty Drive
Bloomington, IN 47403
www.iuniverse.com
1-800-Authors (1-800-288-4677)

Because of the dynamic nature of the Internet, any Web addresses or links
contained in this book may have changed since publication and may no longer be
valid. The views expressed in this work are solely those of the author and do not
necessarily reflect the views of the publisher, and the publisher hereby disclaims
any responsibility for them.

ISBN: 978-1-4401-5293-1 (sc)
ISBN: 978-1-4401-5295-5 (dj)
ISBN: 978-1-4401-5294-8 (ebook)

Library of Congress Control Number: 2009931025

Printed in the United States of America

iUniverse rev. date: 07/17/09

To my patients

Contents

◄○►

Preface

I FOUND THE PRACTICE OF MEDICINE to be a very rewarding career. In the present atmosphere of managed care, decreasing reimbursement (private insurance, Medicare, and Medicaid), and increasing costs of maintaining an office, the financial rewards are decreasing. For me, the human aspect will always remain the most significant reward of medical practice.

I grew up in a small town in Illinois, the second son of a general practice physician. At home, I absorbed many things about the general practice of medicine. By the time I was in high school, I knew the prescription for paregoric: "Paregoric, drams two in Water, Q. S. ounces four, one tablespoon after ..." I had heard my father say that over the phone to the local pharmacist many times.

My father thought that my older brother would follow him into medicine, but after one year of premed, my brother switched to a major in languages. Because of this, my parents did not want to pressure me into medicine, so I tried engineering. Engineering led me to Purdue University, where I did well, but decided I wanted to be more directly involved in helping people. I discovered that Purdue had a premed curriculum. Before I left Purdue, I met Letha Foss, fell in love, and convinced her to marry me after we finished college.

When it was time to apply to medical school, my father encouraged me to apply to Washington University Medical School, where he had trained. I also applied to the University of Wisconsin

Medical School to increase my chances of admission. My father pestered the chairman of the admissions committee at Washington University until I was accepted.

I was a middle of the road medical student, partially because I am mildly dyslexic. I later learned that being a mediocre student at Washington University made me above average as a physician.

Letha was in psychology graduate school at Washington University, but she decided to apply to medical school after completing everything except her dissertation for a PhD in clinical psychology. She was a first-year medical student during my fourth year. I stayed in St. Louis for my internship so that she could finish the two basic science years of medical school before transferring.

My third and fourth years of medical school were comprised of clerkships on the various services in the hospital and clinic assignments for all the major specialties of medicine. As I rotated through each clerkship and clinic, I eliminated them from a list of specialties that I wanted to practice. I had built HO gauge model trains from the time I was eight years old and enjoyed the meticulous work that the small models required. I thought that general surgery would demand this skill, but I soon learned that general surgery was far less demanding.

The rotations through otolaryngology (ear, nose, and throat) and ophthalmology (eyes) did appeal to me, especially the middle ear and eye surgeries. When I asked for an elective in ear surgery so I could watch the surgery, I was told that I could work in the clinic, but I would not be allowed in the operating room to watch surgery. I took an elective on reading electrocardiograms instead.

Rotating in ophthalmology, I was fascinated by cataract and eye muscle surgery. The delicate nature of eye surgery really appealed to me. I was also impressed that the ophthalmologists were the best-dressed doctors on the faculty. They wore three-piece suits with monogrammed shirts and rarely appeared outside of the operating rooms wearing surgical scrubs. I began applying to ophthalmology residencies during my fourth year of medical school as I applied for an internship.

I did what was then called a rotating internship. This involved rotations of four months each on internal medicine and surgery, and two months each on obstetrics/gynecology and pediatrics. This added a well-rounded experience to the general medical knowledge I had learned in medical school and better prepared me for the diverse field of ophthalmology. My internship was the time when I began to know my patients well enough to appreciate their diversity and complexity.

The call-up of physicians for the Vietnam War was at its height at the end of my internship. I had applied for a medical training deferment to complete my ophthalmology training before being drafted to serve. Through the deferment process, I was assigned to the army. I did not get the deferment, but the army told me that they would not need me for several months, or maybe a year. I tried to enlist in the air force and the navy, but they would not take me because I was assigned to the army.

I applied to the Public Health Service (PHS) and was accepted for duty at the U.S. Food and Drug Administration (FDA). This was a desk job in Washington, DC, but there were three medical schools in the area where Letha could continue medical school. She transferred to George Washington School of Medicine and graduated with honors two years later.

At the FDA I evaluated research studies on drugs to determine whether they were safe and effective enough to be put on the market. This activity taught me the design of good studies and made me think and write as a bureaucrat. I was able to take advantage of the many opportunities in the DC area for professional development in ophthalmology.

The Medical College of Virginia had accepted me for a residency in ophthalmology before I joined the FDA. They delayed my start for two years so that I could serve in the PHS.

My residency experience was split, and I spent half of my time in the clinic and the other half in the research laboratory. Letha and I had naively decided to pursue academic careers so that we could have a life outside of medicine. This research and clinical residency was perfect preparation for an academic position. The clinical side exposed me to the wonderful world of patients and their problems.

I did several corneal transplants during my residency and found that it was my favorite kind of surgery. I decided that I wanted to do more training in corneal transplants and mentioned it to my father. His reply was, "Enough education; go treat some people!"

My parents came to visit during the holidays while I was a senior resident, and my father had the opportunity to watch me remove a cataract from a young woman. He was a general surgeon and had never seen eye surgery. He told me that it was some of the slickest surgery he had ever seen.

I was accepted for fellowship training under Dr. Claes H. Dohlman at the Massachusetts Eye and Ear Infirmary (MEEI), which is part of the Harvard Medical School. The Harvard connection pacified my father, who had always read the *New England Journal of Medicine.*

My two years there in the clinic and research laboratories were the most influential years of my training. Association with Dr. Dohlman was a life- and career-changing experience. Dr. Dohlman taught throughout his two weekly clinics and then went to lunch with the fellows to discuss anything and everything with the group. He was the epitome of "a gentleman and a scholar." He was brilliant, patient, humorous, and extremely humble. If he thought you were wrong, he would reason with you, but never argue. He is now well over eighty years old and still actively teaching and practicing ophthalmology.

I began looking for a job at a medical school during my second year of fellowship. As I looked for a faculty position teaching corneal diseases to residents, I realized that I had sub-specialized to a very limited area of medicine where there were few jobs available. Of the three open positions, I chose the University of Texas Medical Branch in Galveston. The research opportunities fit my training, and the chairman was likable and supportive.

I fit into the department and quickly became very busy. I taught surgery to the residents and gave lectures to students and residents. All faculty members saw private patients two or three half days and supervised the resident's clinic two days each week, leaving little time for research. I was soon promoted to associate professor and began doing research on an artificial cornea with funding from the National Institutes of Health (NIH).

After nine years in Galveston, I started looking for a position as chairman of the ophthalmology department at another medical school. The dean learned that I was looking and called me into his office. He told me that he was having difficulty with the current chairman and was planning to ask him to step down. He wanted me to become the new chairman. After the usual outside search by a committee, I was appointed chairman and served for nine years.

Chairmen of departments served on executive committees for the hospital and the medical school. These committees were often called upon to address problems. These discussions were open and often contentious. I often found myself on the opposite side of the Dean on issues, but I was caught off guard, after eight years as chairman, when he asked me to step down from the chairmanship. He would not give a reason, but I supposed that it was so they could get someone who was more cooperative and less scrupulous. He wanted me to stay and teach and treat patients.

I began looking for another position when they named my successor. I knew I did not want to work for the person they chose. I discovered that St. Francis Medical Center in Pittsburgh was looking for a full-time director for their ophthalmology residency program. This appealed to me because my wife's mother lived about thirty miles from Pittsburgh and was at an age where she occasionally needed someone to help her. I interviewed for the position and was hired.

When I took the position, the residency was on probation and needed to be entirely reorganized. I was fortunate to have a wealth of good teaching ophthalmologists in Pittsburgh who were willing to teach their subspecialties to the residents. We had nationally- and world-recognized experts in several fields on our staff. They devoted many hours, for very little pay, to building the program into a well respected, fully accredited, residency. I had more than two hundred applications for the two positions available each year.

While I was building the program, the Sisters of St. Francis struggled with inadequate reimbursement from Medicare and private insurance and a decreasing endowment caused by invading the principle to cover losses. They were in a downward spiral, which led to loss of the hospital and transfer of all of the residencies to the University of Pittsburgh Medical Center (UPMC). I was director of medical education at St. Francis and supervised the transfer of the seven residency programs, but UPMC did not offer me a job when I finished.

I had recently performed several corneal transplants when the hospital closed abruptly. I joined a group at Western Pennsylvania Hospital so that I could follow these patients for a year until the transplants healed and the sutures could be removed. One year later, I stopped doing surgery and retired after the next year.

For all but the last two years, I practiced in the academic world. My contact with patients came predominantly through the clinics of major health care facilities, often with patients from the lower third of the financial strata. This emphasis has given me a wealth of exposure to life's problems and how these problems interact with the ability to maintain good health. Socioeconomic problems may often cause or at least complicate problems with health. Forty years of dealing with the complex problems that tend to gravitate to medical centers has been a rich experience with human emotions and with the joy of being able to ameliorate some of the pain and misery of the people with whom I came in contact. I had the advantage of colleagues with similar experience and broad knowledge. This was augmented by the stimulus of residents at the height of their training experience who would keep me abreast of the latest information and techniques for treating these patients.

Ophthalmologists rarely deal with life-threatening disorders, but I was often able to restore or save vision, which many consider our most important sense. I saw the impact of visual loss on people, many of whom could not have their vision saved. I also saw how restoration of vision to some of these patients affected their lives.

I decided to compile this collection of the stories of patients that I saw so that young men and women, who may be contemplating a career in medicine, may learn the lessons these patients taught me. It should also demonstrate the impact that they might have on the lives of people they might serve in the medical profession. Over the years I have had many patients who came to me for medical care, and left with very little thought about any benefit to their health or their lifestyle. Others were profoundly affected by what those of us at the medical centers had done for them.

I have long held to the theory that doctors are at the height of their book knowledge at the end of their formal training. Physicians must constantly read and learn of new things in their field to keep current and provide up-to-date medical care, but they often forget the biochemical reactions or anatomical minutia that came from medical school. On the other hand, the experience they have gained from internship and several years of residency is minimal compared to that which they will obtain through years of medical practice treating countless patients from all walks of life. As I look back at the patients I remember best, it is the experience of interacting with patients that has taught me the most about life and the effects of illness and medical care. I hope that these stories of patients will show the reader some of the things I have learned from my patients.

This book is not primarily about specific surgeries or treatments or some unusual or unique solution to a medical problem, although there are some of those. It is about the patients and how they, or I, reacted to the results of that care. At times I describe the particular cure, or surgery, so that the reader may understand the complexity, or, sometimes, the lack thereof, of the treatment. This book is not about the specifics of the care, but about the people and their stories.

In my years in academic medicine, I played a role in the training of more than ninety resident physicians at the University of Texas Medical Branch in Galveston and the St. Francis Medical Center in Pittsburgh. As program director in both residency programs, I was responsible for creating the curriculum, attracting the teaching faculty, and orchestrating the selection of the resident physicians for the programs. Much of the joy I derived from my years of doing this was the interaction with these young men and women and the pride I have in the ophthalmologists who completed these two programs. I also spent many hours discussing career choices with medical students and helped those who wanted ophthalmology as a career to obtain residency positions, in our programs or others. I have included tales about some of the interesting episodes with these young people. They kept me young and alert and up to date with medicine.

I am well aware of the admonition in the Hippocratic Oath not to disclose the details of people's lives that I learned through my privileged position as a physician. The medical profession has long adopted principles to avoid this in medical publications. I have used initials and fictitious names to prevent the recognition of the individuals discussed. Perhaps the patients themselves may recognize their own stories and take pride in the fact that they are included in this book, written to inspire and teach young people. To any who might be offended by inclusion in this book, I offer my sincere apology.

I hope that you, the reader, enjoy these episodes of medical practice and the stories of the people involved. I also hope that as you see the scope and variety of these narratives that you are able to obtain some insight into medical care. I would like to share with you the joy, disappointment, satisfaction, and humor that I have experienced in my years of practicing medicine.

I have lived and practiced medicine in various capacities and in several parts of the United States. In doing so, I have found that people in the Midwest, New England, Texas, and Pittsburgh have different attitudes and lifestyles. I have chosen to divide the stories into those treated during my training, the people in Texas, and those in Pittsburgh. I have also grouped the children and the prisoners into separate sections. Within each section, I have attempted to arrange the stories in chronological order as much as possible. Some patients spanned long periods of time.

I find that it is impossible to describe medical problems and their treatment without using some anatomic and physiologic ophthalmological terms. Therefore, I have included an introduction to familiarize the reader with these terms and their use.

Introduction to Eye Anatomy and Physiology

I TRIED TO WRITE THIS BOOK so that anyone can read and enjoy the stories about my many interesting patients. A short introduction of basic eye anatomy and the function of the eye may help the reader to understand the stories without a medical dictionary.

When the open eye is viewed from the front, the most noticeable part is the iris, which is the colored structure inside the eye. The black spot or hole in the center of the iris is the pupil, which allows light to enter the eye. The muscles within the iris can make the pupil larger (dilation) or smaller (constriction). Directly in front of the iris is a space filled with

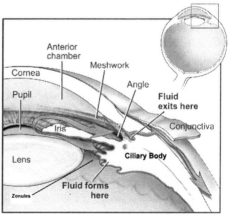

a watery fluid called aqueous humor. This space is called the anterior chamber because it is in front of the iris. The space behind the iris is called the posterior chamber and extends from the back of the iris, around the lens, to the back of the lens or the front of the vitreous body (fig. 1).

Immediately behind the pupil, in the posterior chamber, is a clear, Jello-like structure called the crystalline lens, or simply, the lens. The lens is composed of layers of cells forming a flattened ball, like an onion, which is surrounded by a membrane called the capsule. With the passage of time, the lens becomes translucent and then cloudy. The cloudy lens is called a cataract. Cataracts can form before birth or at any age. They are most common after age sixty, but people can live to ninety or older without having a cataract that needs to be removed.

The clear window in front of the iris is called the cornea. It should be crystal clear and optically smooth. The cornea has several layers (fig 2). The main layer, which makes up 90 percent of the corneal thickness, is called the stroma. The stroma is a layer of interwoven collagen bundles that crisscross

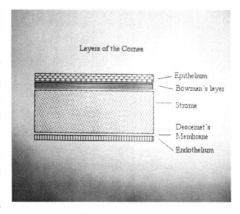

the cornea. The space between the bundles is filled with a substance that cancels the light scattering of the collagen bundles, making the cornea clear. Healing of damage to this layer causes scarring that can interfere with vision. On the front surface of the stroma is a tough layer called Bowman's layer. It consists of collagen fibers that are more tightly compacted than those of the stroma. On top of this layer is the epithelium. It is several cells thick and creates the smooth optical surface of the eye. It can be scratched off to form an epithelial defect, and it can heal to become perfectly smooth. On the back of the stroma is a strong sheet of tissue, like cellophane, called Descemet's membrane. On the back side of Descemet's membrane is a single layer of cells called the endothelium. The cells are tightly bound together to form a watertight barrier. The function of the endothelium is to control the flow of the aqueous humor into and out of the cornea.

The cornea is in a state of perpetual dehydration to keep it clear. The dehydration is accomplished by the endothelium, which pumps water from the cornea into the anterior chamber. At the same time, the endothelium transports nutrients from the aqueous humor to the endothelium, stroma, and epithelium. Failure of the corneal pump leads to swelling, or edema, of the cornea, with blisters of the epithelium, called bullae. The cause of corneal edema can be genetic, as in Fuchs' dystrophy, which is primary failure of the corneal endothelium that leads to swelling of the cornea with blisters on the surface, or it can be from damage during surgery or trauma.

At the edge of the cornea, the tissue becomes white and is called sclera. The sclera is made of the same collagen fibers as the cornea, but its pattern is not the same, and it doesn't have the substance that makes the cornea clear. The transition zone from clear cornea to white sclera is called the limbus. This landmark is often used for surgical incisions (fig. 1).

The sclera at the front of the eyeball is covered by clear tissue called conjunctiva. This tissue is loosely attached to the underlying sclera, allowing the eye to move. The conjunctiva follows the surface of the eyeball to the corners of the eye and behind the eyelids. It reflects upon itself and lines the back side of the eyelids. Conjunctiva contains many tiny tear glands and mucus glands that secrete tears and mucus to lubricate the front of the eye to keep it moist and slippery.

The peripheral edge of the iris is attached to the inside of the sclera and the ciliary body at the limbus, limiting the anterior chamber and preventing aqueous humor from flowing between the inside of the sclera and the iris. There is a porous mesh in the sclera where the iris attaches to the sclera. This mesh covers a network of outflow channels that extend from the anterior chamber into the sclera. (fig. 1) Aqueous humor in the channels flows into the canal of Schlemm, a tube that circles the cornea. This canal connects with veins in the sclera and carries used aqueous humor to the blood stream. When this filter, or mesh, called the trabecular meshwork, becomes collapsed or blocked, the aqueous humor cannot flow from the eye, so the pressure rises. This condition is called glaucoma.

The inside of the sclera is lined with a vascular tissue called the choroid. On the inner side of the choroid is the retina. (fig. 3) The retina is the sensory layer or the film in the camera. When light hits the rods and cones of the retina, a chemical reaction takes place, which causes an electrical impulse to be sent through the nerves of the retina and optic nerve to the back of the brain, where it is interpreted as a picture.

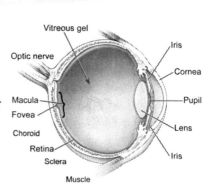

The part of the choroid at the junction between the base of the iris and the front edge of the retina is a specialized tissue called the ciliary body. It controls the lens within the eye, enabling the eye to focus in and out from distance to near. The lens is suspended within the ring of the ciliary body by tiny threads called zonules (fig. 1). The ciliary body pulls these zonules to focus the lens. The surface of the ciliary body has a special tissue that makes the aqueous humor. Aqueous humor is rich in nutrients, amino acids, and vitamin C. The aqueous humor flows around the lens, through the pupil, and around the anterior chamber. It nourishes the lens and the cornea. (The lens and cornea do not contain blood vessels.)

The electrical messages from the retina are carried by the optic nerve. The nerve exits the eye on the back side. The nerve carries more than a million nerve fibers, which will not regenerate like a nerve in the hand or leg. Once cut, they cannot be repaired. At this time, a transplanted eye cannot be attached to the nerve to transmit visual signals to the brain, because the nerve cannot be reconnected.

The central artery for the retina enters the eye in the center of the nerve and spreads over the surface of the retina. Elevated pressure in the eye, known as glaucoma, pinches the nerve and capillaries where they enter the eye. Damage to the nerve from this pressure will cause loss of peripheral vision, which may progress to total loss of vision. This loss of nerve fibers is seen as a pit in the surface of the optic nerve as it exits the eye. As this pit grows, it is known as cupping of the optic nerve. This pressure-related nerve loss is called glaucoma.

Closing of the central retinal artery or central retinal vein usually causes profound loss of vision. The retina will tolerate loss of blood supply from arterial blockage for only ten to twenty minutes before the retina dies permanently. Occlusion (obstruction) of the central retinal vein causes stagnation of the venous blood flow, which backs up the arterial flow, causing less dramatic visual loss.

The eyelids serve a valuable function in protecting the eye and spreading the tear film over the surface of the eye to keep it moist by blinking. Drooping of the eyelid is called ptosis, which may be either congenital or from trauma or disease. The eyelids retract in thyroid disease and certain neurological diseases. The eyelids may appear to be retracted when the eyes are pushed forward by thyroid disease or by tumors behind the eye.

The eyes sit in bony pockets in the front of the skull. These pockets are called the orbits or eye sockets. The muscles that move the eye are attached to the apex and walls of the orbit. Fractures of the bones around the orbit can cause problems with eye movement and also cause distortion of the face.

The inside of the eye behind the lens is filled with a substance, called vitreous, that looks and acts very much like the white of an egg. It is attached loosely to the retina and more firmly to the ciliary body and the optic nerve. As the eye ages, the vitreous shrinks and pulls loose from the retina. Often a ring of vitreous attachment pulls loose from the optic nerve and creates a shadow or floater. This separation may cause micro hemorrhages into the vitreous, which appear to the patient as swarms of gnats. Traction on the retina may cause the rods and cones to discharge, causing flashing lights. These phenomena are referred to as "flashes and floaters." If the vitreous is stuck to a spot on the retina, it may tear a hole in the retina as the vitreous separates from the surrounding retina. This hole allows the retina to detach, which will lead to blindness if it is not repaired immediately. Hemorrhages in the vitreous from diabetes or high blood pressure may organize into opaque membranes, causing blindness.

Feedback from the brain allows the muscles attached to the eye to align the eyes so that the pictures from the two eyes fuse into one image with a three-dimensional view. Some children are born with crossed eyes or without the ability to fuse the two images. Surgery to move or shorten muscles may be successful in straightening the eyes. If the brain can fuse the two images, the eyes will stay straight. If the brain cannot fuse the images, the eyes will drift after surgery.

This brief summary should give the reader sufficient familiarity with the eye to be able to read and understand this book. To review: The cornea is the clear window allowing light to enter the eye. The colored iris contains the pupil that is the opening within the iris, which controls the amount of light that can enter the eye. The anterior chamber is the space between the cornea and the iris. The Junction between the iris and the sclera is a meshwork that allows aqueous humor to escape from the eye. The white outer coat of the eye is the sclera. The sensory tissue that lines the inside of the eye is the retina, which acts like the film in a camera. Between the retina and the sclera is a vascular tissue called the choroid, which brings oxygen and nutrients to the back side of the retina. The front edge of the choroid is the ciliary body, which focuses the lens and produces aqueous humor. The eyes sit in orbits or sockets and are moved by the muscles that attach to the eye and to the walls of the orbit. The optic nerve and central retinal artery and vein enter the back of the eyeball together.

Part I
Training Years
1963–1973

I BEGAN SEEING PATIENTS CLINICALLY AS a third year medical student in 1963. In medical school I largely practiced what I was being taught about interviewing and examining patients. I was not in position to learn personal things about most of the patients I saw. In medical school students were assigned patients to take a history or examine them and then present what we found to the professors. As we progressed, we were given more responsibility for patient care, and so we needed to know the patients' entire history and physical findings and know the results of the laboratory tests.

I continued formal training through my internship, residency, and fellowship, which ended in 1973. The internship year was devoted mainly to care of hospitalized patients, where there was time to study and go back to the patient for more information. Interns were given great responsibility, but we could always turn to the residents or faculty for advice. When I became a resident, I had much more decision-making responsibility under the supervision of the teaching staff. Ophthalmology residency has evolved to more clinic or office patients, with fewer patients being hospitalized. Surgery was performed on hospitalized patients when I was a resident. During my training years, the days of hospitalization decreased from weeks to days. Patients I saw during my residency were all from Virginia, with the majority from Richmond.

My fellowship was different from residency training. I was there to learn the techniques of a master clinician and teacher. I would spend several hours each week seeing patients with several expert physicians. In this way I could learn their techniques. Time between clinics was spent reading about the diseases I was seeing or doing laboratory research on my projects. With rare exception, surgery was done on hospitalized patients. I often operated at night because the tissue for transplants could not be kept more than twenty-four hours before being transplanted. Massachusetts Eye and Ear Infirmary drew patients with complicated eye diseases from all over the world, where previous treatments by ophthalmologists had failed, so we had many difficult and unusual patients.

These ten years of intense training were filled with interesting patients and great learning experiences.

1

Worms in Her Eyes

IN MEDICAL SCHOOL, WE WERE encouraged to read widely about diseases and not to limit ourselves to diagnosing only common diseases. I did some extra reading, but being a slow reader, I did not read too far afield. I did, however, get into a funny situation from reading about a rare disease.

As a junior student I was rotating on the orthopedic service and was assigned to the arthritis clinic one afternoon. As students, we would see the patient and take the history and perform an examination. We would then present the patient to the resident or an attending physician, who would check our findings and then determine what treatment was appropriate.

A small, elderly black woman came into the clinic for treatment of her rheumatoid arthritis. Her fingers were stiff and distorted and her feet bothered her when she walked. Sometimes her other joints would flare up with pain and swelling. After we talked about her joints, she told me that she had another problem. She had been bothered by little white worms in her eyes. Sometimes she felt the worms crawl from one eye to the other across her nose, although she had never seen one on her nose.

She produced a small glass vial from her purse and proceeded to show me the worms. These were little round balls of grey-white material which were adherent to the sides of the vial. She said that she would see these in the corner of her eyes and pull them out. Sometimes they stretched to as much as an inch long as she pulled them from her eye. As soon as they came loose, they would curl up in a ball, which she would put into the vial. All of the things in the vial were round in shape, not elongated.

I remembered reading about a disease that is most often found in the South Pacific Islands, called Loa Loa. In this disease, thin white worms are found in the conjunctiva (the mucous membrane that covers the scleral portion of the front surface of the eye). The worms are known to migrate from one eye to the other across the nose, especially during sleep. When I presented this lady to the attending physician and the other students, I included my diagnosis of Loa Loa. I was almost laughed out of the clinic.

They were sure that Loa Loa never occurred in the United States and that this was a true medical student diagnosis. Word of my bizarre diagnosis spread all over campus, and it took awhile to live it down. I learned that the worms were probably just mucous strands that collect in the corners of the eye in patients with dry eyes and that dry eyes were common in arthritis patients. We sent her to the ophthalmology clinic for treatment of her dry eyes to get rid of the "worms."

I now know that people with rheumatoid arthritis often have dry eyes. The disease attacks the tear glands, and the watery part of tear production decreases. There are three layers of the tear film. A mucous layer coats the eye surface, a watery layer keeps the eye wet, and an oily top layer holds the tears by surface tension and retards evaporation of the watery layer. When there is not enough watery layer to separate the top layer of oil from the bottom layer of mucus, the oil and mucus mix, creating a gummy film. Blinking rolls up the film into strands, which are carried by tears to the nasal corner of the eye, where they accumulate.

This patient had rheumatoid arthritis with dry eyes and developed mucous strands that she thought were worms. She did not have Loa Loa or any other kind of worms. I have since had many patients with dry eyes who have told me about the worms in their eyes. I now know that they are not Loa Loa worms or any worms at all, but mucus strands.

This patient taught me not to believe everything that the patient told me and to reserve judgment on such stories. She also taught me that rare diseases occur rarely, so I must think carefully before diagnosing a rare disease that does not fit the circumstances. This case also illustrates the desire of patients to explain diseases to themselves so that they can understand their signs and symptoms.

2

The Belly Dancer

THE OUTCOMES OF SOME MEDICAL care can be very ironic. I had one such patient encounter while I was an intern, rotating through the obstetrics and gynecology hospital service.

A woman came to the free clinic that was operated by St. Luke's Hospital. She was performing as a belly dancer in St. Louis, at the same club where the Smothers Brothers and Phyllis Diller performed when they made their first breaks. She was not a resident of St. Louis, but she had continued to perform in St. Louis, so she came to the clinic.

Her complaint was that she felt a dragging sensation in her lower abdomen and pelvis while she was belly dancing. She felt that something was bouncing around inside of her. She already had two children who were being cared for by her mother back home while she was on the road. She said that she did not really need any more children, so if we had to take something out of her reproductive tract, it was all right with her.

On examination, we found that she had two masses, each about five centimeters, two inches, in diameter, in her pelvis. They were in the location where her ovaries should be and were nodular in character. This was in the days before diagnostic ultrasound and CT scans were in use to obtain a more definitive diagnosis. Our tentative diagnosis was polycystic ovaries, which could be cancerous or precancerous. She wanted to have them removed, but was concerned about the effects of a large abdominal scar on her career as a belly dancer.

The chief resident, who would be doing the surgery, was a woman from Turkey. She had commented that belly dancing is considered low class in Turkey, at least by the higher class women. She understood the patient's need for a scar-free abdomen, so she suggested a Pfannenstiel incision. This incision is also called the bikini incision because it follows the upper edge of the pelvic bones and can be hidden by a bikini, or a belly dancer's costume.

There are two ways to do a bikini incision, and both require a horizontal skin incision along the pelvic rim. The skin incision is spread upward to expose the vertical muscles of the abdominal wall. These muscles are then split vertically, between the muscles, to enter the lower abdomen and pelvis. The other approach involves the same skin incision, but the muscles are cut free from the bone horizontally and retracted to allow entry to the lower abdomen and pelvis. This latter approach is said to give better surgical exposure, allowing the surgeon to see better and providing more room for surgical instruments.

One of the gynecologists on the teaching staff was known for doing this incision on the society women who could still wear bikinis (it was a more expensive operation). He agreed to help the chief resident do the procedure. Because this was the resident's first Pfannenstiel procedure, she chose the horizontal muscle cutting approach because of the better exposure.

The surgery went well, and we removed two large polycystic ovaries. The incision was closed nicely, with sutures holding the severed muscles to the pelvic bones and a good plastic surgery skin closure. The patient was in the hospital for about one week after the surgery.

On the day of discharge, the chief resident went over the discharge instructions with the patient while we were on rounds. She told the patient that she could walk around, drive a car, carry one bag of groceries, and do light housework. She went on to say that she should not do any belly dancing, not even practice, for at least six months, because this activity might tear open the wound. I could feel a sense of righteousness coming from the chief resident. I learned later that the other incision would have caused disability from belly dancing for only six weeks to two months, but the chief resident did not tell her that.

The patient asked, "Can I walk around and do light exercise?"

The resident answered, "As much as you like."

The patient replied, "Good, then I can strip, and that pays only five dollars less a performance than belly dancing."

The resident was stunned. Instead of keeping her from belly dancing with her costume on, she had forced her to strip and take it all off. No great moral victory!

This patient was discussed long after she left the hospital and our care. When I learned in those discussions that the chief resident had intentionally chosen the incision she did, because it would have a longer healing time and not because it gave the best pelvic exposure, I thought that it was wrong. The doctor had let her own feelings and prejudices interfere with the proper treatment of the patient. She had inflicted her own moral values onto the patient, which was inappropriate. By choosing a procedure for moral reasons instead of the one that was best for her patient, she did not serve her patient well.

3

Man with a Heart Attack

DURING THE MID-SIXTIES, WHEN I was doing my internship, new drugs and therapies were becoming available every week. Off-label uses for older medications were being discovered and disseminated through journal articles, often with little more that anecdotal justification and very little good research. Today many doctors accept only evidence-based medical conclusions founded on quality research.

We had a patient who had suffered a major heart attack and was admitted to the intensive care unit (ICU). He was alive, but he had developed severe heart failure. His cardiac rhythm was ventricular tachycardia, which meant that his heart did not beat from top to bottom as it should, but simply quivered. He was not moving his blood through his lungs and to his body very efficiently.

He was restless and semiconscious. His circulatory system had collapsed so much that it was difficult to find a vein through which to give him fluids or medications. We had done a "cut down" incision on his right ankle to establish an intravenous access. His level of consciousness and blue color told us that his circulation was very poor.

The resident on the case told all of the doctors in the ICU that he had just read a medical journal article in which Valium was used intravenously on several patients to stabilize the cardiac muscle to control cardiac arrhythmias. He had written down the dose that the journal article recommended. The house staff in the ICU agreed that the patient would not live very long in his present condition and elected to try the Valium.

The senior resident on the case gave the man the recommended dose of Valium by injecting it into his intravenous cut down port in his ankle. We waited and watched the electrocardiogram (ECG) for any changes, realizing that it might take awhile for the Valium to travel from his ankle to his heart. After five minutes, nothing had happened, so the resident repeated the dose of Valium into the intravenous port.

We continued to watch the electrocardiogram. After a few minutes, the ventricular pattern changed to a normal configuration, with a very rapid heart beat. After a few minutes of this electrocardiogram rhythm, he began to develop a better color—less blue, more pink. He also started to slow his heart rate. The rate decreased from about one hundred forty beats per minute to one hundred beats. His color continued to improve, which was an indication of the improvement in his circulation. As we watched, his heart rate slowed to seventy beats per minute, and his rhythm was regular and without abnormal beats.

The Valium was stabilizing his cardiac muscle membranes and controlling his heartbeat. The more regular his heartbeat, the better his circulation became. The Valium that had been injected in his ankle had taken ten minutes to arrive at his heart and start to work. The better the heart worked, the faster the Valium moved from his ankle toward his heart. As we watched, the Valium had more and more effect on his heart. The electrical heartbeats became further and further apart. Over the next few minutes, his heart rate slowed to forty, then thirty, and then twenty beats per minute. The ECG configuration looked good, except for the evidence of his massive heart attack. As we continued to watch, the heart rate slowly decreased to an occasional beat and then a straight line. His cardiac muscle membranes had been completely stabilized, stopping his heart all together.

Because he had not been in the hospital for more than twenty-four hours, Missouri state law required that an autopsy be performed. The results of the autopsy showed that the heart attack had killed about 80 percent of his heart muscle. People with this extent of myocardial infarction do not survive more than a few hours. Our therapy may have hastened his demise, but he would have died within hours if we had not intervened. The pathologist thought that the damage to the heart was too extensive for anything to have saved the life of this patient for more than a few hours.

This was a case of applied science. Valium was known to stabilize cell membranes, so it was used on several patients to stop cardiac arrhythmias. Damaged cardiac cell membranes do not conduct the signal that causes the heart to beat. Our patient had damage to his cardiac cells, resulting in an arrhythmia.

Valium did stabilize the patient's cardiac cell membranes and stop his arrhythmia, but it was delayed in reaching the heart because his circulation was so poor. This resulted in a second dose by the impatient resident. The second dose stabilized the membranes even more and stopped his heart. The theory worked too well because of the overdose. However, as noted earlier, the autopsy revealed that this patient would have died anyway.

The patient taught me that acting on theories involved risk. This case is a good argument for fact-based medicine, which is the current standard. As a rule, treatments that have been used on only one or a few patients without further study are no longer considered appropriate unless other therapies are not available and a last-ditch effort is required to try to save the patient from certain death. That was essentially what we were doing that night in 1965. Unfortunately for the patient, the Valium treatment would not have worked even if we had done it correctly.

As I gained more experience, I sometimes broke this rule with some success.

4

The Coach

I WAS ON MY NEUROSURGERY ROTATION during my rotating internship when a high school basketball coach was brought in after complaining of a severe headache that had come on very suddenly while he was arguing with a referee. Shortly after his headache began, he passed out and collapsed.

At the hospital, a lumbar puncture showed blood in the spinal fluid, so a cerebral angiogram was performed that demonstrated a ruptured aneurysm at the base of his brain. The aneurysm was actually located at the junction of the frontal artery and the anterior communicating artery that connects the two frontal arteries as part of the circle of Willis, a ring of connected blood vessels that surrounds the base of the brain. It allows for blood flow to all parts of the brain when one of the major arteries is blocked below the ring. The circle is supplied by all of the major arteries to the head, making it hard to stop bleeding from a hole anywhere on the circle. This aneurysm was at the exact center of the skull, beneath the brain, making it very difficult to approach surgically.

The neurosurgeons planned surgery to clip this leaking aneurysm where it budded off the frontal artery. The approach was to enter the skull from the side while the patient was positioned lying on his other side. The bone plate was removed from the skull, and the dura mater, the tough, fibrous membrane that envelopes the brain, was opened, exposing the brain. The brain was retracted toward the top of the skull to expose the vessels lying in an area beneath the brain.

The aneurysm was visible between the two frontal arteries where the short anterior communicating artery connected the frontal arteries. The neurosurgeon took a clip loaded in a clip holder and attempted to clamp off the base of the aneurysm. As he applied the clip, it sheared off the aneurysm where it attached to the frontal artery. This left a hole in the side of the frontal artery, which immediately started spewing blood. The blood immediately filled the area and obscured the view of the artery.

One of the other neurosurgeons in the practice group, who was in the room observing the surgery, saw what had happened. Since he was not sterile, he ducked under the surgical drapes and quickly placed his thumbs on the two carotid arteries and squeezed them closed. This allowed the suction tube to catch up with the flow of blood from the broken artery and to clear the area of blood. The surgeon could see the hole in the artery, but there was no aneurysm stump to clamp. The only way to stop the bleeding was to clamp the frontal artery. The surgeon loaded a large clip and placed it onto the artery, closing the frontal artery on that side. The neurosurgeon who had stepped in to help stop the bleeding then released the pressure on the carotid arteries. The clamp held, and the artery did not leak. Now that the bleeding was stopped, the membrane around the brain was closed, the bone plate was replaced, the scalp incision was sutured, and head was bandaged.

In medical school, I had learned that one way of stopping certain kinds of psychiatric illness in the early days of neurosurgery had been to put a long needle through a small hole in the temporal bone and to slice the frontal lobe from the rest of the brain. This was called a frontal lobotomy, and the procedure left the patient with no personality. I wondered whether clamping off the blood supply to the frontal lobe of the brain would have the same effect.

I was anxious to see this patient the next day on rounds to see if he had a flat personality. When we entered the room the next morning, the patient was awake and propped up in bed. He greeted us with a cheery hello and immediately asked when he might be able to go home. He said his head was still sore from the surgery, but otherwise he felt fine. We kept him in the hospital for five days. He did not show any signs of a frontal lobotomy and said that he wanted to return to coaching as soon as the neurosurgeons would permit him to do so.

I had another neurosurgery patient who passed out at work. He was the CEO of a major company and worked under a lot of pressure. He was brought, unconscious, to the hospital by ambulance and examined by a neurosurgeon in the emergency room. Ultrasound showed a large blood clot in the brain on only one side. He was immediately taken to the operating room, the skull was entered, and the blood was removed from his brain. The surgeon checked thoroughly to see that there were no bleeders in the brain before closing the skull. The next day, the patient was demanding to go home, saying that he had a business to run and could not stay in the hospital.

In those days, neurosurgery required very bloody incisions and was often imprecise. The surgeons used an instrument called cups to scoop out brain tissue and tumors, and the skin closures were not very aesthetic. Because of this, I decided that eye surgery was much more precise and far more aesthetic.

5

Dr. Bricker

ONE OF THE MOST SKILLED general surgeons that I have had the pleasure to observe and assist was Dr. Eugene Bricker. Before I met Dr. Bricker, my father had told me stories about when they both lived in the Phi Beta medical fraternity house at Washington University. Dr. Bricker liked to wrestle with his roommate for a study break. The banging used to disrupt the whole fraternity house at ten o'clock at night.

When I first met Dr. Bricker, he was an attending surgeon at St. Luke's Hospital in St. Louis. He usually made rounds at about six in the morning and did not expect the house staff to go on rounds with him. He often had to visit several hospitals every morning and evening to check on his patients.

I had seen him at the medical school, but had not met him personally. I was the intern assigned to assist him at surgery. There was also a resident assigned, so I was second assistant, which meant that I would hold retractors and watch.

Randolph was a young man in his mid twenties whose lower bowel was obstructed. We determined by X-ray that the large intestine was constricted for all but the last few inches. At his age, this was probably not cancer, but an inflammatory disease. He had several diverticula that could be seen on X-rays, so the surgeon was expecting extensive diverticulitis.

The planned procedure was to open the abdomen with an incision from the sternum to the pelvis, examine the large bowel, and possibly do biopsies. The type of surgical procedure required would depend on the findings of the exploration.

Dr. Bricker made a long abdominal incision and opened the abdomen. He located the large bowel and found it to be a solid mass consisting of hundreds of little pus pockets (abscesses). These were outpouchings (diverticula) of the intestinal lining that had herniated through the wall of the intestine and had been trapped there. The body reacts to these sacs, which contain fecal matter, by walling them off with inflammation and scar tissue (diverticulitis). The patient's large bowel was a large mass of inflamed scar tissue. The scar tissue constricts the bowel similar to the way a cancer would.

Cancer destroys the lining of the bowel, but diverticulitis does not. Dr. Bricker opened the lumen and found the lining to be normal rather that cancerous. Randolph had diverticulitis with confluent abscesses. With this massive abscess and the related adhesions, it would be impossible to restore the colon to its original shape and function, so Dr. Bricker elected to remove the diseased part of the colon and reconnect the remaining normal ends.

Dr. Bricker cut the small bowel from its attachment to the large bowel and tagged it with sutures so he could find it later. He then cut the large bowel at the sigmoid flexure. He placed two sutures in the cut edge of the remaining stump to pull it up to the lower end of the incision, where he clamped the sutures with hemostats.

The mass of abscesses was stuck to the abdominal walls so that there was no zone of separation between the colon and the abdominal wall. This meant that the diseased tissue would have to be cut out by sharp dissection following the abdominal wall as closely as possible. In about one hour, Dr. Bricker had removed all of the diseased tissue. Before he started to reconnect the cut ends of the intestine, he stopped to be sure that everything was as it should be.

He noticed a large clot of blood that had collected in the pelvic area. He said that he did not want to leave blood in the pelvis because it would be a site for infection and would cause irritation until it reabsorbed in several weeks. He reached down into the pelvis and grabbed the clot to pull it out. As he pulled his hand out of the pelvis, the back of his hand brushed the rectal stump where it was held by the hemostats. There was a gush of brown water from the stump which sprayed all over the abdominal cavity. Dr. Bricker began swearing. He had forgotten about the rectal stump, which still contained some water from the preoperative enemas. This water had just sprayed all over the contents of the abdomen, contaminating the entire surgical field. I could not believe that an experienced surgeon like Dr. Bricker could have done this, but the stump was out of sight and probably out of mind. I also realized immediately that this was a possible disaster.

After about thirty seconds, he stopped swearing and apologized to everyone in the room for his language. He explained that he was cursing himself for the dumb move he had just made. He explained that he was concerned about peritonitis (infection of the abdomen), which could cause sepsis (blood dissemination of the infection that could shut down the kidneys, lungs, and liver). Peritonitis could cause massive adhesions of the intestines and possible death. Before antibiotics, this would usually be fatal.

He then turned to the resident and asked him which of the latest antibiotics would be the best to use to treat the contamination. The resident thought of the two strongest antibiotics he knew and suggested penicillin and chloromycetin. Dr. Bricker then turned to me and asked if I agreed. I did not want to disagree with the resident on my hospital team, but I had attended a conference a week before in which we were told not to use those two antibiotics together. One is a static antibiotic that slows down bacteria so that white blood cells can eat them; the other is a bactericidal antibiotic that kills the bacteria directly. If the one drug slows the metabolism, the other cannot kill the bacteria as easily. At the conference, we had been told to use penicillin with streptomycin, which is what I told Dr. Bricker. Dr. Bricker had heard the same message and agreed with me.

The young man had a normal recovery from his surgery. The loss of almost his entire large bowel would take months to get used to and require many adjustments in his diet and lifestyle. He was fortunate to have had one of the best surgeons in the country to save him from a tremendous blood loss by his skilled and rapid surgical technique. I decided then and there that if I ever needed general surgery, I would have Dr. Bricker do the surgery.

I learned a number of things from this case. Even the best surgeon can make serious errors during a procedure. I learned the benefit of having a fast but skilled surgeon to avoid blood loss. I was surprised to learn that peritonitis could be successfully treated with the correct selection of antibiotics.

This case gave me all the confidence in the world in Dr. Bricker when he performed a complicated surgical procedure on my brother several years later. I was able to pass this confidence on to my sister-in-law.

6

<o>

A Mentally Challenged Pregnant Woman

DURING MY INTERNSHIP, WHILE I was rotating through the obstetrics and gynecology department, I encountered a twenty-five-year-old, very obese woman who was admitted for delivery of her third child. The delivery of her baby girl was uneventful, and the baby was healthy.

While taking her history prior to the delivery, I had learned that the patient was unmarried and had two children at home. She lived with her parents, who helped her care for the children. She had never been in a clinic or hospital except for the delivery of her children. She had only recently discovered that she was pregnant. I also learned that she knew very little about the facts of life and did not know how she had become pregnant. She told me that her mother often fixed her up with dates and that she enjoyed going out with men and "having fun." She did not seem to know that what she did on those dates resulted in her pregnancies. She thought that having babies was just part of being a woman and that there was no cause/effect between contact with men and having babies.

I met the woman's mother, who was also very obese and resembled her daughter. Later I met her father, who was also very obese. This, and her lack of comprehension, made me think that she might have a genetic metabolic disorder that caused her mental problems and obesity. My teachers agreed but could not name a genetic disease that fit this picture. The family may have simply eaten an obesity-prone diet.

She and her mother decided that three babies were enough, and her mother asked us to do a tubal ligation to prevent further babies. The woman agreed that she had enough children and consented to the sterilization procedure. In 1965, all surgery resulting in sterility had to be presented to a hospital committee for approval before it could be scheduled in the operating room. The committee agreed that, under the circumstances, it would be inappropriate for the woman to have more children and gave its consent for the sterilization procedure.

This was before the development of laparoscopic surgery, so the procedure was done through a ten-centimeter, midline, lower abdominal incision when she was about one week postpartum. It was a fairly simple procedure that was complicated only by the obesity of the patient. On the third day after the surgery, she was discharged from the hospital, with instructions not to do house work or lift her children, including her baby. She was to have the baby brought to her to nurse.

A week later her mother brought her to the emergency room. Her surgical wound had opened superficially, but fortunately it was still closed in the deeper layers. When I asked her how this had happened, she told me "It just split open."

I asked her, "What were you doing when it split open?"

She said, "I was walking through the house yesterday, carrying my two-year-old on this hip and my three-year-old on that hip, that's all. It just popped open."

Because of the amount of fat in the walls of her incision and the length of time that had elapsed since the wound opened, my resident elected to allow the wound to heal by second intention. That meant that the wound would not be resutured but would be allowed to fill in with granulation tissue from the bottom up until it healed. Closing a wound again with sutures after it has been open in nonsterile conditions may trap bacteria within the wound. Bacteria grow well in fat, causing wound abscesses that must be drained by opening the wound again. Allowing the wound to heal with granulation tissue takes more time, but it is a safer method.

She was admitted to the hospital and the wound was packed with gauze to encourage granulation tissue to form. Every day it was my job, as the intern, to change the dressing and to irrigate the wound with a dilute solution of peroxide. We knew that it would take two to three weeks for the wound to heal and told the patient and her family to anticipate a hospital stay of that length.

Each morning when I would irrigate the wound and change the dressing, the patient would ask if this was the day she could go home. I would patiently explain to her that it would take about three weeks for the wound to heal and that she could not go home until that happened. She would then ask if she could go home tomorrow. At first I explained to her about the three weeks, but eventually I just replied that we would talk about it again tomorrow, when I came into see her. I talked with her mother whenever she was in the room while I redressed the wound. She explained to me that her daughter had never had much concept of time in days, weeks, or months. Her mother was happy to have her daughter in the hospital while she bottle fed the baby at home.

Hearing their thoughts about the baby, the wound care, and other topics, and observing their vocabulary and grammar, I concluded that none of them appeared to have an IQ of more than 90. They were on permanent welfare and lived in public housing. When this case was discussed among the doctors, we agreed that the members of the family had such strong similarities that it was probably an endocrine or genetic syndrome, but we could not name the syndrome.

We thought that the actions of the mother in arranging dates for the daughter that ended in sexual activity and not teaching her daughter the rudimentary facts of life were not appropriate. The chief resident, who was a woman, sat down with the patient during this hospitalization and explained reproduction to her. Several days after this conversation took place, I asked the patient if she knew now how babies were made and she told me that they just happened to women. I was not sure whether she still did not know, or if she was too embarrassed to tell me what she knew. I suspect that she still did not comprehend what had been told to her by the chief resident.

After her discharge from the hospital, she did not return to the clinic and disappeared from our care. I sometimes wonder if her children developed normally or if one or more developed the same syndrome as their mother and grandmother.

I thought that it was unfortunate for this woman that her mother had not taught her the facts of life and that she had unknowingly produced children. I assumed that the family would care for these children, whose mother could not adequately raise them by herself. This patient raises many moral questions that made me rethink my opinions about birth control, abortion, and mental retardation.

7

The Jaundiced Woman

WHEN I WAS AN INTERN, I learned a lot about the power of the confidentiality that exists between doctor and patient. One night I was called to the emergency room to evaluate a patient who had severe jaundice of undetermined origin. She had been seen by the surgery intern on call, who decided that her jaundice was not of any origin that could lead to surgery.

When I saw the patient, Jane, she was with her sister, who was a nurse from our hospital. The nurse told me that before she left the house that morning, her sister had seemed well and showed no sign of jaundice, but when she returned home that afternoon, her sister was very sick. She had a fever and a headache and felt miserable, and her skin was very yellow.

I took a history from Jane, who denied any history of gastrointestinal problems. She had never experienced a gall bladder attack and had no family history of gall stones. She was not at a usual age for liver cancer. And she was not taking any medications that might cause a hemolytic anemia, which would cause the jaundice.

About two weeks prior to this, the hospital's medicine "grand rounds" was on the topic of jaundice of pregnancy, a slow-developing jaundice related to liver impairment from pregnancy. This patient's jaundice, however, did not fit this picture. She was single, but I did ask the patient if she was pregnant. She was very adamant in stating that she was certain that she was not pregnant.

During her physical examination I noticed that Jane's conjunctiva and her fingernail beds were very pale, but her skin was very yellow.

I drew some blood to determine whether she was anemic, and we later learned that she was very anemic and was probably destroying her red blood cells, creating the jaundice.

I returned to Jane and her sister and told them that I thought blood hemolysis (destruction of red blood cells) was causing her jaundice. The nurse turned to her sister, "You promised to tell the doctor the whole truth."

I asked the patient if she had something else to tell me.

She explained, "I answered you truthfully when you asked me if I was pregnant. I was pregnant this morning, but I had an abortion this afternoon. I am sure that I am not pregnant now."

My presumed diagnosis became sepsis (blood poisoning by bacteria) caused by an abortion with severe blood loss, and jaundice caused by destruction of red blood cells (hemolysis). I called one of my favorite obstetricians and presented the patient to him. He confirmed my diagnosis that she was having a septic abortion with hemolysing sepsis. He made it to the hospital in about fifteen minutes. In the meantime we set up the operating room for an examination and possible surgery under anesthesia and obtained informed consent. I turned over the case to the obstetrical resident.

After the examination, the resident told me that they had seen bubbles coming from the cervix and made the diagnosis of septic abortion from probable Clostridium botulinum bacteria. Clostridium botulinum is one of a few gas-forming bacteria that is a known cause of septic abortions. This disease is almost universally fatal. The obstetrician made the immediate decision to perform a dilation and curettage (D&C) of the uterus to remove as much infection as possible.

Botulinum is very susceptible to penicillin, so a high dose of intravenous penicillin was started immediately. Blood cultures were taken and later proved that the cause of the sepsis was Clostridium botulinum. More than half of her red blood cells had been destroyed, and her kidneys were beginning to fail. After the surgery was complete, the resident on medicine pulled out all of the stops to save her life.

The patient was still alive three days later, but her kidneys had failed and had not begun to function again. Because her kidneys were not working, toxins were accumulating in her blood, causing uremic poisoning. She continued to be very sick.

When this happened in 1965, renal hemodialysis (the artificial kidney) was in its early stages and was not available in our hospital. It was available at the university hospital, so we transferred the patient there for hemodialysis. Typical of some university hospitals, they would not take our word with regard to her condition. They proceeded to work her up all over again for two days, and then presented her to renal conference to determine whether she should be placed on dialysis. Fortunately, during this delay her kidneys began to function again, and the doctors decided not to give her dialysis.

By Saturday morning that week—five days after her admission there—she was well enough for her case to be presented to the medical center Grand Rounds for discussion. The previous ten cases of clostridium septic abortions in St. Louis were also reviewed. Of these cases, one had been treated by D&C and nine had been treated by hysterectomy. The one who had the D&C, like our patient, survived, while all of the women treated by hysterectomy died of their sepsis. This was a real lesson on how this disease should be treated.

After the discussion, one of the faculty physicians got up from his seat and approached the patient. He told her that what she had done was a criminal act and grilled her for the name of the person to whom she had gone for the abortion. She declined, so the physician continued to berate her and demand that she tell him who it was. She refused to name the person and was finally escorted from the amphitheater and returned to her room. She immediately signed out of the hospital against medical advice and returned to our hospital, where she stayed until she was recovered sufficiently for discharge. In cases like this, I was taught to remain amoral in judgment, but to treat the patient to the best of my ability.

This patient makes the case for legal abortions so that they will be done in a suitably sterile environment to avoid infection and sepsis. "Back alley" abortions, done with questionable sterility, more often result in this outcome, often killing young women.

I feel that the grilling from the doctor at the conference is the type of behavior that leads women to secretly seek abortions and puts them at risk of disease and death. The need for secrecy that this patient felt caused delay in the diagnosis, which could have been fatal.

All patients do not understand professional privilege and the confidentiality that it imparts. This patient was reluctant to reveal her history to me: perhaps it was my youth at age twenty-five. Doctors, conversely, tend to assume that the patients know that they have protection of confidentiality. I could have explained this to her and possibly had more cooperation from the patient. After this I made it a point to explain the confidentiality situation to my patients whenever I thought it might apply. The actions of the physician who questioned her at the Grand Rounds session were contrary to the doctrine of doctor-patient privilege.

It should be noted that this case occurred before *Roe v. Wade,* and the atmosphere in most hospitals was very different from what it is today. All surgical procedures that could result in termination of a pregnancy or permanent sterility needed prior approval of a hospital committee, which included private citizens and sometimes clergy. Most doctors would refuse to perform a termination of pregnancy unless it involved rape, incest, or threatened the life of the mother. The situation that existed then probably led to this bad outcome from an abortion.

8

<o>

Hiccups

WHEN I WAS A FIRST-YEAR resident, it was customary for the first-year residents to do the admission histories and physical exams on all of the patients hospitalized for surgery. I went to the ward to work up a patient who had been admitted for cataract surgery. The patient had a case of the hiccups that he said had been going for two days. He also complained that he was having waves of flushing of the skin and a feeling of warmth that lasted for several minutes each time. These occurred several times a day. His wife remarked that the spells reminded her of when she had hot flashes during menopause.

While I was doing the physical exam, Dr. Waller Taylor, the surgeon, came into see the patient and was worried that the patient had the hiccups. If the patient continued to have the hiccups, the surgery would have to be cancelled. Hiccups increase the pressure in the eye and cause the head to move. Under the microscope, this movement would be gigantic and very disturbing to the surgeon. At that time, we did intracapsular cataract surgery, where the lens is removed in one piece, leaving nothing in front of the vitreous. If the eye is open when the patient hiccups, the vitreous could be expelled from the eye, which is a bad complication of cataract surgery.

Waller admitted that he did not know of any medical way to stop the hiccups and asked if I knew of anything that would stop them. During my internship I had cared for a patient who had intractable hiccups. That patient had responded to a dose of Thorazine. I told Waller about him and he told me to try Thorazine for his patient. I gave the patient a therapeutic dose of Thorazine, and the hiccups stopped in about two hours.

Waller did the cataract surgery the next day without the interference of hiccups, and the surgery went smoothly. At the time, patients were kept in the hospital for about five days for cataract surgery. On the third day, I was on hospital call when I was called at about 4:00 PM to see this patient again. The nurse told me that the patient was short of breath and that his pulse was about 120. I was concerned that he had suffered a heart attack or possibly thrown an embolism from his legs to his pulmonary artery.

I ran from the clinic to the hospital, two blocks away. When I arrived on the hospital floor, the nurses were having report, where they turned over the patients to the next shift, so they just pointed toward his room. He was breathing about forty times per minute, (the norm is sixteen to twenty), but having no pain. His pulse was 120 per minute (the norm is seventy to eighty). I listened to his heart and lungs, which were normal except for the rapid rates. I also performed an ECG, which was normal, except for the rate, and showed no sign of heart attack.

He was cold and slightly clammy. I noticed that his conjunctiva and his fingernail beds were both very pale and that he looked anemic. He had not looked anemic when I examined him three days before. I knew that he would have lost only a few milliliters of blood during his cataract surgery, so I needed to find some other cause of blood loss. The most likely cause was gastrointestinal bleeding.

I drew blood to check his hemoglobin and hematocrit to see how much blood he had lost. I then did a guaiac test for blood in his stool. The test was positive and his hematocrit was low. I immediately put in a call to the medicine service to have them evaluate him for the source of gastrointestinal bleeding. The resident in charge told me that they did not have any beds, but they would call me when they did. Meanwhile, I was to take care of him on the ophthalmology service.

I had the patient's blood typed and cross-matched and proceeded to give him three units of blood that evening and later at night. His pulse and breathing rate slowed and he became comfortable. His bleeding appeared to have stopped.

I called the medicine house staff several times over the next two days, and they continued to tell me that they had no beds and could not transfer the patient. On the third day after giving him the transfusions, I came into morning rounds and asked the resident, who had been on call for the previous night, how the patient was doing. He told me that the patient had become short of breath again, so he had called in the surgery residents, who had obtained an emergency upper gastrointestinal barium study. The study showed a large ulcer on the posterior wall of his stomach that had eroded through the wall of the stomach. They had taken him to the operating room and removed the half of his stomach that had the ulcer, and that stopped the bleeding. They discovered that the ulcer had eroded into the pancreas, which lies behind the stomach.

A few minutes later, the chief resident on the medicine service called to tell me that they finally had a bed for my patient who needed evaluation for bleeding. I told him that they could find the patient in the recovery room, but the surgeons had already diagnosed and treated his bleeding problem.

The surgeons had found the cause of his hiccups and his hot flashes. When his large stomach ulcer had eroded through the wall of his stomach, he began leaking stomach acid underneath his diaphragm. The irritation of the diaphragm by the acid caused his hiccups. When the acid eroded his pancreas, it released bradykinin into his blood stream periodically, causing his hot flashes. Had I been able to put this together from his clinical history, I could have predicted the source of his bleeding. I was consoled by the fact that no one else had been able to put it all together either.

Sir Thomas Osler, a famous diagnostician and teacher, had a rule that all of the symptoms of the patient should fit one disease. This case is a perfect example of that rule. The blood loss, hiccups, and hot flashes were all caused by the stomach ulcer. By triangulating the three parts of the disease, it should have been obvious that he had an ulcer, which could cause all three. Had we diagnosed the ulcer, the cataract surgery would have been postponed until after the ulcer was repaired. As it worked out, his cataract was removed before he had the abdominal surgery, and he was able to recuperate from both procedures simultaneously. Ophthalmologists would prefer that any necessary additional surgery be completed before the eye surgery, because the additional surgery could cause an increase in his ocular pressure, either by the positioning of the patient or by putting pressure on his abdominal organs.

He returned for his postoperative visits and did well visually. He did not have any recurrence of his stomach ulcer during the time we followed him. I was able to keep him alive when he was bleeding by giving him blood. Patients who need blood transfusions are rare in ophthalmology, but the Medicine Service was of no help to me with this patient.

9

The Cataract Matriarch

M OST PEOPLE ARE SO DEPENDENT on vision that they cannot imagine what it would be like to be without it and would take all possible steps to prevent or restore it. This is not always the case.

When I was a first-year resident, I was assigned to the screening clinic from time to time. All patients who walked into the clinic without appointments were seen that day as soon as possible. If they had a routine problem that would take some time to examine and start therapy, they would be given a return appointment for that specific problem. If their problem was an emergency, evaluation and treatment were done that day. It was the job of the first-year resident to triage all of the walk-in patients.

One day Mable, an elderly black woman, came to the clinic, with two daughters and three granddaughters accompanying her. I called her back to the screening room, and her entourage came with her. She was constantly requesting that someone do something for her: help her find the chair, get her a tissue, hold her coat, hold her hand, and so forth. The women with her fell over each other to do her bidding.

As she walked into the room, it was obvious why she was almost blind. I saw that both of her pupils were white. Mable had dense cataracts in both eyes, which were probably the cause of her blindness. I examined her, but could not see into the eye through her dense cataracts. She needed to be examined with the indirect ophthalmoscope through dilated pupils, which was beyond the scope of the screening exam. I knew that the senior residents were looking for patients who needed cataract surgery, so I grabbed Dr. Page, the chief resident, as he walked by the screening room. He saw the cataracts and said that he would see her as soon as he finished examining his current patient.

About an hour later I saw him come down the corridor with Mable and her family. I asked him if he was going to take out one of her cataracts. He waved me off and told me to talk with him later.

At lunch that day he explained that she did have dense cataracts, but that everything else in her eye was normal. She was a good candidate for surgery, and he told her that he could probably restore her vision to normal with surgery. She told him that she was eighty-three years old and that she had seen a lot of things in her day. She told him that many of the things that she had seen she would not want to see again, so she just wanted to stay blind and have her family take care of her.

I discussed this with my wife, who was a clinical psychologist and a pediatrician. When I told her about the patient's denial of cataract surgery and described the way the woman manipulated her family, my wife told me it was a classic case of using a disability to manipulate the people around her.

If her vision was restored, Mable would not have a disability with which to manipulate her family. She was comfortable with her life the way it was. It is hard for me to imagine that controlling the people around me would be more important than being independent and able to see the world. But then I am not eighty-three years old with a large family to look after me.

I feel that the sense of vision is so important that I would do almost anything to regain it. I suppose that the power that this lady wielded over her family was enough gain for her that she chose power over independence. I have had only one other patient who refused surgery with a high probability to restore vision.

I learned from these two patients that it is the patient's choice, regardless of my opinion, whether to have vision-restoring surgery.

10

My First Cataract Operation

NOTHING REMAINS IN YOUR MEMORY as much as the first time you do something, especially if it does not turn out well. This was certainly true of my first cataract extraction operation.

In my residency, performing cataract surgery as the first surgeon, not the assistant, was reserved for the third year of residency. To learn surgery, we assisted the senior residents with their cataract surgeries during our second year and were often given one or more of the parts of the operation to do. We were encouraged to practice the techniques of cataract surgery in the laboratory on pig eyes from the slaughter house.

Our graduating residents all attended the "Maine Ophthalmology Course" in Colby, Maine, which was conducted by faculty from Harvard and elsewhere. The graduating senior residents left for the course in mid-June, and responsibility for cataract surgery was passed to the incoming senior residents. By alphabet, I was designated chief resident for the first four months. Therefore, the first cataract would come to me in a rotation with the other two senior residents.

A fifty-five-year-old indigent man came to the clinic with a red, painful eye and very poor vision. He had been bothered by poor vision in that eye for several years, but had not seen a doctor about it. He walked on crutches, having lost his right leg below the knee in a train accident many years before.

He had cataracts in both eyes, but his left eye was red all over the conjunctiva, (the loose tissue that covers the front of the sclera allowing the eye to move). His cornea was slightly hazy. He had a snow-white cataract that filled the pupil. After glycerin was placed on the cornea to remove the haze, large clumps of white blood cells could be seen floating in the aqueous humor between the cornea and the iris. The hazy cornea was caused by elevated intraocular pressure because the clumps of white blood cells had blocked the outflow channels from the eye.

I made the diagnosis of phacotoxic reaction, which is caused by proteins leaking from an "over-ripe" cataract. These toxins cause an inflammatory reaction. Treatment requires removing the cataract, which is the causative agent. I scheduled the operating room and enlisted Dr. King, from the faculty, to assist me.

That afternoon, we took him to the operating room and prepared him for surgery on the eye. Because of the elevated pressure, we massaged his eye and gave him Manitol intravenously to osmotically shrink the vitreous gel and lower the pressure. The pressure dropped to fifteen millimeters of mercury (mm Hg), which is within the normal range, but higher than one would like when opening the eye. Rapid decompression of the eye upon opening the eye can cause a hemorrhage in the eye that expels the contents of the eye.

Since the pressure was as low as Manitol and ocular massage could get it, we decided to proceed with the cataract extraction. A conjunctival flap was turned down toward the cornea, and a groove was made along the limbus from three o'clock to nine o'clock above. Two sutures were placed in the groove to close the wound, but they were left untied and looped out of the bottom of the groove. The eye was entered slowly at twelve o'clock from the bottom of the groove, and we were careful not to allow any fluid to escape the eye. Pressure was slowly lowered by releasing aqueous from the eye, which was done by placing gentle pressure on the posterior lip of the incision.

Once the eye was soft, scissors were introduced into the opening, and the opening was extended to three o'clock and nine o'clock through the groove. At this point the front of the eye collapsed, leaving the iris against the back of the cornea. I was worried that this collapse would complicate the cataract removal because the space to work in had been obliterated. If the space could not be restored, we could not remove the cataract. I had to recreate the anterior chamber space.

The two preplaced sutures were drawn up and tied to close the incision, which was starting to gape open. Attempts to irrigate fluid into the eye and re-establish the space between the iris and cornea were unsuccessful. Dr. King thought that there was vitreous pressure and suggested that we remove some vitreous. So we made a small incision in the sclera (white part of the eye) about four millimeters from the limbus (edge of cornea). A large (15 gauge) blunt-tipped needle was introduced through this incision, and one milliliter of vitreous gel was aspirated. The pressure was immediately relieved, and we were able to reform the front of the eye by injecting saline in front of the iris.

The next step in the operation was to make a hole in the iris at the twelve o'clock location to prevent the vitreous from stopping the flow of aqueous humor out of the eye by blocking the pupil after the surgery. While Dr. King lifted the cornea, I grasped the iris and cut a hole in it next to the incision. When Dr. King released the cornea, the eye would not close because the pressure had returned to the eye. Dr. King suggested removing more vitreous to relieve the pressure. When we aspirated from the center of the eye again, all that came out was bright red blood, not clear vitreous. This told us that the eye was hemorrhaging internally, which was a disaster. These hemorrhages usually arise from the choroid tissue, behind the retina. I realized that the hemorrhage could fill the eye from the back, forcing the normal contents out through the open wound, destroying the eye.

I immediately placed a third suture to close the center of the wound. We already had two sutures tied to close the incision.

The pressure in the eye caused the iris to bulge out of the wound between the three sutures. I repositioned the iris using a thin spatula, and put sutures between those already there and succeeded in closing the eye. I had read about this complication, so I suggested draining the choroidal hemorrhage through the sclera; but Dr. King overruled me, saying that the increased pressure would stop the bleeding and the eye would soften again after the bleeding stopped. I closed the conjunctiva and placed a firm patch on the eye to control the bleeding.

The patient complained of pain in the eye for about twenty-four hours. The pain was probably from the increased pressure in the eye from the hemorrhage. I presented this patient to the Grand Rounds session two days later to discuss the management of an expulsive choroidal hemorrhage. His vision had gone to no light perception, meaning that the pressure had probably closed his central retinal artery. Closure of the central retinal artery would kill the retina within fifteen minutes. The eye was permanently blind.

One of the ophthalmologists attending the session thought that we should have anticipated the hemorrhage because the patient had such bad vascular disease that he had lost a foot to vascular disease. I pointed out that the foot had actually been lost in a train accident many years ago. The cataract-induced inflammation and high pressure did probably contribute to the likelihood of an expulsive choroidal hemorrhage. The discussion then centered on the proper treatment if hemorrhaging occurs. The latest thinking was that the pressure should be relieved immediately by draining the hemorrhage through the sclera until the bleeding vessel clots and the bleeding stops. I was criticized roundly for not doing so during the surgery. Dr. King did not speak up to take responsibility, and I did not want to get him in trouble, so I sat back and learned that I had wanted to do the right thing.

Since this was my first cataract surgery as primary surgeon, I could have been severely traumatized by the outcome. However, I learned that the incidence of expulsive hemorrhages during cataract surgery was about one in ten thousand routine operations. At that rate, I rationalized, I had 9,999 cataract operations until I would have another expulsive hemorrhage. I have found over the years that the cataracts done by residents in training and the complex surgery that I would do in the future had a much higher incidence of hemorrhage than the usual cataract operation.

I have been present for five more intra-operative expulsive hemorrhages and managed them all, as I was taught in the Grand Rounds session, by draining the hemorrhage through the choroid and sclera. The eyes in all of these cases survived, with vision from 20/25 to 20/100.

The patient returned for several postoperative visits. When we explained that the vision would not return in his operated eye, he refused surgery for the cataract in his other eye, and we did not see him again. When his remaining cataract became overripe like his first one, he may seek care again. I hope he had a better outcome with his second eye.

11

My First Corneal Transplant

I CAN VIVIDLY REMEMBER THE FIRST patient on whom I performed a corneal transplant. I had just been to an outstanding course on corneal transplants that was taught by the most prominent corneal surgeons of the time in South Hampton, New York. I was sent to the course at the beginning of my senior year of residency by the Old Dominion Eye Bank, because I had done so much work preparing tissue for the eye bank. There were twenty students and eleven faculty members. I met several students there who went on to become corneal surgeons and lifelong friends. For the laboratory practice sessions, we had five teachers on each of two days. The other five would be at the Meadow Club playing tennis with our host and teacher, Dr. Townley Paton, the professor and chairman emeritus from Manhattan Eye and Ear Hospital.

When I returned from the course, having just learned the techniques for corneal transplants, I was anxious to perform the surgery on a patient. Since I was the first chief resident, I would be first up for a patient needing a corneal transplant.

A young black man, we will call him George, about twenty-two years old came to the clinic. He had a history of several years of poor vision, which was slowly getting worse. He had been to see an optometrist, who could not improve his vision with glasses. The screening resident saw that he had a problem with the shape of his corneas and brought him into my examination room in the clinic.

George's vision was poorer than 20/400 (the big "E" at the top of the eye exam chart) in each eye. I examined him and found that he had an obvious case of keratoconus. In keratoconus, the central cornea thins and becomes elastic. This elasticity allows the central cornea to bulge outwardly from the surrounding cornea and become cone-shaped, rather than spherical. This conical bulge is often asymmetrical and, therefore, produces optical distortion. Since it is asymmetrical, glasses cannot correct the vision. Contact lenses, which rest on the cornea and make a new anterior surface, sometimes succeed in correcting vision. In this case, however, the keratoconus was too advanced and the corneas too pointed to fit a contact lens on either eye. The only satisfactory treatment would be to do a cornea transplant on his worst eye.

I explained why glasses and contacts would not work and offered him corneal transplant surgery on his right eye. George agreed, because he wanted to get a driver's license and could not pass the test with his poor vision. He was placed on the waiting list for corneal donor tissue.

George was indigent and unemployable because of his poor vision, so when I sent him to the hospital for preclearance, the university hospital told him that he would have to make a large deposit before he could enter the hospital. The custom for corneal transplants at that time was to admit the patient for three weeks of absolute bed rest after the surgery. He could not afford this, and social services would not approve him for surgery with a long hospital stay. I learned that the private Richmond Eye and Ear Hospital needed to admit a certain number of indigent patients each year to qualify for the Hill-Burton funds that they received for indigent care. The administrator told me that they would be glad to admit my patient for his three-week stay, completely free of charge.

When tissue became available, we called the patient and learned that the patient's phone had been disconnected. His case worker suggested that we send the county sheriff to find him and bring him to the Richmond Eye and Ear Hospital. Corneal transplants were sufficiently novel at that time, so the sheriff was willing to cooperate to bring the patient ninety miles from southern Virginia.

Dr. Walter Mayer was my attending surgeon. He had trained with Dr. Arruga, in Spain, and did many of the corneal transplants in Richmond. At his suggestion I sutured the transplanted tissue into the hole in the cornea, using 9-0 twisted black silk for suture. This suture was twisted because braiding the three strands together would make it too large. The silk was coated with a material to make it slide through the cornea more smoothly. This coating flaked off in little brown crystals that scattered all over the cornea and had to be constantly irrigated away. The suture was so coarse in the cornea, even at the 9-0 size, that a knot to tie the stitch ends together would be very large. However, the roughness of the suture held the tension on the stitch without a knot. The ends of the stitch were cut flush with the surface of the cornea and left with no knot.

The patient was left in bed with no bathroom privileges, only the bed pan, for nineteen days. Every day we changed the patch on the eye by cutting the tape holding the patch, leaving the tape on his face. The pad was slowly peeled from the inner corner of the eye, and a drop of anesthetic was instilled into the eye to prevent the patient from squeezing his eyelids. Then the eye pad was removed and the mucous was cleaned from the lashes. The eyelid was slowly opened, and the eye was examined for signs of infection or wound shift. When neither was seen, a drop of antibiotics and a drop of steroids were placed in the eye and the eye was patched again, placing new tape over the old tape on the skin. We were afraid that pulling the tape from the skin would make the patient squeeze the eye and shift the wound edges.

Two days before his planned discharge, he was allowed to use a bedside commode, and orders were written for the nurses to walk the patient in the hall three times each day. This was to build up his strength, after lying in bed for three weeks, so that he could walk from the hospital to the car and again from the car into his house when he arrived home.

His postoperative course was very smooth, and his cornea healed rapidly. At two months, Dr. Mayer told me to remove the stitches so that the corneal transplant would not vascularize. The silk causes a reaction which hastens healing. After I removed his suture, I told him to return in two weeks to be fit with glasses for his operated eye.

When he returned, I was impressed that his cornea had healed with very little scarring where the two tissues met. I checked his vision and was very surprised that he read all the way to the 20/20 line without stopping, with no glasses or correction of any kind. It is extremely rare to have a corneal transplant heal so round and evenly stressed that the patient can see that well without any glasses. I think that out of the several hundred transplants that I have done, only three or four were able to see 20/25 or better without glasses or contact lenses.

I was thrilled by the outcome. I told the patient that he could go back to work.

He replied, "What do you mean go back to work? I don't have a job. I have never had a job. I am on welfare."

I replied, "You can go get a job now, because you can see as well as everybody else." This made him mad. He yelled at me that I had ruined his life. He had been legally blind and had been set for life on welfare. Since he was blind, he never needed to get a job. If he could not qualify for welfare because he could see, then I had ruined him. He stormed out that day, and I never saw him again.

I was so proud that George had such a good result, better than most people after a corneal transplant, but he did not appreciate it. In fact, he was upset. It had not occurred to me at that time that becoming a productive member of society would be so foreign and disturbing to George. I was so surprised by his reaction that I forgot that he told me that he wanted to see so that he could get a driver's license.

I thought that it was ironic that my first ever corneal transplant obtained one of the best results of my entire career, but that the patient could not appreciate the wonderful vision that he had received from the transplant.

12

The Lady from San Antonio

DURING MY LAST YEAR OF residency, a lady in her seventies who had lived almost all of her life in San Antonio, Texas, came to see me because she was having pain in her left eye. Her pain had come on gradually and had become much worse over the past several months. It had become so bad that it woke her at night and she could not tolerate bright lights or sunshine.

Rose told me that her husband had died several years before when she lived in Texas. After settling his estate, she had decided to fulfill a lifelong dream of running a Mexican restaurant. San Antonio was full of Mexican restaurants, so she looked around the country for a city that seemed to need a Mexican restaurant. Rose discovered that Richmond did not have a Mexican restaurant. She decided that this was a grievous fault that should be rectified.

She used all of her savings to buy a restaurant to convert to a genuine southwestern Mexican cantina. She discovered why there was no previous Mexican restaurant in Richmond. The restaurant never caught on and she soon lost all of her money. She got out of the restaurant business and was trying to live on the little money she received from selling the building. Rose was deeply embarrassed by having lost all of the money her husband had provided for her and was ashamed to be in the indigent clinic of the Medical College of Virginia.

Her eye problem was primary corneal edema, or Fuchs' dystrophy, and it was worse in her left eye. Primary corneal edema, also known as Fuchs' dystrophy, is a hereditary disease and can cause

43

blurred vision. This disease usually occurs after age fifty. The only lasting cure that can restore vision is a corneal transplant. She was very concerned about paying for the operation, but I assured her that the Commonwealth of Virginia would pay for her surgery. She would have to be in a ward bed and could not have a private or even a double room. Rose was stoic and accepted the situation.

This was my third corneal transplant as first surgeon, so I enlisted the help of Dr. Keith McNeer as attending surgeon, and we performed a routine corneal transplant on her left eye. She did well after the surgery, and it was not long until she could see fairly well with the operated eye. She did not have any more pain in the eye. I followed her for several months before I removed her sutures.

One morning, shortly after I had removed her sutures, I found Rose sitting on the steps of the clinic. She was bundled in a wool coat, but she was obviously very cold. She told me that she was early for her appointment because she had been evicted from her apartment and was living on the street. She could not sleep, so she came to the clinic, even though she knew it would be closed. She knew that she could come in to wait as soon as it opened. After I let her into the clinic, Rose explained that she had run out of money. She had not paid her electric bill for several months and had been living on canned food that she heated with candles. She did not have any heat, but she had several blankets. After three months of not paying her rent, she had been evicted.

When I asked her why she had not applied for welfare, she told me that her late husband would roll over in his grave if she applied for assistance. Her family simply did not do that. I told her that the utilities would also give her assistance if she explained her situation, but she gave me the same reason for not asking for help.

I had a long talk with Rose about overcoming her pride and accepting assistance. She finally agreed to work with one of the hospital social workers to obtain assistance. She was a very gracious, genteel, and proud lady from an old Texas family. Her husband had been a good provider and had left her enough money to live respectably in San Antonio. She was a very feisty lady who did not want to sit at home and dwindle away, so she took a risk to pursue her dream.

I was unaware of the Mexican restaurant and had never been there. Apparently most of the Richmond populace, in a town that reveres ham biscuits and gravy or peanut cured ham, shared my ignorance of the Mexican restaurant. She had failed to do the necessary market research for Mexican food in Richmond, which left her destitute. Because of her prior life, Rose did not have the "welfare mentality" to deal with her situation.

Her husband had paid social security throughout his business career, but had been too proud to apply for it when he retired. The social worker helped her to receive her husband's social security, so she was able to rent an apartment and pay for her utilities and food. When I left Richmond to go to my fellowship in Boston, I lost track of her.

This was a case of treating the "whole patient." I had to become her financial advisor and confidant to convince her to accept her situation and change her attitude about receiving assistance. Rose showed great strength in trying to live by her own means to maintain her pride; it took courage for her to admit that she needed help, and humility to actually accept it. I think that I helped her to understand her situation and accept assistance.

13

<hr>

Results of a Hunting Accident

THE PATIENT WHO INSPIRED ME the most was my father. He was my patient from the time of my residency until he died. My father grew up on a farm in Missouri along the Missouri River, about thirty miles from Kansas City. He was hunting at seventeen years old when he set his shotgun down over a fence before climbing the fence. He told me that it was an inexpensive Sears shotgun with a defective safety, which was set to "on." The gun discharged, tearing off his left thumb and leaving a buckshot in his left eye. This was before the discovery of the first true antibiotic, sulfa, so he lost his left eye. I did not find out until I was about fifteen that he wore a glass eye.

Because of his academic ability, his father let him skip the work on their farm so that he could go to high school his entire senior year, rather than work on the farm with his brothers in the fall and spring. This enabled him to take algebra so he could meet the requirements for graduation from high school. After graduation he attended summer school at a state teacher's college to obtain a teacher's certificate. He returned home and taught at the Fitch one-room school for three years. He lived at home and saved his money to go to college.

He enrolled in the premed curriculum at the University of Missouri. He sold aluminum ware from door to door during the summers, waited tables at a boarding house, and read electric meters during the school years to pay his way through undergraduate school. He met my mother while he waited tables at the boarding house, where she lived as a student at the University of Missouri.

He was admitted to the University of Missouri Medical School, which was only for the two preclinical years at that time. In the summer after his first year, he managed to get a job helping to lay a pipeline across Missouri. Whenever the ditch-digging machine could not dig the ditch, men would dig it with shovels. After his first day he had huge blisters on his hands, so he asked the foreman if he had any suggestions on how to care for them. The foreman noticed his pale, smooth hands and asked him what he had been doing before this job. When my father told him that he was a medical student, the foreman told him that he was looking for someone smart to carry the dynamite and offered him the job. My father agreed, but he immediately separated the blasting caps from the dynamite sticks and made two trips every time he moved the explosives.

His second summer of medical school, he obtained a job working at a state hospital in Missouri. His job was to draw blood from patients and make specially stained slides for the pathologist to read. This was long before penicillin was invented, so there was no drug available to treat Syphilis. One of the ways they treated syphilis then was to give the patient malaria. The spirochete that causes syphilis is very sensitive to temperatures above or below normal body temperature. The high fevers of malaria will kill the spirochete and sometimes cure syphilis. The hospital used more than one variety of malaria to treat these patients. The pathologists examined blood smears to determine if the malaria was active and to verify which form the patient had. Then they discarded the slides.

My father knew that the pathology department at Missouri University did not have good slides for malaria in the pathology teaching sets, so he saved a collection of slides for the different stages of malaria for each type. There were hundreds of slides that summer, so he saved enough for each pathology slide box at Missouri University and presented them to the professor of pathology at the end of the summer.

After the first two years of medical school, he transferred to Washington University Medical School for the two clinical years. Getting from Richmond, Missouri, to St. Louis was a problem. His Uncle Young, who had been a physician, had died the year before and left Aunt Sally with a Model A Ford, which she did not drive, along with a comfortable sum of money. She offered to pay my father's tuition to medical school and loan him the car to drive back and forth. He was not to drive it any place else except to school and back.

On a fine spring day, my father decided to take my mother-to-be, his fiancée, on a ride in Forest Park. My father's cousin, who was also in medical school there, saw them and reported it to Aunt Sally. She was so upset that he had broken the rules that she took the car back and refused to pay his tuition for the fourth year. My father was devastated and did not know how he would complete medical school. He had been dating my mother-to-be for several years, and her father had taken a liking to him. Her father found out how much the tuition and living expenses were and gave my mother the money to give to my father so that he could complete medical school.

He graduated from medical school in 1930 and went directly into an internship at Missouri Baptist Hospital in St. Louis, making twenty-five dollars a month and living in the hospital. At the end of his internship, in the middle of the Depression, he could not afford more training, so he joined the medical practice of Dr. Ferdinand McCormick in Normal, Illinois. He took all of the evening and weekend calls and worked alongside Dr. McCormick in the practice, earning one hundred and fifty dollars per month. During that first year he married my mother. At the end of the year, Dr. McCormick told my father that he had decided he would be a good surgeon if he had some surgical training. He sent my father to Philadelphia to do six months of surgical residency at the University of Pennsylvania Hospital.

At the end of the six months, he returned to Normal to rejoin Dr. McCormick and began doing surgery with him. Three months after his return, Dr. McCormick died of a heart attack. My father took over the practice and did the surgery by himself or with assistance from one of the other doctors in town.

My father had a very successful practice going when World War II came along. He was still in the draft age range for doctors and was concerned about being drafted and sent, as a general practitioner, to the front lines. He learned that he could volunteer for "non-overseas" duty, but if he waited to be drafted, he could be sent anywhere. He was a young married physician with two children, aged three and six, and decided to play it safe. He went down to the draft board office and enlisted. Unfortunately, he had not convinced my mother. She never forgave him for volunteering. Shortly after he volunteered, the city was declared to have a critical number of physicians, so no one else would be drafted. The doctors who stayed home were very busy and prosperous and were often paid in ration coupons instead of cash. Since my father was in the military, we did not share in these benefits.

My father spent a year at Camp Grant in Rockford, Illinois, so we saw him every few weeks. The service allowed him to pursue one of his favorite pastimes, travel. Every troop train was required to have a doctor or two on board. He rode through every mountain pass in the U.S. Rockies and followed the Mississippi to Mobile and New Orleans several times.

After a year of this he received orders to prepare for a cold damp climate. He immediately went to the Post Exchange to buy two fishing rods, one for casting and one for fly fishing. When he boarded the troop ship in Taunton, Massachusetts, his buddies were lugging all of the liquor they could carry. They ribbed my father because he was carrying his fishing rods. Once they were at sea he was told that he was going to Greenland. He spent thirty days zigzagging in convoy to avoid submarines in the North Atlantic to reach his "non-overseas" duty post.

The army had a string of hospitals along the east coast of Greenland to repair wounded soldiers. These hospitals were considered "within the battle theater," so the soldiers could return to battle when considered fit for duty. Captain Barber worked for one year as a general surgeon, repairing war wounds. He was then promoted to major and transferred to another Greenland hospital to run that hospital and continue to do surgery. Many of his favorite medical stories were from his two years in Greenland.

He told the story of a planeload of soldiers arriving at the hospital airstrip in a DC-4. This airplane sat high above the ground and required steps or a ladder for people to deplane. It taxied near a snow drift and stopped. Some of the soldiers could not wait for the ladder and began to jump into the snow drift. The snow drift was actually a mound of ice with an inch of snow over it. The first soldier broke both heels when he landed. Before they realized what was happening, seven other soldiers had jumped and broken both heels. My father pinned all sixteen heels and had the patients lined up in a row of beds on the ward. The army sent an orthopedic specialist to check the results. After the specialist reviewed the X-rays and examined the patients, he told my father that he had done a beautiful job on all eight patients. Then he admitted that he had not operated on eight bilateral heel fractures in his career in orthopedics.

The maximum tour of duty in Greenland was eight months. His first replacement managed a transfer before reporting. The rules were that you did not leave your duty post until your replacement had arrived. He stayed another eight months. The same thing happened with his second replacement. At the end of twenty four months, his commanding officer told him that he did not need to wait for his replacement, but to get on the first plane out on his last day. When his relief time came, he threw a stack of gunnysacks in the back of a transport plane that was flying south and curled up on them to sleep on his way to Goose Bay.

His next duty assignment was Ashford General Hospital in West Virginia, better known to most of us as the Greenbrier Hotel in White Sulfur Springs. He arrived a day early and was not expected. All of the bachelor's officer quarters rooms were occupied so they put him in the VIP suite above the front door of the hotel. Somehow, they forgot that they had put him there, and he spent the whole year in that suite. This was after the war, but many of the injured soldiers were still in rehabilitation or had to undergo corrective surgery to restore function after war injuries.

Since he had been gone for two years and did not get home leave between assignments, my mother put my older brother and me in her two-door, two-seat, blue Chevy coupe, and we drove from Illinois to West Virginia. We stayed in an apartment in town and visited my dad at the hospital. I remember "helping" my dad carry his golf bag around the White Course on his afternoon off. There were men caring for the gardens and golf course wearing khaki pants and shirts with big letters on the front and back. At age six, I did not know what POW meant.

After the military, he would arise in the morning and go to the hospital after breakfast for 8:00 AM surgery. He would do one or two surgical cases and then go to the office to see his postoperative patients. Then it was home for lunch and back to the office to see patients until 5:30 or 6:00 PM. He would have dinner at home and then head out for house calls, which usually took until 10:00 PM or later. If he got home in time, he would watch the ten o'clock news while perusing the latest journals. Often he would fall asleep, so my mother would wake him after the weather and sports and send him to bed. He made house calls on Sunday morning and would sometimes slip into the back pew with us during church. When he could, he took Sunday afternoon off to work in the garden or take us for a boat ride on Lake Bloomington. I decided that I did not want to be a doctor because I would not have any time of my own.

When I was ten years old, my father started taking my brother and me fishing in Canada for a week each summer. He would show us the way he could tie knots and hold a surgical instrument in his left hand that did not have a thumb. He had developed a very strong grip between his index and middle fingers of his left hand. When asked by someone how he could do surgery with only one thumb, he would reply that he had known people who tried to do surgery who were "all thumbs."

When he was fifty-nine years old, he had a gallbladder attack in the middle of the night. My mother woke my brother and had him get my father's black bag from the back seat of the car. My father gave him instructions on putting together the syringe and drawing up a shot of Demerol. Then he proceeded to tell my brother how to give him the shot in the arm, believing that it might encourage my brother to go into medicine as a career.

The next day he went to see Dr. Ben Hoopes, a fellow surgeon and close friend, and told Ben that he wanted his gallbladder out. Dr. Hoopes insisted on a proper workup and then agreed to do the surgery. During the recuperative period, my dad was besieged by phone calls from families of sick patients who demanded to be seen. He was under medical orders not to work for three weeks. He had closed his office for three weeks and had given his nurse a vacation. He did not want to go to the hospital to see patients or open office hours at home, so my mother packed their bags and they left for three weeks of R&R in the Ozarks. My mother liked the area of northern Arkansas so much that she bought a house with a beautiful view of Bull Shoals Lake—supposedly for vacations.

By the time my father was sixty years old, my mother had convinced him to retire. He sold his practice, and they moved to the Ozarks to make a clean break from his practice. It took him two years to adapt to not having to go to see patients every day. He did not like to watch TV except for a few favorite shows. He would get up from his recliner and head for the garage, where he would straighten and restraighten his tools, shred coconut with his coconut grater from the Fiji Islands, or work on his fishing tackle or guns. He had a floating boat dock that had to be moved every few days because of the changing lake level. He mowed the grass, chopped wood, smoked fish, and picked wild berries. My mother immediately taught him how to make his own jelly with the berries he picked. He managed to keep busy.

During my third year of residency, my parents came to Richmond, Virginia, for the Christmas holidays. We three senior residents split call nights evenly for the two weeks of holiday break. I had the days between Christmas and New Year's. Now that I was in ophthalmology, my father asked me to help him find someone who could make good glass eyes for him. Technology was changing from hand-blown, hand-colored glass prostheses to machine-made and -printed plastic eye prostheses, but my father could not tolerate the plastic and still wanted glass. The man who had made all of his prostheses for years had retired, but I was able to find him a prosthesis artist in Chicago.

On that visit, my father came with me to the operating room to watch me remove a cataract from a young woman. He watched the entire procedure through the assistant arm of the microscope. The whole operation took about ten minutes. On the way home he told me that it was some of the slickest surgery that he had ever seen. Up to that point he had not understood why I went into ophthalmology and specialized in such a small part of the body. Now he understood.

My father was seventy when I finished my fellowship in Boston. My parents came to visit in New England before we moved to Texas. While they were there, my dad suddenly developed rather severe angina and could not walk a block without sitting to rest. Back home in Arkansas, he went to see his doctor, who told him that he needed coronary artery bypass. My father's doctor recommended either Dr. Shumway in San Francisco or Dr. Cooley in Houston. At that time, my brother lived in the San Francisco area and I had just moved to Galveston. Since my wife and I were both doctors and my brother was in business, my father chose to come to Houston so I could make the arrangements. Denton Cooley had a rule that he would not do CABG (coronary artery bypass graft, pronounced cabbage) on anyone over age sixty-five. My father was in such good shape, however, that he waved the rule and did the CABG procedure. My dad spent six weeks with us in Texas after surgery and did very well after that.

In their fifteenth year of retirement, they were part of a close group of fourteen couples who partied together and formed a tight group of friends. During that year, however, one member of each couple died, except my parents. The surviving spouses all moved back to wherever they had lived before retirement. My parents were left with many younger people with whom to associate.

Life was hard in the Ozarks—groceries were fifteen miles away, the mail was one mile away, boat docks had to be moved frequently, and the winters were cold and dreary. They decided to try Phoenix in the winters, and Colorado in the summers. Dad could fly fish for trout and enjoy the mountains in the summer, while my mother read and explored the shops. In Phoenix, he took up lapidary work at the community center at their retirement community. He still kept very busy. My parents had several close friends from Normal who retired to Phoenix who formed their social group.

My mother died of leukemia when I was forty-five years old. She was seventy-five and my father was eighty. Both my brother and I tried to get our father to move close to one of us, but he decided to live on as a bachelor in Phoenix, socializing with friends and his rock shop buddies.

A year later, he came to visit us in Galveston, so I took the opportunity to check his eyes. He was getting a cataract in his remaining eye, but could still see well enough to drive. I hooked him up with an ophthalmologist in the Phoenix area who followed him for the progression of the cataract. I began thinking about who I would send him to for the cataract surgery. I received reports from Phoenix that his cataract was not progressing.

Three years after my mother died, when my father was eighty-three, my brother was diagnosed with carcinoma of the bile ducts. My brother lived only three months after the diagnosis. This was a severe blow to my father, who was battling prostate cancer that had spread to the bladder and may possibly have metastasized by that time.

Three months after my brother died I went out to Phoenix to be with my dad for surgery on his prostate. He insisted that we have a steak dinner on the night before his surgery. After dinner, while we were watching TV, he told me to get his stethoscope from his bedroom and listen to his abdomen. He had become distended and uncomfortable. As he suspected, he had developed an ileus, which is paralysis and distension of the intestines. Since he was scheduled for surgery the following morning, I tried to call his urologist. I reached his partner, who told me he did not know my father and that I should just take him to the emergency room.

When we arrived at the emergency room, my father was so distended that he could not bend at the waist to sit in a chair. He was only comfortable when he was lying on his back. I finally convinced the receptionist that he could not sit in the waiting room, so she let him lay on a gurney. When they took him into the emergency room and hooked him to monitors, he had a heart rate of about 140, but no chest pain or other major cardiac symptoms. The EKG looked great except for the rate, and especially for someone who had undergone quadruple bypass surgery. He was passed back and forth between the internists and the surgeons, neither of whom could determine why he had the ileus. He was admitted to the hospital at about 1:00 AM, and they started treating him with enemas.

I went home to get some sleep and returned at about eight o'clock in the morning. There was an empty catheter bag on the side of the bed. When I asked the nurse when the bag was last changed, she checked the chart and found that it had been attached at 1:00 AM and had not been emptied. I pointed out to her that he had not put out any urine for seven to eight hours. She called the doctor. She returned with a hypodermic syringe and gave my father a shot. I asked what it was, and she replied "Lasix." It seemed obvious to me that he had renal obstruction and I thought a diuretic would only make things worse. In about half an hour, he suddenly started putting out a stream of urine and put out more than a liter in about ten minutes. The Lasix had blown him open. It could have ruptured one of his kidneys or ureters.

When the results of the CAT scan came back, it showed that he had blockage of both ureters at the bladder, with dilated ureters and kidneys. His cancer had spread to involve the area where the ureters entered the bladder. This was the cause of his ileus. They still treated him with enemas. When the doctor came in on rounds, I took him out to the hallway to ask him why they were not using a nasogastric tube to treat the abdominal distention of the ileus, as I had been taught to do. He said he had never heard of using an N-G tube for ileus. He then remembered that my father was a physician and suggested that we ask him what he thought. When the doctor asked my father if he would mind an N-G tube in the morning if he had not improved by then, my father's reply was "What in the hell have you been waiting for, put it in now! That's the way to treat ileus!"

The nurse came in about two minutes later to pass the tube, and within an hour his distention was gone and he was comfortable. One of his doctor's partners told me that they planned to put stents in the ureters to keep the cancer from obstructing them, but that they would wait a week or so for the tissues to quiet down and shrink to normal size. At no time had I seen his named doctor, only his partners. I went back to Texas to await a call before they put in stents to keep him open. They thought it might be about two weeks.

On the following Sunday, Easter, I got a phone call about 7:00 AM from friends of my father's in Phoenix, who told me that they had been called to the hospital because my father had taken a turn for the worse. I immediately called the nursing station at the hospital. I held for about five minutes while they tried to find the nurse, but I was cut off. When I called back, the nurse was there and told me that he had taken a turn for the worse. I reminded her that I was a physician and asked what had happened. She told me that they had found him about thirty minutes before with no vital signs (no pulse, blood pressure, or respirations). In other words, he was dead. I asked what had been done, and she reminded me of his living will specifying no resuscitation. They were waiting for the intern from the emergency room to pronounce him dead. I asked her to have his urologist call me in Texas when he made rounds.

About two o'clock in the afternoon, the physician called me. He started off the conversation with the statement that he "was sorry to hear that my father had died." I thought that summed up the level of involvement he had experienced with my father—that he had only heard that my father had died.

I asked that an autopsy be performed and that the report be sent to Dr. Denton Cooley in Texas. I knew that my father was the oldest patient to have bypasses by Dr. Cooley, and that he would want to know about the condition of the bypasses thirteen years later. I also wanted to know if they were sure that he had prostate cancer rather than bladder cancer. My father had smoked all of his life, and smokers are susceptible to bladder cancer. I think the doctor felt guilty and was worried that I was going to sue him over my father's death, because he told me that autopsies were no longer performed. The pathologists were afraid of AIDS. I asked him if he had any reason to believe that my father had AIDS, and he admitted that he did not. He said that an autopsy could be done if the body was embalmed, but he knew that my father wanted to be cremated. Embalming was not necessary and would be an extra expense. Also, the cost of the funeral would pay for the transportation of the body from the hospital to the mortuary, but not the trip back and forth for embalming. By this time I was feeling very frustrated and told him to have the embalming and the autopsy done and send me the bill. We flew out to Phoenix the next day to hold a memorial service and see my fathers ashes scattered, by airplane, on Red Mountain, where we had spread my mother's ashes three years before.

I never received a report of the autopsy, and I doubt that Dr. Cooley did either. My father's death, in a quiet way on Easter morning, when he knew he was dying of cancer, was a blessing. He told me on the way to the hospital that he would probably not come back to his home. If he left the hospital at all it would be to a nursing home. He pointed out the one he wanted on our way to the hospital.

He had a full life. He had cared for hundreds of good people and was very proud of that. He sat in the audience at high school graduations and told my mother, "I delivered that one," or "I set her fractures when she fell off a horse," and many more. Many of the people he repaired during the war never saw him again and may not have recognized that he saved their life or a limb for them.

He was proudest of his work in the military, an assignment for which my mother never forgave him. He practiced before Medicare came into being. He had many patients who had retired and had limited income. When they needed surgery, he performed it and sent them a bill for the usual amount, but when they came to him saying that they would have difficulty paying the fee, he told them to pay him what they thought they could afford. Then he would "charge the rest of it to the dust and let the rain settle it."

I thought of this many times during my practice years. Although my patients had Medicare, there were two ways to do Medicare billing. One is to bill the patient directly. The patient usually has to pay the doctor more than the co-pay.

The other method of billing is called "accepting assignment." Medicare sets the price and pays 80 percent. The doctor bills the patient for the co-pay of 20 percent of the Medicare allowable, and absorbs the difference between his fee and the Medicare allowable. Had I ever gouged the patient by not billing directly, I am sure that my father's ashes would have become a dust devil on Red Mountain.

I was relieved from deciding who I should send my father to for cataract surgery. He died before his vision, in his only eye, decreased to what he needed to drive a car or read for pleasure, so he did not need surgery.

I learned a lot caring for my father. I have always had difficulty intervening in the care of family members. When I see that the care given is different from what I would have done, I want to speak up, but I am not the doctor treating the patient. This happened with my father, my mother, and my brother. Usually my patience wore thin and I spoke up. My brother did not want my help, but my mother and father welcomed it.

My father was an old-time private practitioner who knew his patients. He always did what was best for them. He was dedicated to them in a way that was sometimes a detriment to his wife and family. I strove for this commitment to my patients to follow his example. I also tried to minimize the inconvenience to my family that a medical career requires. I was glad when my wife, Letha, entered medicine, because it gave her a better understanding of the requirements of medical practice. The longer I practiced, the more I appreciated what my father had done—he came from a rural farming family, put himself through years of school, and cared for thousands of patients.

14

<o>

Bad Trifocals

IT IS GENERALLY CONSIDERED POOR practice for a doctor to take care of his or her own family, except for minor ailments. I never did surgery on either of my parents, but I was frequently called upon to fit them with glasses. My parents came to Richmond every year to visit while I was in my residency training, and one year my mother complained that she could not see well with the glasses that she had used for over ten years and asked me to prescribe new lenses for her.

I took her to the clinic after hours and examined her eyes. Everything was normal, but she could only see about 20/40 with her glasses, just legal to drive. I read her old glasses and learned that she had a small degree of astigmatism. However, when I measured her for glasses, I discovered that she had about twice as much astigmatism as the amount in her glasses, and at a different axis. I prescribed glasses for her with the new power and axis that I had determined. With the new correction, she could see 20/20.

She waited until she returned home to Arkansas to get the prescription filled. She called me a week later to tell me that she could not see through the glasses and they made her feel dizzy. I was sure that this was a result of my changing her astigmatism correction. I explained to her that she would get used to it in about two to three weeks. She was not very happy with my instructions, but she did adjust in about three weeks.

Some ophthalmologists will not correct the full amount for high astigmatism and rarely change the axis of astigmatism. They often cut the correction in half and will only move the axis a small amount so they will not get these complaints. I think that is why there was such a big difference between her old glasses and what I had measured for her.

My mother had her glasses changed several times over the years when she came to visit me. When I lived in Texas I examined her for glasses. She was getting early cataracts, which changed her myopia (nearsightedness), and she needed new glasses to keep up with the changes. I carefully refracted her again and gave her a prescription for trifocals, like what she had been wearing.

Again, she waited until she returned home, in Arizona, to get her prescription filled. When we visited Arizona for the holidays, she complained that she could not read fine print and that, at times, everything seemed out of focus. She complained that she could not read the stock quotes in the paper. She had gotten stylish new frames. The upper curve of the frame followed the curve of her eyebrows and she liked them very much.

I examined the glasses and discovered that they had cut the lenses to fit the frames in such a way that the trifocal segments were very low in the lens. She was trying to read through the upper, middle distance, segment of the trifocal part. She had to throw her head all the way back to see through the bottom, or near, part of the lenses. I told her that they were made wrong and that she should go back where she got them and have the lenses remade.

The next day, I went with her to the optical shop. My mother tried to explain to the optician that the segments were too low and that she could not use them. He insisted that they were positioned exactly how they should be. He showed us that the top of the trifocal was two millimeters below the edge of her lower eyelid and told us that the position was exactly as it should be.

At that point I stepped in and showed him that she could not see through the lower segment when they were positioned that way, making the near segment useless. He argued that they were as they should be. I told him he should remake the lenses to position the top of the top segment at the level of the pupil edge, two millimeters *above* the lower eyelid. He said that he would not remake the lenses, but he would bend the nose pieces to raise the frames and the segments to the lower eyelid.

My mother lifted the glasses and looked in the mirror. She declared that they looked ridiculous. Her eyebrows were visible through the lenses and the frames were up on her forehead. This solution was unacceptable. The optician said that he would not change the glasses.

At this point I lost my usual restraint. I took out my business card and gave it to the optician. It told him that I was chairman of the Department of Ophthalmology at the University of Texas and that I knew what I was talking about. I explained to him that I was perfectly willing to explain to his boss that he did not know how to fit either bifocals or trifocals and that we could see if his boss believed his employee or a chairman of a department of ophthalmology at a major university. I also warned him that it might cost him his job, because I was sure that I was correct. I suggested that he might need to go back to his textbooks and read up on the subject.

At this point he capitulated completely and asked me to mark her present lenses to show where I wanted the segments to be located. Two days later we picked up a pair of glasses that were made correctly. My mother wore those glasses until she died.

Refraction (measuring for glasses) is part art and part optical science. It is necessary to know how the patient uses the glasses to get it right. Many people are unhappy with their new glasses. Some have to adapt to the correct glasses. Sometimes I made a mistake and had to correct it. The optometrists and opticians who work with ophthalmologists often change the glasses for free to keep the referrals.

I learned several things from taking care of my mother. First, that it was a mistake. I learned that family members are not very forgiving when you practice medicine on them. Her expectations of my abilities were so high that she did not expect to have to get used to her new glasses. My mother was unhappy the first time I changed her glasses, although the new glasses contained the correct prescription. I think that she thought that I had made another mistake on her last pair. I proved to her that I knew what I was doing when I forced the optician to change her glasses and the new glasses worked beautifully after that.

15

The Shakespearian Actor

M R. M. CAME TO THE Massachusetts Eye and Ear Infirmary to learn if anything could be done to restore his vision. He had lost all vision in his right eye several years before. More recently he had gone through a series of problems with his left eye that had left him with very little vision. He had first undergone cataract surgery. After the cataract extraction he had developed the complication of epithelial down growth, wherein tissue from the surface of the eye grows down through the incision and invades the eye. The tissue spreads around the back of the cornea and over the surface of the iris. This eventually covers the trabecular meshwork where the aqueous humor escapes from the eye. Once half of the meshwork is covered, the fluid backs up into the eye, increasing the pressure. This is a form of secondary glaucoma that will eventually destroy all vision.

Once this complication was discovered, he was given radiation therapy to destroy the invading tissue. Destroying the layer of epithelium, which covered the back surface of the cornea, also damaged the normal corneal endothelium on the back surface of the cornea and may also have caused radiation necrosis (tissue death) of the retina.

When I first saw Mr. M. he had no vision in the right eye and only questionable vision in the left eye. When I waved a hand in front of his left eye and asked him which way the hand was moving, up and down or left and right, he could not tell me. However, he insisted that he could see his own hand when he moved it up and down or left and right in front of his eye, and he always got it right.

He could accurately tell when a light shining in his left eye was turned on or off, which meant that he had some visual function. His cornea was white with corneal edema and bullous keratopathy (corneal blisters), so the retina could not be seen.

Mr. M. was a ninety-six-year-old retired itinerant Shakespearian actor. He had lost his first wife many years ago, but had married his assistant and secretary two or three years ago. She had helped him write a novel before he married her. Writing the book and marrying his assistant had both taken place after he had lost his vision. Dr. Dohlman determined that Mr. M. had never seen his wife and wanted to see again just so he could look at her.

That motivation was enough for Dr. Dohlman to agree to do a corneal transplant to try to restore his vision. He was put on the waiting list and was soon called into the hospital for his corneal transplant. Mildred, the cornea service secretary, received a call from the admissions office saying that Mr. M. would not come into the hospital because they told him that his wife could not sleep in the same bed with him while he was in the hospital. The hospital reached a compromise by putting a rollaway bed in his room for her. We all speculated about whether she actually slept in bed with him anyway.

The corneal transplant surgery went well, and the pathology study of the recipient button (the part of the cornea removed) showed that the epithelial down growth and the normal corneal endothelium had been killed by the radiation and that the down growth would not be a problem for the new cornea.

Following surgery, Mr. M. was seen in the clinic for several days during his hospitalization. On the first day, his wife brought several copies of his book to the clinic and passed them around to everybody who worked in the cornea service. When she came in on the third day, she asked everyone to whom she had given a book to pay twenty-five dollars for it or give it back. Several people had taken the book home but did not want to keep it and pay for it, so there was a mad scramble to bring the books back to the clinic and give them back to his wife. Dr. Dohlman bought a copy to keep her happy.

Once the cornea had cleared after the surgery, we could see the retina and found it to have significant degenerative changes because of the radiation he had received. Once again, he could see light, but he was correct in determining which direction a hand was moving in front of his face only when it was his own hand.

About one month after the transplant, when the graft was clear, Dr. Dohlman asked Mr. M. whether he had seen his ninety-year-old "bride." His only reply was "Yup." He did not elaborate further. We all thought that this was a very short answer for a Shakespearean actor to make.

I thought that Dr. Dohlman had been right in deciding to operate on this gentleman who had come from a long distance to try to restore his vision. The poor, but present, vision that he demonstrated before surgery could have been caused by his cloudy cornea and might have improved significantly following surgery if the retina had not been damaged by the radiation. We could not determine whether the retina had been damaged before doing the surgery. Because of this experience, I later operated on several people who had lost almost all of their vision, and I was successful at restoring vision to most of those people.

16

A Conflict of Interest

IT IS THE DUTY OF a physician to try to alleviate pain and suffering and to treat the disease of the patient in such a way as to shorten the illness as much as possible. I can recall one case where we may have had a conflict of interest with doing this.

One of the patients we treated at the Massachusetts Eye and Ear Infirmary had a severe infection of his cornea. He had been treated at the infirmary for several years for recurrent bouts of herpes simplex of the cornea. One day he came in with white infiltrates in his cornea that extended from the front surface to deep within the cornea. His eye was very red and pus was coming from it. He had developed a bacterial or fungal infection secondary to his viral herpes.

We started him on antibiotic eyedrops, every two hours, and had him return in two days. When he returned two days later, he showed some improvement, but still needed intensive treatment to get rid of the infection. When he was ready to leave, he called the fellows over to where he was sitting and asked if anyone could use two tickets to see the Boston Bruins play hockey at the North Station Arena that night. He told us that he had been to a hockey game two nights before, but that the lights in the arena were so bright that he could not open his eyes to watch the game. He wanted us to have the tickets because we were taking care of him.

One of the fellows took the tickets and took his wife to the game. When the fellow came into the clinic the next morning, he could not wait to tell us what great seats they were. He was in the first row of the balcony at center ice. When the patient returned several days later, he was improving, but he was still light-sensitive. He offered us two more tickets to a hockey game. The fellow who had taken the first tickets asked him how he had obtained such great tickets. He told us that he worked in the ticket office for the Boston Red Sox, so he was able to get very good seats for hockey.

At that time, the Bruins were leading the league, and it was impossible to get seats at the box office. People would sleep overnight in sleeping bags on the floor of the North Station to be first in line to purchase tickets for obstructed seats so they could get into the game to stand or hop seats. We were getting front row center seats. It took him over two weeks to get over this infection sufficiently to be comfortable with the lights in the North Station Arena. We joked among ourselves that we were working against ourselves by trying to treat his infection, but we did not decrease his treatments.

Once the infection was treated and sterile, we fit him with a soft contact lens so that he could tolerate the pain and go to the hockey games. He was a big hockey fan, so as soon as he could tolerate the lights, the supply of hockey tickets dried up. I did get to see Bobby Orr and Phil Esposito play when it was my turn to get the tickets.

I cannot recall another time when I was ever tempted to prolong the treatment of a patient because I was receiving some secondary gain. Some physicians will continue to see patients more often than necessary so that they can bill for the visits. I did have patients try to bribe or browbeat me to write false letters for them so that they could get out of work, avoid fines, sue for damages, or collect insurance payments that they did not deserve. I lost several of those patients who probably went looking for a doctor who would lie for them. A physician must maintain integrity in all cases so that he can be trusted when recommending various forms of treatment, especially surgery.

Although we joked about a conflict of interest, no one did anything to prolong this patient's pain so that we could see more hockey. I was proud of the fellows that I worked with at MEEI. I was sure that Dr. Dohlman would never have approved of any delay in this man's treatment. Some ethicists feel that we should have turned down the tickets to avoid the appearance of a conflict, but I don't think we would have changed our therapy. Only the guilty need to hide.

I rarely recommended surgery to a patient the first time I saw him or her because usually all of the possible nonsurgical treatments had not been exhausted. This also gave patients time to get used to the diagnosis and consider the alternatives before they were asked to decide on surgical intervention.

There are too many physicians practicing today who are more concerned about their house, car, or yacht payments than morality in patient care. Some are ego-involved and feel that if they, "the best surgeon around," do not do the surgery before it is needed, that someone "less qualified" will do the surgery anyway. This is self-serving and egotistical.

17

The Miraculous Unveiling

THERE IS AN ONGOING CONTROVERSY whether religious faith has anything to do with healing. My mother was a Christian Scientist until she married my father. She was a great believer in religious faith and wellness being related. I worked for twelve years in a Catholic hospital and learned that the nuns certainly believed in the power of prayer to heal the sick. Most religions pray for the sick. Long before my years in the Catholic hospital, I had a case, involving a possible miracle, which made one patient a very evangelistic Christian.

I saw Christine after her miraculous event, but she was more than happy to tell me about it. She and her father both had Fuchs' dystrophy, and they both had developed corneal edema, which decreased their vision. Consequently, they were both scheduled for corneal transplants. Two donor corneas became available to their surgeon at the same time, so father and daughter received back-to-back corneal transplants on the same day.

Both transplants appeared to go very smoothly, and success was anticipated for both patients. However, on the day following surgery, the daughter was found to have a very unusual complication. When the diseased cornea was removed from her eye, the posterior layer, Descemet's membrane, was still attached to the cornea in three places, so it peeled loose from the rest of the cornea as the tissue was removed, and the membrane remained in the eye. It was suspended by three points of attachment that formed an equilateral triangle. Descemet's membrane is very thin and is optically clear, so the fact that it remained in the eye was not noticed during the surgery.

The surgeon sewed the new cornea into place over the patient's original Descemet's membrane and did not discover the remaining membrane until he saw Christine at the slit lamp in his office the following morning. Because of this case, I proceeded to always grasp the iris gently with a micro forceps after removing a diseased cornea. If Descemet's membrane is still in the eye, it would prevent the forceps from touching the iris and I would know that the membrane was still there and must be removed before putting the donor button in the cornea.

Tension on the membrane caused it to tighten and wrinkle, disrupting the optical pathway of the light entering the eye. This decreased her vision considerably, but the surgeon did not tell her the reason, only explaining that it took a while after the surgery before her vision would clear. The transplant itself was doing very well and remained clear in front of the wrinkled membrane. The surgeon planned to wait several months until the grafted cornea had recovered from the surgery before removing the wrinkled membrane, using a needle knife to cut one or more of the three attachments.

Christine was a religious person and went to church several times a week. Her church occasionally showed religious movies on Wednesday nights, which she usually attended. One night she attended a movie depicting the life of Christ. As she relates her miracle, when the story of Jesus reached the resurrection, her vision suddenly became very clear. She covered her eye that had not been operated on and discovered that she saw clearly with the operated eye. She believed that a miracle had happened.

As soon as she arrived home that night, Christine called the surgeon to tell him about the miracle of healing that she had experienced. He told her to come to the office the next morning so that he could examine her. When he saw her at the slit lamp the next day, he saw that the superior attachment had come loose and the membrane had scrolled to a compact tube across the lower edge of the transplanted tissue. It was below the level of the pupil, so her optical pathway was clear and free of any distortion. She did not need any further intervention to restore her vision.

When I saw Christine a year after the unveiling, the scroll of Descemet's membrane was still attached in two places at the lower edge of the transplant. Her vision was very good with glasses, and she was extremely pleased with her vision and her physician. Most importantly to her, she was pleased with her Lord and Savior, Jesus Christ. She offered me a Bible, but I told her to give it to someone who did not have one, since I had several Bibles and I was already a believer.

Throughout college and medical school, I thought a lot about the incongruity of science and faith. I had studied science and had learned about evolution and Darwin's theories. My wife took a graduate school course in the evolution of the nervous system taught by the Nobel Laureate Dr. Rita Levi-Montalcini. The course taught that the nervous system evolved through a succession of species, adding functions and adapting existing systems to serve the increasingly complex organisms until reaching near perfection in the human species.

I was told that Dr. Levi-Montalcini lived in Italy during the beginning of World War II. Because of persecution of her Jewish faith, she was brought from Italy to St. Louis by a Jewish German anatomist who had escaped from Germany. He taught her English, which she spoke with an Italian and German accent, and she did brilliant research at Washington University. I never heard how she reconciled her Jewish faith with the theory of evolution that she taught.

As I began to practice medicine, I saw many things happen to patients that I could not explain scientifically, and I began to believe in divine intervention. The more we uncover molecular biology and the complexity of biological systems, from DNA to Nano tubes, the harder it is not to believe in an intelligent design by a divine being. Whether that being is called God, Messiah, Christian Trinity, Allah, or some other name remains a mystery of faith to me.

Many years after my father retired from the practice of medicine he told me that he had developed a deep faith and belief in God because of the things he witnessed during his thirty-plus years in treating patients.

Christine was a believer before her surgery and continued to attend church functions after her transplant. When her Descemet's scroll broke and cleared her vision while she was watching the resurrection of Jesus, her religion became deeply personal for her.

People of faith would say there is a connection between the movie and her miracle.

One of my patients gave me a barn wood sign that said, "God heals, the doctor takes the fee." I often looked at it that way.

Part II

Children and Young Patients
Ages: Newborn to Twenty-five

1969–1991

CHILDREN AND YOUNG PATIENTS HAVE always been a special interest for me. Some of my most interesting and rewarding cases were children.

The visual system is not fully developed at birth, but reaches full anatomical form before the first year of life. The visual ability continues to develop connections to the brain until age six to eight years. Interference of vision from one eye, like a cataract or crossed eyes, may lead to a "lazy" eye, known as amblyopia. Each eye develops its own representation in the occipital cortex (back of the brain). This representation continues to improve until the age of six to eight years. If vision is blocked in one eye, growth of this representation is stopped and withdrawal begins. If vision is reestablished, the representation recovers unless the child is past the age for it. If vision is not restored before this critical age, vision is permanently impaired in the affected eye, a permanently "lazy" eye. The clock is always running in children until visual connections are permanently established at somewhere between age six and eight.

Our major learning years are between birth and twenty-one. Interruption of vision during this time often leads to life-changing defects in knowledge and physical abilities. Therefore, restoring vision in children, teenagers, and young adults takes on a special meaning and urgency.

The innocence of small children also makes taking care of them more rewarding. My wife, the pediatrician, often reminded me that children are fragile, developing diseases very rapidly. They can go sour in moments, but they can also recover just as fast with the right intervention. This exuberant healing of childhood is often counterproductive to good visual function. When children are injured or have surgery, they pour out large amounts of fibrin or epithelium to heal the wound. This excessive fibrin forms large scars that later contract, causing distortion. When these scars occur in soft tissue in the eye, such as the retina or the cornea, the contraction may tear the tissue or distort the optical properties. Excessive growth of epithelium may grow into the wound, delaying healing and causing other problems. Fibrin may deposit on either side of a detached retina and later shrink, pulling the retina away from the choroid again.

Extra steps must be taken to avoid these complications. For these reasons, I have placed these cases in a separate section of the book.

18

◄○►

The Little Cross-Eyed Girl

I WAS WORKING IN MY EXAM room one day during the second year of my residency when I received a call from one of the pediatric residents. He told me he was seeing a six-year-old girl who had very crossed eyes and asked if I could see her. Since the second year of residency is the year for learning surgery and other treatments to straighten eyes, I was more than happy to oblige. I had her sent immediately to the clinic.

When I saw her, she was accompanied by both parents. They were very concerned by her crossed eyes and wanted to know if she needed surgery. I examined her and determined that much of her crossing was because she was farsighted. Children who are very farsighted are focused beyond the moon and must accommodate (focus) from far to near just to see at far distances. The brain combines focusing the eyes with turning them inward to fuse the vision from the two eyes into one image. The pupil also constricts to improve depth-of-field. These three actions combine to form what is called the synkinetic near response. When the child purposely looks at anything within range, the eyes focus. The near response is then focused for near, and the child's eyes cross. The eyes appear crossed at all times that the child is focusing on something. This can be combined, in some children, with misalignment of the eyes from a different cause.

To determine whether there was underlying permanent crossing, I put drops into her eyes to paralyze her ability to focus so that I could measure all of her farsightedness. Children who are farsighted

77

focus partially all of the time. To determine how farsighted the eye really is, it is necessary to paralyze this permanent focusing using eyedrops.

Without the drops, she measured two diopters of farsightedness in each eye. A diopter is a measure of the strength of an optical lens. I made up these glasses in trial frames. With this power of glasses, about half of the crossing went away. Once the drops were effective, she had four diopters of farsightedness in each eye. Four diopter glasses made her eyes perfectly straight. I had a cure for this little girl. All she had to do was wear glasses. No surgery was necessary.

When I explained this to her parents, they told me that they had taken her to see a local optometrist who specialized in children. He had told them that she was farsighted and needed glasses, but that they would not straighten her eyes. The parents had already paid for the glasses and did not want to buy another pair. I knew that optometrists were not allowed to use eyedrops in Virginia, so he had not determined the full amount of farsightedness. I also knew that a partial correction would not straighten her eyes. She would still be at risk of developing a lazy eye that could become permanently blind when she became eight years old. I asked the parents for the name of the optometrist who had examined the child so I could talk with him.

I called the optometrist to tell him what I had found so that he could give her the correct power to straighten her eyes. He was clearly offended to be called by a resident and proceeded to "teach me" about children with crossed eyes. He told me that these children were brain damaged and would never be straight. He went on to tell me that she would never tolerate the prescription that I proposed and would not wear the glasses. He explained to me that he had the child wear the frames for several weeks without lenses. He would then put lenses with 0.5 diopters of power in the frames and have her wear the glasses for three months. Then he would add 0.5 diopters to each lens every three months, selling a new pair of lenses each time. At about one year he would have the full 2.0 diopter correction in place, but she would probably need more by then because they always did. (I knew that as part of the far sightedness is corrected by glasses, they relax some of the permanent focusing, accepting more correction).

When I asked him about his refraction technique and whether he had used cycloplegic drops to paralyze her accommodation, he told me he used cartoon movies to keep the child focused at distance and did not need drops. When I tried to explain the residual accommodation that the drops would uncover, he dismissed me as an inexperienced resident who did not know what he was talking about.

This was very frustrating to me, because I knew more about the problem than this optometrist, who did not understand the pharmacology and physiology of accommodative esotropia (crossed eyes due to farsightedness). Optometrists, not being physicians, were not allowed to use drugs and did not understand their use in this disease. Not being able to uncover the full amount of farsightedness, he explained away his incomplete cure as "brain damage." I knew that the eyes could be completely cured because the full, 4.0 diopter lenses did straighten the eyes when the little girl was in the exam chair. We usually use atropine ointment for several days to block accommodation (focusing) when we dispense the glasses. The child cannot see without the glasses, but can see perfectly well with the glasses. By the time the atropine wears off in three weeks, the child has adapted to the glasses and there is no residual accommodation, because the glasses do all of the focusing. The eye accommodates normally for near vision and the eyes turn inward the appropriate amount for near vision.

I tried to explain this to the parents of the little girl. Even though I could show them that her eyes were straight with my correction, they maintained that the other "doctor" was older and in a private office; they had paid good money for his advice, and they had already purchased glasses from him. I told them that they could return to the clinic if the glasses they had purchased did not straighten her eyes the way the glasses I had put on her had. Unfortunately, I never saw the little girl again.

There are three levels of eye care providers in the marketplace: the optician, who makes and fits glasses and contacts lenses; the optometrist, who can refract for glasses and contacts and sells them to patients; and the ophthalmologist, who is a physician who is licensed to prescribe medications and do surgery. Optometrists have two to four years of optometry school after high school or some college. Ophthalmologists have three or four years of college followed by four years of medical school, a year of internship, and at least three years of training in ophthalmology. Training in optometry is improving, but it is still less rigorous than training for ophthalmology. In many states, optometrists are trying to get legislative approval to prescribe drugs and do surgery, even though they have not been trained as medical doctors or surgeons. Many states allow them to prescribe some, but not all, medications. Oklahoma allows optometrists to do laser surgery, and other states are trying to allow this. Ophthalmologists believe that only people who have been trained to be physicians should be allowed to do surgery and prescribe prescription drugs.

This patient taught me that some people are more impressed by age and appearance of physicians than objective proof of a needed prescription—in this case that the glasses I wanted the little girl to have completely straightened her eyes. This also taught me that the pediatric optometrist did not know how to treat this common problem in children. He was also ripping off the parents by selling them multiple pairs of glasses while not giving them the appropriate correction.

I think the fact that the parents had already paid for glasses also influenced them to make the wrong decision. I often wondered if I should have exposed the optometrist for not knowing what he was doing. I discussed this with Dr. McNeer, our faculty pediatric ophthalmologist. He advised me that I could get into legal trouble and be sued for restraint of trade for criticizing the optometrist.

This was the first time that I had a patient, or in this case the patient's family, tell me that medical advice or medications that are paid for are better and worth more than free advice or free medicine. Later, I saw that patients who received free medications, courtesy of the State of Texas, considered them ineffective since they were free, and did not bother to take them.

I was sorry for the little girl that I could not help her by straightening her eyes and thus avoiding the possibility of a lazy eye. When her eyes crossed, she would suppress one to avoid double vision. The suppressed eye could become lazy unless she had one eye patched, alternately, to make her use each eye part of the time to maintain the representation of that eye in the brain.

19

The Baby with a Congenital Orbital Teratoma

I RECEIVED A CALL FROM MY wife one day when I was a chief resident. She was a pediatric intern serving on the wards. She wanted me to come to the ward immediately to see a baby girl that she had just admitted. She called me directly so I would respond to the case before the written consult arrived at the clinic.

I went immediately to the children's hospital two blocks down the hill to see this child. She was less than a day old and had been sent up from South Hill, Virginia, because one of her eyes protruded from the eye socket, causing deformation of her face. It was obvious that there was something behind the eye pushing it forward and to the side. The other eye appeared normal. Because the eye was pushed forward, it was difficult for the baby to close that eye, especially when she was asleep. This caused the front of her eye to dry and lose the sheen on the surface.

The most common tumor in the eye socket in a newborn is a rhabdomyosarcoma, which is a malignant tumor that metastasizes early and is often fatal. I worked up the case and presented her at Grand Rounds that week. After much discussion it was decided that we needed to know what kind of tumor this was before deciding what major surgery to perform. When she was one week old, we took her to the operating room and put her under general anesthesia to do a biopsy and possible removal of the mass if it appeared to be a simple procedure. General anesthesia was risky in a week-old child, but the chance that this was a rhabdomyosarcoma, which might metastasize early, forced our hand.

We made a skin incision in the lower eyelid over the spot where the tumor pushed out below the eye. We immediately exposed a blue-black, round mass. Dr. Geereats, my supervising surgeon, suggested that I take a biopsy from the mass. When I cut into the mass to remove a piece of it for microscopic examination, it suddenly spurted clear fluid. The mass turned out to be a cystic space from which clear fluid continued to drain. We collected some of the clear fluid and sent it to the laboratory to be analyzed. We were afraid that we had entered an encephalocele or meningocele. These would be bulges of brain or meninges (the membranes that cover the brain,) through a hole in the orbital wall. Either one would contain clear cerebrospinal fluid. We decided to stop with only the biopsy, close the incision, and wait for pathology to tell us what the biopsy showed.

The fluid contained protein, sugar, and a few white blood cells, which was typical of cerebrospinal fluid. The biopsy was reported as neurological tissue. To determine if this was from the cranial vault (i.e., brain or meninges), we needed to demonstrate a connection between the cranium and the eye socket. This was before CT scans and MRIs. Bones in newborns are poorly formed and are not calcified, so stereo X-ray would not work. The only technique in use at that time was a pneumoencephalogram. In this procedure, sterile air is injected into the space between the brain and the meninges at the base of the brain to create a bubble. The patient is then positioned in various postures to make the bubble float around certain parts of the brain to outline them for x-ray. If there is a communication between the cranium and eye socket, the air should enter the eye socket and be seen on the X-ray. The radiologists turned the baby every way they could to get air to flow into the eye socket, but could not make air go into the eye socket or even show a dimple from a bulge in the cavity wall.

These results made us believe that the tumor was not connected to the brain. It was becoming larger, causing more distortion of the face and pushing the eye further forward. If it was malignant, it should be removed as soon as possible. If it was benign, it should be removed before it damaged the eyeball and permanently deformed the face. Another presentation at Grand Rounds resulted in the conclusion that the eye socket should be explored and the tumor removed if possible. The location and attachments of the tumor could give us valuable information as to the type of tumor she had. Dr. D. Dupont Guerry, III, the department chairman, suggested that I have Dr. Bob King assist me with the operation. When I asked Dr. King, he told me that he had never done or seen an orbital exploration and suggested Dr. Chip Morgan, another attending, who had spent time at the National Eye Institute. He had never done an orbital exploration either, and he told me that the only ophthalmologist in town who did orbital explorations was Dr. Guerry.

I called Dr. Guerry and asked him to assist me. He said he was busy and could only operate on Wednesday morning, when he would usually be at Grand Rounds. I called the operating room to schedule the case and was curtly told that ophthalmology only had operating time on Monday and Friday. I went back and forth between the OR and Dr. Guerry. Neither would budge. I decided to discuss it with Dr. Guerry at Grand Rounds and possibly bring enough pressure from the other attending physicians to get him to operate on Monday or Friday.

Because my wife was the intern on the pediatrics inpatient ward and she was following the case closely with me, she managed to talk the pediatric attending physicians into giving us permission to operate when the child was three weeks old. The baby was otherwise healthy and on frequent feeding of formula. Only two hours notice was necessary for the pediatricians to prepare her for surgery if we could get a time.

On Wednesday, as I was walking through the back door of the clinic to attend Grand Rounds, Dr. Guerry hailed me from the parking lot next door. He said something like, "Where's your kid? We need to get her to the operating room." He had prevailed on the operating room to let us operate that morning. I called my wife to prepare the baby for surgery. I called the anesthesia department to request MD-only anesthesia because of the age of the child. The pediatricians had requested that we have only MDs (no students or nurse anesthetists) to put her to sleep as a condition to their allowing us to operate. The anesthesiologists agreed to have

MD-only anesthesia. Since this was such a rare case, all of the senior eye residents were excused from Grand Rounds to watch and assist.

Within an hour, four surgeons were huddled around the small head of this baby, who was asleep under the direction of two MD anesthesiologists. I had read extensively on doing orbital (eye socket) explorations, but Dr. Guerry was the only one in the room who had done one. He had never done one on a child this age, but he was the most senior and probably the most experienced eye surgeon in Virginia. I proceeded to do the operation under his direction and with his assistance. We made an incision from the corner of the eye to the ear and exposed the lateral rim of the eye socket. Since it was only cartilage, not bone at this age, we easily opened the lateral wall and exposed the contents of the eye socket.

We found a two-by-two-by-three-centimeter bluish-black mass, which was smooth and not attached firmly to the eyeball, the muscles, or the optic nerve. It was located behind the eyeball, and, except for a small extension below, it was between the four rectus muscles and mostly within the muscle cone. The lateral rectus muscle was stretched thinly over the mass, but it was easily freed. Tracing the mass posteriorly and nasally in the eye socket, we determined that it was attached to the bone of the nasal wall of the eye socket. We dissected it from the bony attachment and removed the tumor. Dr. Guerry was anxious to determine what kind of tumor it was, so he placed it on the Mayo stand and split it lengthwise with a scalpel. It was a cyst with hair inside of it. That meant that it was probably a dermoid cyst or teratoma. Both are benign tumors that would probably not recur if adequately removed.

As soon as the tumor was out and we knew what it was, Dr. Guerry said that he had to leave. He told us to close the eye socket, suturing the orbital (eye socket) rim together where we had cut it, and then close the skin incision.

After he left, as we were repositioning ourselves around the head of the table, I turned to the person administering the anesthesia. She was a woman who appeared to be about twenty years old, probably a nurse anesthetist student. I asked her how the patient was doing. She said, "OK, but she doesn't fill the gas bag very well."

I had done a student rotation on anesthesia and knew something about it, so I suggested that she check to see if the endotracheal tube was still in position. She looked under the drapes to check and immediately called for the MD anesthesiologist, who came in and discovered that the tube was out of the trachea and only the tip was in the baby's mouth. He quickly began to intubate the trachea again. As soon as he tore off the drapes, I grabbed a stack of four-by-four gauze squares from the sterile Mayo stand to hold them over the open incision to try to protect the surgical field from contamination during the intubation process.

Once the tube was back in place and the baby was back asleep, we redraped the surgical field, removed the four by fours, and resumed closing up the patient. We sutured the eye socket rim back together and closed the incision without further incident, and sent her to the recovery room in good condition. We sent the specimen to pathology for a definitive diagnosis of congenital orbital teratoma, a benign tumor.

When she was fully awake the next day, her eye turned inward on the operated side. We knew that the lateral rectus muscle, which pulls the eye outward, had been stretched over the tumor. We hoped that it would shrink back to a normal size to pull the eye into the normal position. If it did not, a tuck could be taken later to shorten it to a working length.

About three days after surgery, the stitches were removed. Babies heal very quickly, and leaving the stitches in the skin too long can leave stitch scars. The next day there were beads of yellow pus at the suture holes. These were cultured and grew staphylococcus bacteria sensitive to the antibiotic gentamycin, which was very new at the time. To give the antibiotic intravenously, the pharmacy measured the powder at the pharmacy and placed it in a sealed sterile bottle. On the hospital floor, the intern injected saline into the bottle to dissolve the powder. The solution was then injected into the intravenous bottle. My wife, the intern, had to move the intravenous needle to a new site every day while the baby received the drugs. The infection dried up, and the wound healed completely in about three weeks. The child had spent her entire life in the hospital until she was six weeks old and was finally ready for discharge.

The social worker tried to contact the mother, but was unsuccessful. She did find the grandmother, who told the mother to come get the baby. The mother said that she did not have a baby;

the baby died at birth. My wife, who was a psychologist before becoming a physician, explained to me that when babies are taken away from their mother immediately at birth, there is no chance for bonding and that the mother sometimes denies that the baby lived or that she had a baby at all. Apparently this mother was in complete denial. The social worker and the grandmother came to retrieve the baby and take her home. Reports from the social worker told us that the grandmother was raising the baby and the mother would have nothing to do with her.

We were anxious to learn how the baby was doing: whether the face returned to normal symmetry and whether the eye functioned and aligned itself. We made numerous return appointments through the social worker, but the child was six months old before the social worker brought the baby in by herself. They arrived at the back door of the clinic at about 4:30 in the afternoon, and I was the only one in the clinic. The nurse had just left. Fortunately, I had my own clinical camera and took several pictures of the baby. The baby was fussy and there were only two of us to hold, examine, and photograph her. The eye was still turned inward, but the pupil responded to light, telling us that the eye could still see light. The pupils were equal in size, so the light input from both eyes and the third nerve pathways to the eyes were still functioning. I could not get a photograph with both eyes open to check alignment or make any measurements.

That was the last time I saw the child. I hope that she grew up to be a healthy child. I doubt that she received the attention she needed to have the eye straightened, so it probably became a lazy eye, which would not have responded to treatment if she attempted to address the problem when she was older.

I wrote my first medical paper about this case. There were over twenty cases of congenital orbital teratoma reported in the world literature, but ours was only the third case in which only the tumor was removed. Because of fear of malignant tumors, everything in the eye socket was usually removed, including the eyeball and its muscles. We made a case for a thorough evaluation and conservative surgery when indicated. Because of the hard work that my wife, Dr. Letha Barber, did to get this baby through the postoperative infection, she was an author on the paper along with Dr. Guerry, Dr. Geereats, and me.

I learned that the anesthesiologists on this case were not as concerned about having "MD-only" anesthesia as the pediatricians or the ophthalmologists. The probability is high that the endotracheal tube coming out during the time that the MD anesthesiologists were out of the room was the cause of the incision infection. The infection prolonged the recovery of the child and delayed her return to her mother and family.

This baby's case taught me about the results of separation of a mother and baby at the time of birth. If the mother did see the child immediately after she gave birth, the appearance of the deformed face may have caused her to reject the child or to not recognize the child after the tumor was removed.

We also demonstrated that it was possible to remove a tumor from the eye socket of an infant without removing the eye, optic nerve, and muscles, saving the appearance of the child and leaving a growing eyeball in place to cause the eye socket to grow normally to create a symmetrical face.

20

An Infant with Aniridia

I HAD JUST STARTED MY FELLOWSHIP at Massachusetts Eye and Ear Infirmary (MEEI, The Iron Ear) when I was asked to scrub with Dr. S. Arthur Boruchoff, one of the leading attending physicians on the cornea service. An infant, Bobby, who had been born with a hazy cornea, had been referred to him. The boy was three months old and the cornea had not cleared, so an ophthalmologist in western Massachusetts had referred him to Dr. Boruchoff for evaluation under anesthesia.

Bobby had been given a preoperative evaluation by one of the MEEI residents on admission. The exam was recorded as unremarkable, except for the hazy cornea and inability to see into the eye to evaluate it further, which is what we would try to do under anesthesia. The examining resident noted that the child was crying throughout the exam, which meant that he could not evaluate the heart, lungs, or abdomen very well, but he thought they were normal.

Once the child was under anesthesia, we tried to see through the cornea with an indirect ophthalmoscope. This instrument floods the eye with light and focuses the reflected light from the retina into an upside down virtual image outside of the eye so that it is not necessary to look "through" the hazy cornea. As soon as we directed the light through the pupil, we noted that the light reflected from the retina filled the entire cornea. This meant that the pupil was more than ten millimeters in diameter without dilation. Everyone agreed that this child had no iris, or only a rudimentary iris structure. This is called aniridia, a condition in which the iris does not develop or is only a rudimentary rim of tissue.

Dr. Boruchoff asked me what I thought of when I saw a child with aniridia, and asked the nurse for the tonometer to measure the intraocular pressure. I had reported on two journal articles during my residency that detailed the relationship of nonfamilial aniridia with Wilm's tumor near the kidney. I immediately answered "Wilm's Tumor." He ignored my answer and asked again. Then I replied "glaucoma," which is what he wanted to hear. Glaucoma could also have caused the cloudy cornea. After we determined that the pressure was normal, Dr. Boruchoff asked what I had said before "glaucoma." I replied "Wilm's Tumor." He asked me to explain, so I told him about the journal articles about aniridia and Wilm's Tumor.

Since the child was under pretty deep anesthesia, we took the opportunity to examine his abdomen under optimal conditions, with total relaxation of the abdomen. We immediately found a three- to four-centimeter round mass in the area of the left kidney, a possible Wilm's Tumor. My wife, a pediatrician, had told me about a child she saw with an abdominal mass near the kidney during her internship in pediatrics, so I knew that this constituted a pediatric surgery emergency because Wilm's tumors metastasize so early. Once pediatricians found an abdominal mass, they gave themselves twenty-four hours to determine if it was operable or if there had been too many metastases to permit a surgical cure.

I told this to Dr. Boruchoff and suggested that we immediately refer the child to Massachusetts General Hospital or Boston Children's Hospital for evaluation. He told me that the "unwritten rules of referral" made that quite impossible. He would have to send the child back to western Massachusetts to the referring ophthalmologist, who would have to tell the local pediatrician, who could refer the child wherever he wanted. About four days later the child was admitted for workup and surgery at Massachusetts General Hospital to remove what turned out to be a Wilm's Tumor.

As we returned to the locker room after the original examination, we encountered Dr. Henry Allen, the chief of ophthalmology at the MEEI and the editor of *Archives of Ophthalmology,* one of the two most important journals in the field. Dr. Boruchoff asked Dr. Allen what he knew of the association of aniridia with Wilm's Tumor. He replied that he had never heard of an association and was interested to learn of one.

I went to the library that afternoon to look up the articles for Dr. Boruchoff. (I could not remember in which major journals the articles had been published.) One was in *American Journal of Ophthalmology*, and the other was in *Archives of Ophthalmology*, the journal that Dr. Allen edited. I have since learned that the editor sets the tone and editorial policies of the journal, but does not personally edit every article, or necessarily read the journal.

Bobby did well after the tumor was removed, and we had the opportunity to see him again at age one year. He had not had a recurrence of his tumor. The cornea remained cloudy, however, so the parents wanted to know if something could be done to save the vision in that eye. Dr. Boruchoff decided that a cornea transplant would probably help, so Bobby was called in when tissue was available. I was chosen to assist again.

As soon as the cornea was trephined (a circular cut made in the cornea) and the anterior chamber was entered through the trephine incision, it was apparent that the lens was adherent to the back of the cornea. In removing the corneal button, the anterior capsule of the lens and part of the cortex was also removed. This would lead to a total cataract within twenty-four hours, which would compromise the new cornea being transplanted. The remaining part of the lens was removed from the capsule to prevent this complication. The power of the lens could be replaced with a contact lens or glasses if the transplant was successful. This condition of the lens, being adherent to the back of the cornea with abnormal iris structures, is an anterior cleavage syndrome of arrested development during the fetal period, which is also known as Peters anomaly.

Bobby did well with his transplant, and his cornea stayed clear until I left Massachusetts. Wilm's tumor has a constant growth rate beginning near the time of conception, so if it has not recurred to the same size that it was when it was removed within the time determined by the child's age at tumor removal plus nine months for gestation, the child is cured. That amount of time had elapsed before I left Massachusetts, so I knew that the tumor would not come back.

I was surprised how this one bit of knowledge about Wilm's tumor made such an impression on the attending ophthalmologists and how it established my reputation at MEEI. I guess it was being in the right place at the right time with the right piece of random information.

We did not accept the examination of this child done on admission and did our own abdominal exam while the child was under anesthesia. That is when we found the Wilm's tumor. We would not have done this if we had not known of the relation of Wilm's tumor to the aniridia. My being familiar with the latest reports paid off for this child.

21

The Swimmer

SHORTLY AFTER ARRIVING IN MY first academic position in Texas, my chairman, Dr. Ed Ferguson, took me to my first Houston Ophthalmological Society meeting. As we were driving to Houston, he told me that he wanted to buy a new instrument that would cut and remove the vitreous gel from the back of the eye. This instrument had just been invented by one of his former Iowa residents, who lived in Michigan. He wanted me to learn how to use the instrument so we could work together. I thought it was a good idea.

Dr. Ferguson found a source of funding to donate the fourteen thousand dollars we needed to buy the suction cutter. In January, Ed and I flew to Detroit and rented a car to drive to Port Huron. We attended three days of courses on the design and use of the cutter. We even had practice sessions and learned to personally disassemble, clean, and reassemble the instrument. We learned techniques for removal of cataracts and the vitreous membranes created by intraocular hemorrhages from diabetes.

Several weeks after we returned to Galveston a young man named Carlos, who was about fifteen years old, was referred to Galveston from Corpus Christi, Texas. He had been on the swim team and was practicing one day, about a year before, when he collided with another swimmer and sustained a large hyphema (a hemorrhage in the front of the eye). The blood had taken several weeks to absorb, and by that time he had formed a cataract. The referring ophthalmologist was worried that there had been a hemorrhage into the vitreous and possibly a retinal detachment.

Carlos could see light and tell which direction it was coming from, but he could not count fingers held several inches in front of his face. He had a dense white cataract in the lens of the involved eye. It was impossible to see through the cataract to examine his retina or the vitreous body in that eye. We decided that the first step was to remove the cataract so that we could see the vitreous and possibly the retina, if the vitreous was clear. We decided to use the suction cutter to remove the cataract because of the problems experienced in cataract surgery in patients under the age of forty-five. We did get preoperative permission to remove the vitreous if necessary.

The cataract was easily removed from within the capsule bag through a small incision using the cutter. Behind the capsule bag normal vitreous should be clear and therefore not visible, but his vitreous had a foamy white texture and looked like white cotton candy. The "cotton candy" was easily nibbled by the cutter and removed from the eye.

The cutter tip is about the size of a ballpoint pen refill. An outer sleeve irrigates saline into the eye, maintaining pressure in the eye and holding the eye in its spherical shape. A tube within the rotating cutter tip connects to a syringe for suction to withdraw the irrigation fluid, which contains whatever the cutter nibbles. The cutting needle rotates within the aspiration tube, taking the razor-sharp needle edge past an aspiration port cutting off anything sucked in through the port.

The posterior surface of the vitreous is adherent to the retina in young people. As the bulk of the "cotton candy" vitreous was removed, the retina became visible, making it easier to remove the remaining vitreous without damaging the retina. All of the vitreous, except a small tuft over the optic nerve, was removed.

The day after surgery, I performed a refraction on Carlos to determine how well he could see. He was correctable to 20/20 with a lens to compensate for the removal of the crystalline lens (the cataract) from his eye. After several days, we fit him with a soft contact lens that gave him 20/25 vision. I was very pleased with the results of the surgery. I discharged him on the fifth day after surgery. He explained to me that he was from a large family in which all of the children who were old enough had to work. He worked as a busboy in a restaurant and wanted to know how soon he could go back to work to help his family pay for his surgery and to support his family.

I was so happy with the surgical results that I had our photographer make a photo montage of his retina, complete with the tuft of vitreous over the optic nerve. I had the photographer make a projector slide of this montage for my lectures on vitrectomy. It was especially satisfying to obtain good results on such a motivated young man.

Carlos had been referred to the medical center because the referring ophthalmologist thought that there had been a vitreous hemorrhage behind the cataract. The ophthalmologist was not prepared to remove the vitreous and knew that we had the equipment to accomplish that part of his care. I learned that it is necessary to be capable of doing all of the procedures needed to restore the eye. Before we removed the cataract, we did not know that we would have to remove the vitreous, but we were prepared to do what was necessary.

Dr. Ferguson told me, after we finished the course on vitrectomy, that he thought the instrument was too dangerous in his hands and that he would probably destroy the eye rather than fix it. By operating on this patient, I learned that the instrument could be safely used to remove all of the vitreous without destroying the eye, and gained confidence using it in Carlos' eye.

22

<o>

The Girl with the Bulging Eye

O NE LITTLE GIRL SURPRISED THE entire faculty by her tenacity
and survival. By the time I was involved in the care of this
eight-year-old girl ("Sandra"), she had already had an exploration
of the orbit (eye socket). Sandra also had the diagnosis of von
Recklinghausen's disease, or neurofibromatosis. Her father also had
neurofibromatosis, which is a genetically transmitted disease.

The exploration of the orbit had been prompted by the presence
of a bulging of her left eye. Glioma, a type of brain tumor, of the
optic nerve is common in von Recklinghausen's disease. Because it
involves the optic nerve, it usually causes blindness in that eye. As the
tumor grows, it pushes the eye forward, causing facial disfigurement.
Once the eye becomes blind, the tumor and the optic nerve behind
the eye are often removed, leaving the blind eye in place to prevent
facial disfigurement.

The initial surgery was done under the supervision of a
prominent ophthalmic surgeon and pathologist. This was done in
the era before CT scans and MRIs, so there was no precise knowledge
of the exact location or the character of tumor. During the surgery,
the surgeons were surprised to find that the mass in the eye socket
was not an optic nerve swollen by an optic nerve tumor, but rather
a meningioma in the eye socket. This is a tumor that arises from
the meninges, the tissue that surrounds the brain and optic nerve.
It can originate from either the portion around the optic nerve or

from meninges around the brain, and it can grow through the optic foramen into the orbit. During the operation, the ocular surgeons removed as much of the tumor as they could and closed the eye socket. This relieved the bulging of the eye temporarily, but did not do anything to improve the vision. Histopathology study confirmed the diagnosis, but could not establish the origin of the meningioma.

Sandra was then referred to the neurosurgeons, who explored the base of the brain and found that the meningioma was wrapped around the optic nerve, the optic chiasm, the pituitary gland, and other vital structures, including the carotid arteries. The neurosurgeons confirmed the diagnosis of meningioma in this tissue with biopsies, but felt that attempting to remove most of the tumor would endanger the structures involved but still not be sufficient to achieve a cure. They decreased the size of the tumor where they could and closed the skull.

The advice of the neurosurgeons was to follow her and give her palliative treatment, like pain medications, to relieve pain and make her comfortable, as the tumor spread around the base of brain to involve the structures there, until she died. Meningiomas did not usually respond well to the chemotherapy available at that time.

The senior resident responsible for this case did not like the idea of doing nothing for this young girl, so he went to the library to review the literature on treatment of meningiomas. He found an article on radiation therapy of meningiomas that reported favorable results in a number of cases. On the next follow-up visit, the possibility of radiation was presented to the patient and her family. They wanted to try anything that might save her life, so she was immediately referred to the radiation oncology department. Sandra was given a course of radiation to the posterior orbit and the area around and above the pituitary gland where the tumor had been seen.

She did well following the radiation therapy, with no evidence of tumor progression for the next year. About one year after the radiation therapy, she moved to Louisiana with her family and was lost to follow-up.

Five years later, when she was fourteen years old, Sandra returned to the clinic because her eye was becoming more prominent and the boys were teasing her about it. She could not see with that eye, so her real concern was cosmetic. I was concerned that the tumor had recurred in the eye socket after the radiation. She was referred to the neurosurgeons, who worked her up and decided to do another exploratory operation to determine whether there was a recurrence inside the head (CT scans and MRIs had still not been invented).

The neurosurgeons explored the base of the brain and found it to be surrounded by scar tissue, but no definite tumor mass was found. Numerous biopsies were taken from the area and examined by pathologists, but no tumor was found. There was only scar tissue from the radiation. This was good news, but did not solve the cosmetic problem and did not answer the question concerning the possibility of meningioma recurrence in the orbit.

Since the eye was sightless, turned out, and bulging forward, I elected to remove the entire contents of the eye socket and do a plastic reconstruction of the eyelids. The most cosmetic way to do this was to clean out the eye socket, remove the outside wall of the eye socket beneath the temporalis muscle, and pull part of that muscle, the chewing muscle, into the orbit to fill the space. The chewing muscle originates on the temporal side of the face above and in front of ear. The other end inserts on the jaw bone, pulling the jaw closed against the upper jaw. Most of the motion created by this muscle occurs below the zygomatic arch, the horizontal bony ridge in front of the ear. The muscle can be split vertically in half, superior to the arch, and the front half can be freed from the temporal bone beneath it. This half of the muscle is then passed through a hole in the lateral wall of the eye socket, underneath where the muscle had been attached. This will fill the socket and cover the front opening of the socket. It is attached to the rim of the eye socket by suturing it to the periosteum, which is adherent to the bone. This fills the front portion of the eye socket to avoid the sunken appearance. Strange as it seems, this does not interfere with chewing.

We did this procedure and Sandra healed well after the surgery. She was pleased with the result. Since she was able to look in the mirror with only one eye, she did not have good enough depth perception to notice the difference from the previous bulging eye to the now somewhat flat eyelids. I was not entirely satisfied with the result because the lids lay flat against the muscle layer at the front of the socket. However, once a built up artificial eye was fit in the conjunctival pocket, the eyelids were pushed forward somewhat and took on a more natural curve.

Sandra was moderately nearsighted in her good eye and needed glasses to see the blackboard at school or anything else more than several feet away from her. When her glasses were on, the result was quite cosmetically pleasant and she was very happy. She was young enough that there was subcutaneous fat over the temple area that hid the defect in the temporalis muscle.

I had an anxious moment while freeing the anterior half of the muscle when I discovered that the neurosurgeons had used the temporal approach to the base of the brain and had not replaced the skull bone behind the muscle. The muscle was attached to the periosteum, which was resting on the meninges covering the brain, and there was no bone in between the two layers to protect the brain. Despite my anxiety, the surgery was a success. The meninges and periosteum remained intact, the brain was never exposed, and there were no ill effects to the brain from the surgery.

Thanks to a resident who would not accept the assumption that there was nothing that could be done for this girl, rather than being left to die from her tumor, this girl received radiation and survived. She reported after her last surgery that the boys did not make fun of her anymore. She may still be alive and reasonably well today, thanks to that resident. She, of course, still has von Recklinghausen's disease, which can be rather benign or may be disfiguring. Other tumors could still occur. It was very important to her at fourteen years of age to have a normal appearance. Fortunately, her von Recklinghausen's disease was not otherwise deforming. I hope she is doing well.

Sandra taught me that I should not quit on a patient until every possibility has been exhausted. If the resident had accepted the advice of the neruosurgeons that nothing could be done except palliative care, she would have been dead within a year. However, he did not give up, which saved Sandra's life.

I also received an education on the importance of cosmetic appearance to a teenaged girl. She was very concerned about her looks and wanted her blind, displaced eye to look better. I searched many surgical books to locate the procedure that would produce the most cosmetically pleasing results, and Sandra's appreciation compensated for the effort.

23

◄○►

The Five-Year-Old Surfer

I AM ALWAYS CONCERNED WHEN A child has an eye injury, especially when I am having difficulty treating the problem. A five-year-old, blond-haired girl was sent to us from Beaumont, Texas. Suzy had been to Galveston several days before, and her mother had taken her to the beach. She was having lots of fun playing in the surf until a larger than expected wave knocked her down and rolled her on the beach. After this she complained to her mother that her eye hurt. Her mother looked at her eye and did not see anything wrong with it. The child's mother did notice that there was a lot of debris in the water and thought it was from some shrimp boats working close to the beach.

Two days later the little girl was still complaining about her eye, so her mother took her to an ophthalmologist in Beaumont. That ophthalmologist put her on antibiotic eyedrops, but the next day she was worse, so he sent her to Galveston to the medical school. Dr. Ferguson saw her and noticed that the iris in her good eye was light blue, but the iris appeared blue-green in her involved eye. He had seen this several times before, and the eyes had always done badly. Since I was the infectious disease person in the department, he sent her to me.

We discovered that she had a very small puncture wound in the middle of her cornea and that there was the beginning of a layer of white blood cells on the inside of the eye at the bottom of her cornea. This was evidence of a bacterial infection within the eye, which we needed to culture. We took her to the operating room, where she

99

was anesthetized so that we could draw some fluid from her eye for the culture. We inoculated this fluid on fresh culture plates that the resident surgeon had brought directly from the microbiology laboratory. We increased her antibiotics and continued to follow her.

The next day her eye was worse and had begun to develop a cataract at the center of the lens, directly behind the corneal puncture wound. The lens was probably perforated by the same object that penetrated her cornea. We watched her for a day and saw that she was getting worse and the cataract was spreading. There were no bacteria growing on the culture plates. Our pediatric ophthalmologist then proceeded to remove the cataract so that it would not swell and cause glaucoma on top of everything else. He had the resident bring more fresh culture plates to the operating room so they could take another culture. The lens extraction went well, but the eye continued to get worse. On the next day, she developed cloudiness of the vitreous jelly that fills the back of the eye.

We decided that whatever was infecting the eye was not susceptible to the antibiotics. Most antibiotics do not penetrate the vitreous well, so the bacteria within the vitreous are protected. By this time everyone in the department was involved in her care. Our vitreous and retina surgeon proceeded to operate again to remove the vitreous to give the antibiotics better access to the bacteria. When he was in the operating room he decided to take another culture, so he sent the resident to get culture plates. The resident looked around the operating room and found some old plates in the laboratory refrigerator.

The next day the laboratory called to ask where we had found this culture sample; it was growing a lush culture of Vibrio cholera. Vibrio is usually only found in saltwater and takes very salty culture plates to grow. Apparently, the old plates were so dehydrated that the salt in them had concentrated to the level of sea water and the Vibrio grew abundantly on them. This would also explain why we had not seen any growth on the fresh plates.

The Vibrio was very sensitive to penicillin, which we almost never use in the eye. We started her on synthetic penicillin, which easily penetrates the eye, and she began improving within hours. We were able to send her home in a few days to have her Beaumont ophthalmologist fit her with a contact lens to replace the focusing power that we had removed by removing her cataract.

The blue green color in her eye was pigment from the Vibrio cholera bacteria. It turned the same color of green on the culture plates. Apparently, the little girl had been stuck in the eye with something like a broken crab shell when she rolled with the wave. She had brushed it away before her mother saw the eye. Shrimpers often discard crabs caught in their nets. The seawater around Galveston Island contains high counts (one million bacteria per milliliter) of Vibrio cholera bacteria all summer. The bacteria do not penetrate skin or mucous membranes, but they were implanted by whatever penetrated her cornea.

Serendipity had played a major role in the treatment of this little girl. Had it not been for the use of the dried up old culture plates, we might not have known what was causing the problem until it was too late. Sometimes serendipity helps in a tough diagnosis.

This patient taught me to look more closely at the conditions surrounding the cause of the problem. She was swimming in salt water. The bacteria that caused her infection probably came from salt water. We should have cultured on saltwater plates and thought of saltwater bacteria.

The discoloration of the anterior chamber that Dr. Ferguson saw when he first saw her was from Vibrio. Now I know what a green discoloration of the anterior chamber means.

24

Bottle Rocket

DURING MY SECOND SUMMER IN Galveston, I was called into the emergency room on the Fourth of July by the resident on call. A six-year-old boy ("Jimmy") was visiting the family's beach house with his parents and his brother. Beach houses on Galveston Island are built above the ground on stilts because of the frequent hurricanes. His brother was setting off fireworks on the ground below the house. Jimmy was standing on the deck of the beach house, leaning over the railing, watching the fireworks. His brother set off a bottle rocket that shot up into the air and struck Jimmy directly in the right eye.

The rocket was flying at considerable speed when it hit his eye. Besides the force of the rocket, it was burning at about four thousand degrees and contained a number of very caustic chemicals. The result was a swollen eye with severe thermal and chemical burns of the skin around the eye. He did not have a hyphema, a hemorrhage in the anterior chamber of the eye between the iris and cornea, but his corneal epithelium was abraded, and much of the epithelium was missing. This gave him eye pain in addition to the burns of the skin.

We treated his eye with antibiotic eyedrops and administered burn cream for the skin burns. The corneal defects healed quickly and became more comfortable.

The family lived in Houston and Jimmy's father was anxious to return to Houston, where he ran his own business. On Jimmy's third day in the hospital, I took him to the clinic and did a dilated examination of his retina. The back of the eye looked normal, but the front edge of the retina appeared as a red ring. It looked like the front edge had become torn at the junction with the ciliary body, leaving a red ring for 360 degrees. I explained to his parents that this tear could go on to become a serious retinal detachment and that he should be seen by our retina specialist before leaving the hospital. The father said that he wanted him seen by a retina specialist in Houston instead, so I gave them the name of a retina specialist I knew in Houston.

About a week later, I received a call from the retina specialist, who told me that what I had seen was just hemorrhage and that there were no holes in the retina. He went on to make some disparaging remarks about my ability to examine the retina and reminded me that I was a cornea specialist.

I did not see Jimmy again until about twelve years later when the boy, now a high school graduate, came to see me in my office. He told me that about three weeks after leaving Galveston and seeing the retina specialist, he had suddenly lost all vision in that eye. He had gone back to the retina specialist, who told him that he had a total retinal detachment, which was inoperable. This is typical of the retinal detachment that is caused by a giant retinal tear like the one I thought I saw. I thought that the retinal surgeon had probably given him a cursory exam and missed the giant tear at the far periphery of the retina. This led to the retinal detachment. If he had repaired the tear, the eye might have been saved.

Since then Jimmy had been blind in his right eye, but had adapted to the loss and had learned depth perception. His left eye was normal and did not need glasses for vision. He had been given safety glasses to protect his only eye, but he did not like to wear them.

He had done well in grade school and high school and was very active, although he had not been allowed to play varsity sports in high school because of his one-eye status. He was planning to enroll in the University of Texas at Austin in the upcoming fall and wanted to play football. He was built like a lineman and wanted to play guard. To do that he needed a letter from an ophthalmologist saying that it was safe for him to play football at the college level.

I told him that he should be wearing his safety glasses and that it was not safe for him to play football. He had a limited vision to his right side and was more prone to being injured by being blind sided. I explained that he had lost one of his two eyes and could still see, but if he injured his left eye, he could lose all of his vision permanently. I refused to write the letter and take responsibility for his going blind.

Three years later I was watching Texas play Oklahoma at the Cotton Bowl. When they introduced the starters before the game, there was Jimmy, blind in one eye from a fireworks injury, playing left guard for Texas. I do not know if he got a letter from another ophthalmologist or if the coach overlooked the problem. I have thought about this situation many times and wondered if I was being too protective and should have let him play football. He played anyway, and I never heard of his getting injured in the good eye. This situation came up several times in my practice with young corneal transplant patients and I always told them not to take the risk. They could play in the band or be in the pep squad, but no contact sports.

When the retina expert told me that there was no tear, I began doubting my ability to examine the retina with the indirect ophthalmoscope, which is difficult to use. It had a profound effect on me. I worked long and hard to get better with this instrument, and I regained my confidence using it long before I learned that I had been correct in my diagnosis on Jimmy.

25

Boys Will Be Boys

ALEX, A BOY ABOUT EIGHT years old, was sent to me for possible vitrectomy. He and some other boys had been playing on a house construction site. They found a keg of nails and decided to choose up sides and throw nails at each other. After several minutes, one of the boys decided they should quit throwing nails because someone might get hit in the eye with a nail. They discussed the probability of someone getting hit in the eye with a nail and decided that the possibility of someone actually being hit in the eye with a nail was pretty remote. So they went back to throwing nails.

Shortly after that, Alex had been hit in the eye with a nail. He pulled the nail out and went home to his mother, who took him to one of the local ophthalmologists. The doctor found that the nail had perforated the front of the eye at the lower limbus, where the white and clear parts meet. It had entered the eye part way and left a path of hemorrhage in the vitreous gel. The doctor repaired the puncture wound and watched the eye as it healed. During the three weeks after the injury, a fibrous band formed along the hemorrhage tract. It extended from the inside of the front of the eye all the way to the surface of the retina, just below the macula at the center of the back of the eye. Once this band formed, it began to shrink and pull on the retina. The doctor sent him to me to cut the band and remove it with our new vitreous-cutting machine.

When I saw this young boy, I saw that the front of the eye was in good condition. The nail had missed the lens, so there was no traumatic cataract formation. When the pupil was dilated, a band of brown tissue could be seen extending from the ciliary body at the perforation site, through the vitreous jelly, to attach to the retina below the macula. The retina was tented up by traction from this band, and there was a small localized retinal detachment. Careful examination of the retina did not reveal a hole from either the nail or the traction on the retina.

We knew from past experience that the progression of shrinkage of the band would lead to increasing detachment of the retina, causing blindness. Before the vitreous cutters, there was nothing that could be done to stop this inevitable shrinkage and retinal detachment. The exuberant healing that occurs in a child would lead to the detachment of the retina. I decided that cutting this band with the vitreous cutter and removal of enough vitreous to keep a new band from forming in the remaining vitreous was the only way to save the eye. Since Dr. Ferguson (our retina surgeon) had decided not to use the cutter, we suggested that the parents should take the child to one of the retinal surgeons who was experienced with a vitreous suction cutter.

This boy was one of six siblings, and his father was a busy surgeon who decided that he could not leave town for any extended period. The mother felt that she could not leave her other children to take this child to Houston, St. Louis, or the Detroit area for the surgery. I explained to them that almost all of my experience with our suction cutter was in the front of the eye, but they insisted that I perform the surgery in Galveston. I had been to the courses on vitrectomy and knew how to do the case. So I prevailed on Dr. Ferguson to assist with the surgery in case retinal problems developed; if they did, he could repair the retina immediately. He agreed, and we decided to do the surgery.

We made an incision posterior to the limbus at about 90 degrees from the injury site so that the cutter would be perpendicular to the band. The cutter easily cut through the band. As the band parted and swung to the side, it revealed a small hole in the retina that had been hidden behind the band. The hole opened and immediately the surrounding retina started to detach. The detachment progressed in a matter of seconds to involve most of the retina, and a large tear developed at the edge of the retina. I turned the case over to Dr. Ferguson.

Dr Ferguson located and marked the spot on the sclera adjacent to the hole. We injected a large air bubble to push the retina back into position, and a silicone band was placed around the eye to cinch the eye wall to the retina.

Over the next two or three days, Dr. Ferguson treated the retina around the hole with laser burns to seal it to the choroid so the hole would not leak fluid under the retina. The hole did seal, and the retina went back to its original position. The boy's vision improved to about 20/40, and he was happy with the result.

About one month after the surgery, Alex woke up with no vision at all in the operated eye. When Dr. Ferguson examined him that day, he found a total detachment of the retina. The retina was rolled into a ball attached to the optic nerve, and Dr. Ferguson considered it inoperable.

The exuberant healing in this young boy had caused a membrane to form on the surface of the retina. This membrane shrank and pulled the retina loose. Once it tore loose in one place, the tear extended all around the front edge of the retina, allowing it to retract into a ball of retina. I had not anticipated this response, and I was very disappointed when it happened. I thought we had won.

Alex was philosophical about the outcome. He knew that he should not have been in the nail fight and that it was his fault that he had lost the vision in one eye. Loss of vision in one eye causes immediate loss of all depth perception. My experience with loss of vision in one eye in a young person is that they soon learn other forms of depth perception and lead relatively normal lives. They do have permanent loss of peripheral vision on the side of the injury.

I thought that it was ironic that the boys had stopped throwing nails because they feared that someone would be hit in the eye. As soon as they rationalized this possibility away and went back to throwing nails, someone was hit in the eye.

I had looked for a hole, but it was hidden from me by the vitreous band. I learned to expect the unexpected after this case. I learned that a surgical procedure that had been well planned and well executed could be brought to failure by a hidden cause, such as the hidden hole in Alex's retina.

26

Running with Scissors

EVERY MOTHER TELLS HER CHILD not to run with scissors. Children usually disregard this advice or forget it in the excitement of daily activities. Sissy was brought into the emergency room one night with a perforation of her cornea. The tear, in the middle of her cornea, was ragged, with several triangular points that almost met in the middle. The residents took her to the operating room and placed several sutures to pull the points together to prevent the aqueous fluid from leaking from the eye.

The following day I saw Sissy in the clinic and tested the wound for leakage. There was a slow leak seeping from the wound, but there were already sutures placed at various angles to re-approximate the edges, and a total redo was not indicated. Instead, we placed a soft contact lens over the cornea to stop the flow of fluid from the eye.

The next day, the leak had stopped and the soft lens was removed. Further testing after several minutes showed that there was no leak after the lens was removed. We continued to treat her with antibiotics, but we withheld steroids so that the wound would heal.

About three weeks later we removed the sutures, but the central cornea remained hazy because of the healing process. When we saw her two weeks after we removed the sutures, the cornea had cleared, revealing a membrane with scalloped edges on the back surface of the cornea. This could have been caused by fibrinous deposits on the back of the healing area, or the growth of the corneal epithelium down through the leaking wound and onto the back of the cornea.

Epithelium does not belong on the back of the cornea or inside of the eye. It can destroy the eye. I decided to wait and watch the eye, knowing that fibrinous tissue will shrink and may disappear completely, while epithelium will continue to grow and spread.

Two weeks later the membrane had spread over the central cornea and all of the way to the edge of the cornea below. This told us that the membrane was epithelium, creating what is known as epithelial down growth. The epithelium will continue to spread until it covers the entire posterior surface of the cornea and bridges the gap between the cornea and the iris, blocking the outflow of aqueous humor from the eye. This will create intractable glaucoma, which leads to loss of the eye. Once the epithelium enters the anterior chamber of the eye, it is very hard to eradicate. If 99 percent is removed, the 1 percent will continue to spread and destroy the eye.

We could only save her eye if we could remove all of the epithelium. By careful exam we could delineate the extent of the epithelium. It extended to the edge of the cornea below, between four o'clock and eight o'clock, and probably covered the outflow structures in that area. It did not involve the remaining eight hours of the angle structures (eight o'clock through twelve o'clock to four o'clock). The central and lower cornea was damaged by the epithelium and needed to be replaced. The rest was not involved.

I devised an operation that would remove the involved cornea, the lower angle structures, and the lower iris and replace the cornea and sclera with a transplant consisting of a new cornea and part of the sclera from a donor eye. A trephine was used to delineate a round area in the central cornea that had epithelium on the posterior surface, cutting to about 90 percent of the thickness. Cuts were then made at three and nine o'clock to extend from the trephine cut to the edge of the cornea and about two millimeters into the sclera. Another cut in the sclera was made from three o'clock to nine o'clock, running parallel to the corneal edge. A donor graft in the same shape as the outlined tissue to be removed was prepared from a donor eye.

The involved cornea was excised along the previous cuts. The inferior half of the iris was also removed, along with the ciliary body that was exposed. The new donor tissue was sewn into the eye to replace the damaged tissue. The space in the eye between the iris and lens, and the cornea, was inflated with saline, and the eye appeared relatively normal at the end of the surgery, except for the missing bottom half of the iris. The next day the eye looked even better, and the little girl said that she could see much better. Of course the scar was gone from the center of her cornea, and the stitches were away from the part of the cornea through which she looked.

Unfortunately, about three weeks after the surgery, she told her mother that she could not see from the eye on which we had operated. When we examined her we found that the edge of the ciliary body, where it was cut, had separated from the sclera (the wall of the eye), and the entire retina had become detached. Dr. Ferguson examined the girl and felt that surgery could not reattach the retina. Her eye now looked normal but could not see. We had saved the eye but lost the vision.

We followed her for several months, but her father was transferred out of town and she was lost for follow-up.

In retrospect, we could have sutured the edge of the choroid (ciliary body) to the sclera prior to suturing the new cornea into place to try to prevent the retinal detachment. This would have required that the eye be open for an extended period of time, which could have caused a hemorrhage or loss of the vitreous jelly from the eye, both of which could have been disastrous.

The only way that this problem could have been avoided was for the initial repair to have been watertight to prevent the epithelium from growing into the wound. Removing all of the sutures and closing the wound again might have stopped the epithelium, but it would have meant more time under anesthesia for the child, and it might not have worked. The down growth may have already occurred before a repair was considered.

I learned that an operation that appears to be carefully and completely planned may have flaws in the design or execution. These may even become obvious soon after the operation is complete. I also learned that surgeons may replace one vision-threatening disease with another by doing surgery. The beautiful result of this operation was destroyed by unforeseen complication.

I already knew that children and adults should not run with scissors in their hands.

27

Boy with Peters Anomaly

ONE OF THE RESIDENTS ASKED me to see a six-year-old Mexican boy with cloudy corneas and poor vision. Ricardo was very cooperative and spoke fairly good English, although the woman with him did not. His vision allowed him to count my fingers at one foot, and he verified with the woman who brought him that his vision had always been poor. The woman with him said she was his aunt who often cared for him and that his mother lived in Houston and could not come to the clinic that day.

Ricardo had hazy corneas in both eyes. When viewed with the slit lamp, the lens in each eye was seen to be against or just behind the cornea. When the eye was illuminated through the sclera, there was only a small rim of iris to block the transmitted light shining back through his cornea. He had little or no iris. This reminded me of a child I saw at Massachusetts Eye and Ear Infirmary during my training whose condition turned out to be Peters anomaly. To restore vision for Ricardo, he would need a corneal transplant and possible a lens extraction if the cornea was fused to the lens, as it is in Peter's anomaly.

Tissue was obtained and the surgery was scheduled. Ricardo's mother came from Houston to sign him into the hospital, but she left immediately thereafter, leaving Ricardo's aunt to look after him. His aunt's husband, Ricardo's uncle, was also there throughout the hospitalization.

I performed a corneal transplant and lens extraction on both eyes about six months apart. The lenses in both eyes were adherent to the back of the cornea, and the lens capsules tore when the corneas were removed. Because the lenses were broken, the remaining lens material had to be removed.

Ricardo responded well to the surgery. Because of his age, we could not use intraocular lenses when we removed his lenses, but we did fit him with regular thick cataract glasses, which he wore all of the time.

I continued to follow Ricardo for six years, and his aunt continued to be the one to bring him to the hospital. His uncle often accompanied him and his aunt on their visits, as he did on their first visit to the hospital. Ricardo was extremely bright and would always translate for me and for his aunt and uncle. He said he did very well in school and that he looked after those around him who did not speak English. As it turned out, Ricardo did not reject either corneal transplant, and he proceeded to develop very good vision.

Six years after Ricardo received his corneal transplants, his aunt who always brought him to the hospital brought in her newborn child, a boy named Manual, who had been born with cloudy corneas and aniridia in both eyes. She was pregnant with Manual when she brought Ricardo in for his previous visit, so I knew that she had really just had a baby when she brought in this child. Since aniridia, part of Ricardo's problem, runs in families, our suspicions were increased that she was also Ricardo's real mother. One of our clinic nurses, Mrs. Silvas, was from Mexico and spoke native Spanish. She took Manual's mother aside and had a heart-to-heart talk with her and learned that she was actually Ricardo's mother as well, but that she had only recently become a legal immigrant. She had always been afraid that if she was discovered to be an illegal alien that she would be deported and that Ricardo would not be cared for at the university hospital and could not obtain treatment to give him vision. It was also confirmed that Ricardo's "uncle" was actually his father.

The pediatric department insisted on doing a complete Wilms's tumor workup on Manual as they had on Ricardo, even though we assured them that Wilms's tumor was associated with sporadic aniridia, but not with familial aniridia, which these two boys obviously had.

Several years after I did Manual's corneal transplants, both Ricardo and Manual disappeared from my practice in Galveston.

Since I had followed Ricardo for more than eight years without a rejection episode, the likelihood of rejection is very small, but it never goes to zero. He was extremely bright, fluent in two languages, apparently very well connected in the Houston Hispanic community, and a proven survivor. He was also very good at looking after Manual and telling his mother when he or his brother needed to be seen, and explaining what needed to be done to protect his transplants.

It was obvious to us from a very early time in Ricardo's care that the woman with him had much more than a babysitter's interest in the care and outcome of Ricardo's blindness. She acted like a mother, and her husband acted like a father, even though they both constantly denied that Ricardo was their child. The second child with aniridia finally forced their hand. Fortunately, by that time, the parents were both legal immigrants.

These two boys were a delight to work with, and they gave me a great feeling of accomplishment. I was glad that neither boy rejected his transplants, at least while I cared for them. Children often reject transplants when they develop an immune response to a viral or bacterial disease such as measles, mumps, chicken pox, or pneumonia. Without these transplants, both boys would have become amblyopic (lazy eyed) when they became eight years old, and would not have improved very much if they had transplants after that age.

I learned to trust Ricardo when he was only six years old. I think his blindness had forced a maturity upon him that was far above his age. His ability to go back and forth between two languages and comprehend the technical things that he was told showed me that he had superior intelligence. I am sure that he is doing very well, wherever he is.

I also learned that parents will go to great lengths to obtain good medical care for their children. These boys reinforced the concept that the doctor must remain nonjudgmental and treat the patient, even though we thought the family was in the United States illegally.

28

The Snuff Dipper

ONE OF MY INTERESTS IN Galveston was caring for the many children who were sent to the Shrine Burn Center. This was an eight-bed unit for children with severe burns. Some had been caught in house or car fires; others were burned by gasoline explosions associated with camp or trash fires. One was set on fire by his father, who threw charcoal lighter fluid on him and lit it with a match. The one thing that impressed me most about these children was their wonderful good nature and personalities.

One boy in particular had a very interesting story. Denny was thirteen years old and a big boy for his age. He loved playing basketball, and he also liked to dip snuff. His mother did not know that Denny dipped snuff because he kept his snuff behind the hot-water heater in a storage shed in back of the house. One day as he was retrieving his snuff, he stepped on the PVC gas line and it cracked. Apparently the gas element of the water heater was lighted at the time and the escaping gas ignited immediately. Before Denny could get out of the shed, his clothes were on fire, and he had suffered severe burns to almost his entire body. His feet had been spared because he was wearing shoes, and the part of his body covered by his undershorts somehow had been protected as well.

Denny had particularly severe burns of his face, ears, and fingers. He suffered third-degree burns on his eyelids, nose, and ears, meaning that the full thickness of his skin was destroyed. When the eyelid skin and the muscles just below the skin are severely burned, the dead tissue shrinks, pulling the eyes open. When there is no remaining circular muscle under the skin to close the eye, the deeper levator muscle that opens the eye is unopposed and the eye is constantly pulled open.

I was trained, during my residency, to immediately sew the eyelids closed in a semipermanent manner so that the eye would be protected. For reasons that the burn surgeons could never really explain to me, except not wanting to create sensory deprivation of the patient, the burn surgeons would not allow us to close the eyes. Consequently, on about the third day after his admission, Denny's eyelids started to retract.

The burn doctors excised the burned skin of the eyelids and placed skin grafts over the area in an attempt to allow the eyes to close. This did not stop the levator muscle from pulling the eyelids open, so Denny could not close his eyes. I had the nurses cover his eyes with large amounts of ophthalmic antibiotic ointment to keep them from drying out and becoming infected. Under the circumstances, the ointment often dried out and slid off of his eyes, leaving them exposed.

These severely burned children are very sick. They are often barely conscious and require intensive care for weeks. To the nurses, the eye problems are less critical than tending the large areas of burned skin and the possible pulmonary burns. The huge metabolic demands from fluid loss and evaporative cooling and the massive healing effort demanded by the body add to the distress. After about three days, the patient goes into negative nitrogen balance, meaning that they are consuming their fat and other tissues faster than they can replace it, leaving them no energy for the body healing that must take place. New techniques to conserve heat loss and supplement the diet to maximize available energy have greatly increased the rate of survival from severe burns.

The main cause of death from burns now is overwhelming infection, usually from staphylococcus and pseudomonas, with a high incidence of Candida yeast infection also. All of these microbes are bad actors in the eye. I checked burn patients daily for signs of infection, particularly corneal ulcers. Once an ulcer starts, it is very difficult to keep it from progressing in size and depth.

Denny developed ulcers in both eyes. Fortunately, one eye developed an ulcer several weeks before the other eye. Even though we used the latest antibiotics and covered the eye with Saran Wrap to preserve moisture, the ulcer perforated, allowing the eye to collapse, and possibly permitting the bacteria to enter his eyeball. This called for immediate corneal transplant to close the eye and restore the cornea. To prevent subsequent ulceration of the new cornea, we pulled a flap of conjunctiva from the tissue surrounding the cornea and covered the cornea. By providing a covering tissue with a blood supply to the cornea, the chance of another infection and ulcer was greatly decreased. The flap has the downside of greatly obscuring the vision in that eye. Over time the flap will thin itself and become more transparent, allowing better vision. I have seen patients after conjunctival flaps who obtained vision of 20/40, which is good enough to pass a driver's license examination in most states.

Several weeks after the first cornea received the cornea transplant, the second eye began to ulcerate. A second corneal transplant within one year of the first may cause rejection of the first transplant and may also reject. We did not wait for the ulcer to perforate. We proceeded immediately to pull a protective conjunctival flap over the ulcer to prevent ulceration and better prevent infection. This left Denny with enough vision to identify only the forms of people around him.

Denny did recover from the burns, although he lost the tips of all of his fingers, the tip of his nose, and both ears. He also lost most of the hair on his head and had to wear a pressure mask over his head, face, and upper body to prevent scarring of the skin grafts. He wore a blond wig that looked like it was made of broom straw, but he seemed to take pride in the way it looked.

As soon as his eyelids healed sufficiently to protect his eyes, we did a corneal transplant through the conjunctival flap of the eye that had not had a corneal transplant. This immediately improved his vision. After several weeks Denny obtained vision of 20/50 without glasses. I tried to improve his vision with glasses and found that the transplant was warped, producing six diopters of astigmatism. With this correction in glasses, he still saw 20/50. He did not have a cataract or any other explanation why he could not see better with his glasses. He said that things looked slightly sharper, but he could not read the 20/40 line on the chart. The only rationale that I could provide for this powerful correction not causing a change in vision was that the axis of the astigmatism was at 90 degrees, thus producing symmetrical distortion.

By this time Denny was back in school and doing well. He could hold a pen or pencil between the stubs of his fingers, and he could see well enough to read his school books and see the blackboard. His mother told me that he was making all As and Bs.

Around November, Denny brought in a permission slip from the basketball coach for me to sign, giving him permission to play basketball on the school team. He was less than one year from the corneal transplant, and it had not completely healed. I told him that an elbow or finger to the eye, or even a blow to the head, could rupture the wounds on his corneal transplants and cause him to permanently lose his vision. He told me that he had a basketball hoop at home and had been shooting baskets and was getting very good. The coach really wanted him to play on the team. Even though he was severely stressed during his rapid growth phase, he had grown to a height of about six feet two inches and was bigger than most of the boys in his classes. I did not sign the permission slip.

He told me that once his classmates got over the scarring and disfigurement he had from the burns, they accepted it well, and he had very few problems with comments or teasing. He had a great personality considering that he had been hospitalized with severe pain and disfigurement and that he had fought for his life for many weeks. He just wanted to be treated normally again and go on with his life. He did not dip snuff anymore.

After seeing his hands, with only the first joints remaining on several fingers and none of the joints on the rest, I asked him how he was able to shoot so well. He told me he held the ball in his palms and did not miss his fingers at all when he played. If everyone could accept these severe hardships and disfigurement, the world would be different.

In caring for these burn patients, I learned that it is possible to endure prolonged pain and massive scarring with deformity and still have a great personality. I also learned that they have a strong drive to be treated as normal individuals and want to enjoy the same things that the people around them are enjoying. Denny was able to move past his disfigurement and disabilities to live a relatively normal life.

Part III
Texas Patients
1973–1991

I MOVED FROM BOSTON TO GALVESTON to become an assistant professor of ophthalmology and began my professional career during the summer of 1973. I was thirty-three years old and had finally finished my training. I was now ready to teach in a medical school and residency training program. Instead of asking permission to do surgery, I was now the one to give approval to the residents.

Upon my arrival, there were three physicians and one PhD researcher who were full-time faculty in ophthalmology at the University of Texas Medical Branch. Dr. Ferguson was chairman and retinal specialist, and Dr. John McCrary was a neuro-ophthalmologist and general ophthalmologist. John had been assisting the residents with surgery, but being a neuro-ophthalmologist, he did not like to do surgery, especially with the residents. He was happy to turn that duty over to me.

There were several specialists who were on the part-time faculty. They would come regularly to cover certain specialties in the clinic, and some would do surgeries with the residents. The brunt of the surgical supervision fell to Dr. Ferguson and me.

The medical branch was the sole indigent general care facility for the State of Texas. Our department was the end of the referral chain for the care of all things ophthalmic for indigent Texans. When patients were sent to us for care, we did whatever was necessary to care for them. We could not refer them out to other doctors. Therefore, we did all kinds of eye surgery, including cataract extraction, ocular alignment, glaucoma, retina, orbital (eye socket), or oculoplastic surgery. I had learned the fundamentals of all of these as a resident, but I had specialized in corneal transplants.

Ed taught me the fine points of glaucoma surgery, plastic surgery of the eyelids, and exploration of the eye socket. We had specialists who came to Galveston to see the children with crossed eyes. They would tell the residents and me how much surgery to do. I would go to the operating room to supervise the resident doing the surgery.

The first five years that I was in Texas, we had nine residents, three each year of residency. After that we expanded to four residents each year. This kept us very busy until we slowly added more faculty members, increasing our expertise and spreading the surgical load.

Our indigent clinic volume quadrupled in two years, when the recession of the '80s finally hit Texas.

Shortly before I arrived in Galveston vitrectomy was invented, so I learned that procedure. Several years later, phacoemulsification became popular and intraocular lenses were developed. All of medicine involves continuous learning of new treatments and surgical procedures, and we added these new procedures and equipment to our armamentarium (the equipment, pharmaceuticals, and methods used in our practice).

In my ninth year in Texas, I was named the chairman of the department. By that time I had developed a large referral practice in corneal diseases.

Our department saw more private patients than any other department at the university's medical branch, so there was little time for research. Our faculty saw many private and indigent patients, which gave me a wealth of patient experience. The patients and their cases reported here are only a few of the many interesting cases I experienced in Texas.

29

The Nun Who Could Not Wear Black

S ISTER MARY ELIZABETH WAS PRESENTED to me when I visited Texas to interview for a position on the faculty. I was finishing my fellowship at Massachusetts Eye and Ear Infirmary in Boston and was being interviewed for a position as an external eye and corneal disease expert. Sister Elizabeth's problem fell within my realm of expertise, and I was asked to see her.

Sister Elizabeth was a postulate in the convent at St. Elizabeth Hospital in Beaumont, Texas. She had been assigned the job of cleaning out the old pathology laboratory of the hospital. This involved disposing of old specimens, cleaning the specimen jars, and replacing them on the shelves to be reused. As she performed this task, she developed a pus-producing pink eye, which became very severe. She was treated in Beaumont with antibiotics but became progressively worse, so she was referred to Galveston for diagnosis and therapy.

Her eyes had been cultured on every available culture medium, looking for some rare bacteria that could survive years in pathological fixative and remain viable enough to cause an infection. These cultures had all been negative except for one culture plate, which grew one colony of a rare species of Klebsiella bacteria. This colony was not on the culture streak on the plate, but it was the only thing that grew.

Eye cultures are taken by scraping a tiny spatula on the infected area and then wiping the spatula on a culture plate. This leaves a streak on the surface of the plate, where the bacteria should grow. Bacteria that grow anywhere else on the plate except on the streak are considered contaminants, which probably landed on the plate from the air, during the culture process. She was given antibiotics to kill the Klebsiella, but this did not cause improvement.

The presenting resident mentioned that Sister Elizabeth was receiving a lot of attention from the priests and nuns from the St. Mary's Hospital across the street from the university medical center. They would come to pray with her several times each day and bring flowers and candy. This seemed to elevate her spirits, so much so that the residents became suspicious that this whole problem could be caused by self-induced chemical conjunctivitis to obtain sympathy.

They asked the nurses to search her purse for anything that she could put in her eye. The nurses found a jar of Nair, a hair remover. They decided that a nun would not have any legitimate use for this and that she must be putting this into her eye to gain sympathy.

To "prove" this, the residents decided to patch both eyes with eye pads and white adhesive tape for forty-eight hours to see if she would get better when she was prevented from putting anything into her eyes. They even drew lines with a ballpoint pen from the tape to the skin so that if she did peel off the patches to put something in her eye, she would be caught because she could not replace the patches with the lines correctly aligned. After two days of patching, the lines were still perfectly aligned, so they removed the patches. Her eyes were greatly improved. This is when I saw her.

One apparently incidental finding in her history was that she was allergic to black clothing that caused her skin to break out in a rash when it contacted her skin directly.

She was a short, overweight, smiling, pleasant, young woman. She did have a light growth of facial hair. She was complaining of not being able to see for two days, but she was otherwise in good humor. Her eyelids were slightly swollen, and the vessels on her eyes were dilated more than they should have been. There were several areas of white infiltration in the center of her corneas in both eyes, which also appeared very dry and dull.

I had never seen the effects of Nair on the eye, but assumed that it had caused severe inflammation and corneal damage due to a chemical reaction. I suggested that they remove her access to the Nair, admonish her not to put anything in her eye, because it could make her blind, and to give her nothing in the eye except artificial tears to treat the dryness. I recommended some new tears with the Burton Parsons polymer that was supposed to wet the eye better.

Several days later, when I was back in Boston, I was talking on the phone with Dr. Ferguson, the department chairman, about the faculty position, and I asked about Sister Elizabeth. He told me that she had gotten worse again. He had decided that whatever toxic material had given her the reaction was still in her superficial cornea, so he peeled off the superficial layers and patched her eyes, with no eyedrops to be used. She was slowly improving.

Six months later I arrived in Texas to start my position there. One of my first patients was Sister Elizabeth. Her corneas had healed and her eyes looked normal, but she couldn't see very well. The removal of the superficial layer of her corneas had left her with irregular surfaces on both corneas. It looked clear, but was optically very irregular. Dr. Ferguson thought that if I fit her with hard contact lenses, this would overcome the irregularities and improve her vision.

I measured her corneas, tried to refract her, and ordered contact lenses for her. Two weeks later, when the lenses arrived, I called her in to try the lenses so that I could refract her eyes through the lenses to obtain the correct power for the contacts. Remembering how "schizoid" the residents thought she was, I used "comfort drops" on her contact lenses to make it easier for her to tolerate them. Burton Parsons had marketed a new polymer that claimed to make their artificial tears work better than anything on the market at that time, and they made a thicker formula for use on contact lenses.

As soon as I put the lenses in her eyes, she complained of discomfort. I thought that the residents were right; she would be a difficult patient. I told her to just sit there with her eyes closed and get used to the lenses, and I assured her that she would soon be able to tolerate the lenses. She needed to wear the lenses for fifteen to twenty minutes to adapt to the lenses and decrease her tearing so that I could see the fit of the lenses and determine the lens power to correct her vision.

Since I was just beginning to see patients in Galveston, I had plenty of time. I decided to sit with her and talk to her to take her mind off of the contact lenses. We chatted about her life in the convent, and I learned that she had transferred, within her order, to the convent in Galveston for medical convenience. We talked about the weather, the news, and anything else to take her mind off of the contacts.

After about fifteen minutes, she interrupted to say that her eyes were feeling worse instead of better, and she wanted to get the contacts out. I decided that she should be ready to proceed, so I put her at the slip lamp and had her open her eyes. Her eyes were beet red, and they poured forth a white cheesy material. A brief look at the contacts told me that they fit fairly well and that this was not a fit problem. I told her that she had worn the lenses long enough and immediately took them out. She reported immediate relief, but her eyes stayed red and oozed the cheesy material. It was obvious that there was a significant problem.

I decided to take my own history from Sister Elizabeth to figure out why she had responded so violently to the contact lenses. I learned that, until her problem when I had seen her before, she had not had any problems with her eyes other than nearsightedness. She had always been overweight, and she did have a problem with facial hair, which was why she was using the Nair. She had suffered with the "black pox" as a young girl in southern Louisiana. This, I learned from her, was a variation of chicken pox in which the patient has small hemorrhages into the vesicles. The blood immediately turns black, causing a black vesicle on the red chicken pox spot rather than the usual clear vesicle. While she had this illness, the nuns taking care of her in Louisiana thought it might be smallpox, so they sponged her all over with Merthiolate three times a day. Ever since then, she had been allergic to Merthiolate and any black clothing that touched her skin. This was a problem for her, being a nun, but the nuns in the south could wear the white habit at any time, so she was able to avoid black clothes next to her skin.

I discussed this with Dr. Ferguson, who was able to produce the missing links. He explained to me that the allergy to black clothing was probably an allergy to mercury. Most black dyes contained mercury, the element that drove the makers of black beaver hats to insanity and originated the phrase "mad as a hatter." He also told me that Merthiolate was the same thing as thimerosal, the most common preservative in eyedrops at that time. I looked up the formula for Merthiolate and discovered that it contained mercury. We now knew that, basically, she was allergic to mercury. But, what was the original cause of her eye problem? I checked the formula of formalin and determined that it did not contain mercury. Dr. Ferguson suggested that I check the formula for Zenker's solution. Before formalin was used, pathologists used Zenker's solution to preserve specimens. I learned that Zenker's solution could contain mercury.

Putting this all together, Sister Elizabeth was allergic to mercury. She was exposed to mercury while cleaning out the laboratory, and she developed a severe allergic conjunctivitis and keratitis, which progressed to a necrotizing keratitis (inflammation of the cornea, causing death to the tissue). Treating her keratitis and conjuctivitis with antibiotic eyedrops preserved with thimerosal worsened her condition. Patching her eye and not giving her drops allowed her to get better, but prescribing artificial tears, preserved with thimerosal, made her worse again. Removing the superficial layers of her cornea may or may not have been necessary. Stopping the drops again allowed her to heal.

The comfort drops I used on her contact lenses contained thimerosal. They caused her to react once again, which started the resolution of her problem. St. Mary's, the hospital where she worked, was the compounding pharmacy for the city of Galveston. That meant that they were equipped to make up any prescription that was not available commercially. Once they learned of Sister Elizabeth's problem, they offered to make up any eyedrops she needed and make them preservative free. Preservative free eyedrops must be used in a sterile technique and must be discarded and replaced every week. They made her fresh contact lens wetting solution and artificial tears every week, and she did well with the contact lenses.

Her vision was better with the contact lenses, but she only saw 20/40 in her right eye and 20/80 in her left. This was good enough for her to do her job at the hospital. She soon took her vows as a nun and visited Catholic patients in the hospital to pray with and for them.

Several years after she obtained her contact lenses, the mother superior called me about Sister Elizabeth. She had told the mother superior that her vision was rapidly failing, that she could not find the rooms of patients in the hospital, and that she had difficulty reading her large-print Bible. I saw her the next day in the office. Her eyes had not changed from the last time I had seen her. The contact lenses still fit well, the corneas were unchanged, and the back of the eye looked very healthy. Yet, she said that she could only see the 20/200 "E" on the eye chart. Something was not right. I told her things looked all right and that this was probably a temporary change, and that I would need to see her again in a few weeks.

By now I had gotten to know her fairly well, so I asked her how things were going at the convent. Sister Elizabeth replied that there was a lot of excitement in the convent because a team from their mission hospital in Huehuetenango, Guatemala, had been there "enlisting" nuns to go to the mountains of Guatemala. I told her I had been to the mountains of Guatemala and thought it would be interesting to work there for a short time. She said that she was afraid to go there and did not want to be chosen. She thought her present visual problems would prevent her from being effective in the strange environment of Guatemala, and that she hoped she would not be chosen.

With this obvious linkage to her visual problems, I asked her to see a psychiatrist to determine if there was some other reason that she was not allowing herself to see better. She agreed to try that approach, so I referred her to a psychiatrist at the medical school.

About one month later, the psychiatrist called me to report that Sister Elizabeth thought she might be seeing better. I saw her that day. Her eyes looked the same as usual, and she could see 20/40 and 20/80 again. I asked her how things were going at the convent and whether the people from Huehuetenango were sill there. She said that everything was just great at the convent and that the visitors had left about a week before.

I continued to follow her for her contact lenses. She kept saying that she wished that she could see better, especially in her bad eye. I kept telling her that her bad eye was still not bad enough to justify a corneal transplant and the risk of losing the vision she had in that eye. As time went on, she was tolerating her contacts well and had no further problems with her eyes. After several years, as my success rate with corneal transplants improved, I softened to her constant entreaties and agreed to do a corneal transplant on her worst eye.

Her name worked up to the top of the list of waiting transplant patients and tissue became available. The transplant was routine: so routine that I sewed it into the cornea with a 10-0 nylon suture as I always did. We were careful to order prednisilone sodium phosphate, preserved with chlorbutanol, and Parke-Davis chloramphenicol antibiotics without preservative, for her postoperative medications.

The next day the transplant looked great, but the following day we noticed some minimal white blood cell infiltration along the suture lines. On the third day, the infiltrates were very definite and the conjunctiva had become reddened. The new cornea had developed a slight shift forward in the eye, which is very unusual. Something was wrong! I had the resident go to the nursing station and get the eyedrops she was taking. The prednisilone sodium phosphate was correct, but the pharmacist, in his wisdom, had substituted generic chloramphenicol, Opti-chlor, preserved with thimerosal. I also realized at that time that the black suture might contain mercurial dye. I called Ethicon, the suture company, in Summerville, New Jersey, to check on this. They reported back that it had only about one part per million of mercury in the dye.

Since the infiltrates had loosened the sutures and the new cornea was impregnated with mercury, either from the eyedrops or the suture, I decided to replace the corneal button with a new cornea. We obtained a fresh cornea from the eye bank on an emergency basis and redid the transplant—this time with blue Dacron suture and the correct eyedrops.

With this done, she progressed extremely well. In six months she was seeing 20/25 in the operated eye wearing glasses. This eye was now better than her right eye. She was very happy. She knit a two-tone blue afghan for me after calling my wife to find out my favorite color. At Christmas and Easter I received prayer cards. I continued to see her routinely to check the transplant.

Just before the first anniversary of her transplant, she came in to see me as an emergency. She had gone to Texas City with several of the sisters to do some church work on the day before. She said that the smell of the refineries had been particularly bad that day and that the air had burned her eyes. When she awoke that morning her vision on the transplant side had been very hazy.

When I examined her, the conjunctiva in both eyes was reddened. Her right cornea looked as it always did, but the surface of her corneal transplant was hazy and looked like drought-cracked mud. I decided that she must have come in contact with mercury in the air or at least something that could cross-react with her immune system like mercury reacted. I started her on prednisilone acetate forte without preservatives and some antibiotic eyedrops without preservatives and told her to return on the next day.

When I saw her the on next day, the conjunctiva had become more normal, but several of the cracked squares of dried epithelium had fallen off, leaving a defect in the corneal epithelium. Over the next several days she lost most of the corneal epithelium, exposing the corneal stroma to enzymatic degradation (melting), infection, and scarring.

I placed a "bandage" soft contact lens over the defect, added nonpreserved artificial tears, and carbachol eyedrops to try to get the epithelium to heal. This went on for several weeks without obtaining total closure of the defect. After about three months, when the defect was down to about two millimeters in diameter, appearing to have stalled out in the healing process, she came into the office saying that she had great news.

The good news was that the convent had budgeted for new furniture for the common room. When they had asked for bids from the local stores, one of the local stores had donated the furniture, so the convent had money left over. The sisters had voted to spend the money to send Sister Elizabeth, with another sister, to the Mother House in Lourdes, France, to help heal her eye. I gave her enough eyedrops to make the trip and wished her Godspeed with her healing.

Three weeks later, Sister Elizabeth returned from Lourdes and came to see me. When I looked at her left cornea, the defect had healed over completely. There was haze in the cornea beneath the healed epithelium, and she could only see 20/200. Her eye had healed! Over the next several months the haze cleared until she could see 20/80 again. She wanted me to try again with a new corneal transplant, but I convinced her that her chances of success decreased with each subsequent corneal transplant.

She said it was nice while it lasted. I continued to receive prayer cards on special occasions, and she continued to do her good work with patients at St. Mary's Hospital. I saw her there occasionally when I went to see a patient on consult. Several years before I left Galveston, I received word from her that she had been assigned to a hospital in Houston. I referred her to a colleague in Houston and subsequently lost track of her.

Sister Elizabeth was a very pleasant and caring person who was widely misunderstood by many of her physicians, including me. I hope she continues to do well, wherever she is.

I learned from Sister Elizabeth that malingering (feigning or exaggerating an illness to avoid work) is rare and should only be considered after all diagnostic tests have failed and all possible organic diseases have been ruled out. I was also caught ignoring the admonition from medical school to always take a history from the patient yourself, not relying on the work of other people.

I also learned many facts about mercury, Zenker's solution, the "black pox," thimerosal, Merthiolate, and mad hatters. The solution to this problem took more knowledge than basic knowledge of the cornea and corneal diseases.

30

The Lady Who Sat in the Dark

MRS. LAFITTE WAS A WOMAN in her late sixties who came to see me shortly after I arrived in Galveston. She told me that she had a problem with her eyes that had bothered her for about ten years. She had seen other eye doctors in Galveston, but they had told her that the kind of surgery she needed was not done in Galveston, but that she could go to Houston to have it done. She would not go to Houston, so she went home and stayed indoors with the curtains pulled and pressed cold compresses on her eyes to relieve the pain. She stated that sometimes the pain was almost unbearable. Each time a new ophthalmologist came to Galveston she went to see if they could help her. Each one had told her to go to Houston. She had learned that I had come to town, so here she was.

My examination showed that Mrs. Lafitte had bilateral Fuchs' dystrophy of the cornea, with advanced epithelial edema and large blisters in both eyes. As you may recall, this is a hereditary disease that causes the back surface of the cornea to leak, allowing the water-like fluid in the front of the eye to enter the cornea and make it cloudy. It may even cause the surface layer to separate from the cornea and form blisters. She was very light-sensitive and could hardly cooperate with my examination. She also had advanced senile cataracts, but did not appear to have glaucoma. Because of her two problems, the corneal edema and the cataracts, her vision in both eyes was reduced to being able to see a hand waived at six to twelve inches in front of her face.

She obviously needed a corneal transplant in each eye to relieve the pain and improve her vision. She also needed a cataract extraction in each eye to complete the restoration of vision. To relieve her pain, I placed soft contact lenses in both eyes, knowing that this would probably further decrease her vision. This was a temporary fix for the pain only. She was anxious to have any surgery that could improve her vision, so a combined corneal transplant and cataract extraction was to be scheduled as soon as we could obtain a donor cornea. Intraocular lenses were still in the experimental stages at that time, so a triple procedure of corneal transplant, cataract extraction, and intraocular lens implantation was out of the question.

I had just completed my corneal training at Massachusetts Eye and Ear Infirmary, where combined cornea transplant and cataract procedures were the norm, if indicated. This combined therapy had not reached the Texas coast, so I took some grief from other faculty members about not doing them as two separate procedures several weeks or months apart.

Fortunately, we soon obtained a donor cornea, and I brought Mrs. Lafitte into the hospital and performed the combined procedure. I removed the cataract in one piece through the eight-millimeter hole in the center of her cornea where her own cornea had been removed to make room for the donor transplant tissue.

At that time it was routine to keep corneal transplant patients in the hospital for about five to seven days following surgery. Three years earlier, as a resident in Richmond, Virginia, I kept my first corneal transplant patient in bed in the hospital for three weeks after surgery, which was the customary there.

The operation went smoothly, and she was kept on bed rest overnight. I called her down to the examination room the next day and met her sitting in her wheel chair in the waiting room. She looked up at me and said, "Doctor, I am so happy! I'm as happy as if I had good sense! This is the first time in ten years I have been without pain in my eyes." She still had the "bandage" contact lens in her other eye to relieve the pain.

She did well with the operated eye, and as soon as she could see with the post cataract extraction spectacles, about three months later, I did the same operation on her other eye.

Both eyes did very well, and at one year after the first operation she could see 20/20 in her first operated eye, the right eye, and 20/25 in her left eye using her cataract spectacles. I was extremely happy with the outcome and told her what her vision was, explaining that her left eye was not quite as good as her right one. She immediately replied, "That's all right doctor. The left one never was any good."

She continued to do well and I followed her for several years. Her husband always accompanied her on her visits, and we had several conversations about how Galveston was changing. The crime rate was going up, and "undesirable" neighbors were moving into their neighborhood such that they could not go out at night anymore. One day he told me that he was prepared for any shenanigans, because he had bought a big butcher knife that he kept in a box next to the front door. He declared that he was not afraid to use it if the wrong person came to the door. I thought that he sounded a little paranoid, but was probably talking bigger than he would act.

About a year later, I received a call from one of the psychiatry residents. He had just admitted Mrs. Lafitte to the psychiatry unit for acute paranoid schizophrenia and needed to know how she was to use her steroid eyedrops. The resident said Mrs. Lafitte was confused, because she had said that she was to use them differently in the two eyes. I checked the chart and told him that she was correct; they were to be taken once daily in the right eye and twice daily in the left.

I asked what kind of problem she was having and was told that she was brought in by the police, because she called them to report that her husband was chasing her around the house with a butcher knife. I tried to tell the resident about Mr. Lafitte's butcher knife, but he dismissed me with a comment that I should take care of eyes and he would do the psychiatry.

Two days later he called me to tell me that Mrs. Lafitte was being discharged and wanted to know if I wanted her to continue the steroids the same way at home. I commended him on his rapid cure of her paranoia and asked him what he was giving her that worked so well. He sheepishly admitted that the police had brought in Mr.

Lafitte the night before because he was chasing a neighbor around the block with his butcher knife.

Several years later, Mrs. Lafitte came to see me to check on her transplants. She was brought in by a friend and her husband was not with her. It was obvious that her physical and mental status had deteriorated since I had last seen her. One of her transplants had rejected without her realizing it, but her other eye was still very good. Because of her condition, we elected not to do a repeat transplant in the eye with the rejection, especially since she was seeing well with the "good" eye.

At the end of her visit, as she got up from the chair and walked toward the door of the room, she had one long, loud, continuous, escape of flatulence. At the door she turned back to me, smiled, and said, "I'm sorry. I can't help it. I'm old." I knew that she was correct, so I told her to take care of herself, and then I went to get the spray can of "Big D."

I never saw her again after that visit, but I will always remember her beautifully clear corneal transplants and her Texas-style comments to me. I also remember that I knew my patient and her husband much better than the psychiatry resident knew them. I also appreciate the fortitude that it took for the psychiatry resident to call me, a department chairman, to admit that he was wrong.

I learned early in my career in Galveston that many Galvestonians would never leave the island, even for pain-relieving surgery. Houston was only fifty miles away, but many islanders would never go there to shop or attend arts or sporting events. I did not realize it at the time, but she was teaching me how many of the older people of Galveston reacted in situations similar to hers.

When the psychiatry resident called me, I knew Mrs. Lafitte's husband well enough to understand exactly what had happened, but the resident would not listen to me—I was an ophthalmologist, not a psychiatrist.

31

◄○►

A Special-Needs Woman
with a Corneal Transplant

About one month after my arrival in Galveston, Dr. Ed Ferguson called me to see a patient with him. One of the residents had put dilating drops into an elderly woman's eye without checking the chart or the patient's eyes for a shallow anterior chamber. The drops precipitated an angle-closure glaucoma attack in both eyes.

The pressure had quickly risen to above fifty millimeters of mercury in both eyes (normal is 10 to 21). Ed had used pilocarpine eyedrops in both eyes and had given Diamox by mouth to break the attack. In an effort to get the pupil to constrict from its pharmacologically dilated position, Ed had shined the bright light from the indirect ophthalmoscope into her eyes, but it did not break the attack. He wanted me to see the patient and to know if I had any suggestions that might lower the pressure or constrict the pupil.

He had already done what I knew to do to break an attack and it had not worked. The pressure had already come down some after the Diamox, and the dilating drops would wear off in a few hours, so we decided to watch her in the hospital and wait. I was on call that night, and I was to call him if anything adverse happened. Fortunately, her attack broke spontaneously when the dilating drops wore off, so she did not need further treatment.

The lady's son and daughter were in the room, so Ed introduced me to them. The son was a local judge and a good person to know in Galveston. The daughter was married and had several children. She wanted to ask me about her youngest daughter. The daughter, Linda, was born forty years ago with Down syndrome. She lived in a school for special-needs people in Houston, where they visited her several times each month.

The clinic at Baylor Eye Center in Houston provided eye care for the school. The mother told me that they had recently done a corneal transplant on the forty-year-old daughter's left eye, because she had keratoconus in both eyes. Keratoconus is a bulging of the cornea and is often a problem for those with Down syndrome. The woman's mother asked if I would see the daughter in consultation for a second opinion. I agreed to see her.

When they brought the daughter to me, I obtained a more complete history. She had received her first corneal transplant about six months before I saw her. They had not used arm restraints on her after surgery, and she had rubbed her eye and broken the sutures. They had immediately replaced the corneal transplant on the second or third day, and that time they had kept her from rubbing the eye.

About three months after the replacement surgery, her immune system rejected the transplant. Because of her Down syndrome she did not know to tell someone when her vision became cloudy and the eye became light-sensitive, so the treatment for graft rejection was not started until it was too late. The latest information in the chart was that they planned to do another transplant when tissue became available. This time they would try the other eye. The parents wanted to know what my opinion was about further surgery.

It was obvious to me that the grafted eye was not being used and that her useful vision came from her unoperated eye with keratoconus. She looked at me and at her parents when we talked to her. Her mother said that she always sat at the front window of the school residence and watched for them on Saturdays when they came to visit. She was able to spot their car to run out to greet them. She was unable to read because of her IQ, but she could dress herself, find her food, and did not have difficulty getting around the school or her parent's home. She could interact with the other residents and be competitive while playing games. I decided that she was visually functional and did not need to have further surgery. Her operated eye was essentially blind, but stable. That eye could be operated again for a corneal transplant if something happened to decrease the vision in her good eye. In my opinion, any surgery should be to restore vision in the eye with the failed transplant. Any surgery to put her good eye at risk, especially in a patient who is unable to understand what was happening and cooperate with nondestructive behavior, would be irresponsible. This surgery was also unnecessary because she was functioning at her normal level with the vision she had.

This was just what the parents wanted to hear. They immediately asked me if I would assume her eye care, for which they would pay cash. She qualified for free eye care from the State of Texas but had to go to Baylor to get it.

I continued to follow this young woman for many years. The keratoconus had arrested at age thirty-five, and her vision remained adequate for her limited visual demands. Her rejected corneal transplant remained opaque, but did not cause any other problem. She never needed a corneal transplant in her unoperated eye and appeared happy with the vision she had.

The mother later developed combined mechanism glaucoma and became a patient of mine. The father was diabetic and had very high cholesterol, so I followed his diabetic retinopathy.

I continued to follow the mother for many years for her glaucoma. Every time I saw her she would tell me how well her daughter was doing and how grateful the family was that she had not had surgery in both eyes and possibly been made blind.

I used this patient to teach the residents that the need for surgery must be based on the needs of the patient. A disease that is treated by surgery does not automatically mean that the patient needs surgery. They must treat the whole patient and not do unnecessary surgery that might be catastrophic for the patient. This conservative approach was so reasonable to the parents that they both became patients of mine.

32

A Melanoma Survivor

SHORTLY AFTER I ARRIVED IN Galveston, the residents presented a clinic patient to me. Mr. Menendez had been seen in the clinic for a darkly pigmented lump on his left upper eyelid. A biopsy of the lump was performed, and it was determined to be a malignant melanoma of the skin. Under the supervision of an ocular oncologist, six radon seeds had been implanted in the left upper eyelid to irradiate the tumor. After several weeks of radiation, with diminution of the lesion size and firmness, an operation to remove the seeds was performed. Unfortunately, only four of the six seeds could be located and surgically exposed to remove them. The two remaining seeds could be seen on X-ray, but dissection of the eyelid could not locate them, so they were left in place.

In the weeks that followed this attempted removal, the eye became very dry and appeared dull. The corneal epithelium became opaque and then separated from the cornea, leaving a large epithelial defect. I was called in at this point and determined that the radiation had damaged the tear glands and the epithelial layer of cells that cover the cornea. Radiation kills the rapidly growing cells of cancers. It also kills or damages epithelial cells and tear glands because they are some of the fastest growing normal cells in the body.

A white plaque, which formed on the surface of the cornea, was later determined to be caused by calcium deposits. The artificial tears we gave him to relieve the dryness contained thimerosal as a preservative. Thimerosal contains mercury, which has been known to precipitate calcium in damaged tissue. Because of the dryness of the eye, this corneal defect slowly progressed to a deep corneal ulcer in spite of all the tricks I could come up with to stop the ulceration.

At about this time, Mr. Menendez developed a swelling in front of his left ear. The otolaryngologists made a biopsy of the lump and found it to contain malignant melanoma that had probably spread from his eyelid to the ear area through the lymphatic system. They proceeded to perform an excision of the skin and underlying tissues from the left eye to the area just below his left ear. They then performed a radical neck dissection of the left side of his neck, covering the excision area with a skin graft. This procedure was done to remove any lymph nodes that might contain metastases.

He was referred back to the ophthalmology service because of presumed seeding of the melanoma to the left eye socket. By this time the corneal ulcer had perforated, and the eye had become blind. In an attempt to remove any remaining melanoma, we elected to remove the eye and the entire contents of the eye socket, along with the eyelids, which were the source of the tumor.

I assisted the residents in removing the eyelids, eyeball, and all of the contents of the socket. The incision followed the rim of the eye socket for 360 degrees and extended to the bone of the orbital rim. The periosteum (bone-covering membrane) was elevated from the bony walls of the eye socket as far posteriorly as possible. The contents of the socket were dissected free of the tissues at the apex of the eye socket and removed.

The socket was then lined with partial thickness skin from the inside surface of his left upper arm where there is no hair. The skin graft was sutured to the skin edge of the opening and held in place against the walls of the orbit by gauze that was packed into the opening. After one week, the gauze was removed and the skin graft was found to be attached to the walls of the socket and had established a blood supply of its own.

Mr. Menendez was sent home to heal and was told to come back in six weeks to be checked before we could send him to the ocularist to be fit with a prosthesis that would fill the orbit and appear like a normal eye and eyelids.

He returned in six weeks, as requested, and the skin was found to be healed tightly to the bone of the eye socket. However, there was a black, spherical, one-centimeter mass in the back of the socket that was firmly attached at the junction of the roof and nasal wall of the eye socket. It was immediately assumed that this was another recurrence of the melanoma. He was scheduled for the operating room to remove this growth.

In the operating room, under light general anesthesia, this mass was cut loose from the attachments to the wall of the eye socket. Clear fluid, most likely cerebrospinal fluid, gushed from the area where the mass had been, and the patient immediately began to have a seizure. The anesthesia team stopped the seizures by giving him deeper anesthesia.

The neurosurgeons were immediately called to the room to explore the leaking area from inside the skull. They found a hole in the meningeal membranes corresponding with the location in the eye socket where the black mass was excised. They fashioned a patch to cover the hole and restore the meningeal fluid barrier. Their exploration determined that the meninges had protruded through a small hole in the eye socket wall where the contents had been removed. The meninges had bulged through the hole, dried out, and turned black. Fortunately for Mr. Menendez, none of the brain had herniated into the bulge of meninges so that his brain remained intact.

Subsequent to the neurosurgeon's repair of the leak, he remained unconscious for almost three weeks. By the time he awakened from the coma, he had several large bed sores over his pelvis and sacrum. The eye service nurses were not practiced in the treatment and prevention of these bed sores, so the resident in charge of this man visited the neurology and neurosurgery floors and learned from the nurses there how he could treat the bed sores. He treated them several times a day and taught Mrs. Menendez how to irrigate and dress the bed sores. After another week, the patient was discharged home to the Rio Grande Valley for his wife to continue to treat his sores.

He was told to return, after he got back on his feet, to be fitted with an orbital prosthesis to make him appear normal so that he could return to work. Because of his extensive involvement with the tumor and the amount of surgery it had taken to treat it, and also the possibility that he had more metastases scattered through his body, no one at the clinic really expected to see him again.

Mr. Menendez proved us wrong when he walked into the clinic, about three months later, and asked to be fitted for the prosthesis. His bed sores had healed and he was back on his feet. He was referred to the local office of the State Commission for the Blind for authorization. The commission had paid for all of his care to this point. After about an hour, he returned saying that the commission was refusing to pay for his prosthesis.

I was on pretty good terms with the woman who ran the local office of the commission (our sons were in school together), so I called her immediately and asked why they were now refusing to pay for his prosthesis. She told me that they had already spent slightly over ten thousand dollars on his case (this was in 1973) and that they had decided not to spend any more.

I explained to her that all of the expensive care had resulted in a probable cure, but that he could not return to work until the gaping hole in his face was made to be more presentable to the public. I reminded her that the goal of the commission was to rehabilitate people with eye problems so that they could return to the workplace as useful citizens. At this point they had a case on which they had spent ten thousand dollars on what was now a failure of rehabilitation on their records. For as little as $500, for a good prosthesis, they could convert it to a $10,500 success story that would look much better on their annual report to the State Health Department. She relented and asked me to send him back for his authorization papers and to set up his prosthesis fitting.

He returned once more to the clinic to show us his prosthesis. It filled the opening in his eye socket and blended in well with the surrounding skin of the face, so he looked very natural. He told us he had already been back to work for several weeks. He left the clinic with a big smile on his face and thanked us for taking care of him.

Since he lived more than three hundred miles from the clinic and he did not return, we assumed that he did well after that. We do not know if he had further metastases of his melanoma. Many people do survive for five to ten years or longer with melanoma metastases. I hope he survived a long time to reward him for his good fight with his tumor.

I had an early lesson in health care assistance bureaucracies from this patient. This was the first of several of my patients who received assistance of some kind for their care in which the assisting agencies or companies decided to stop paying for the care before the endpoint was reached. They were bureaucratic and short-sighted, imposing artificial limits rather than a good end result in determining the amounts of assistance they would give. Usually I was able to impose reason and logic on them to continue assistance until the resolution of the problem. The duties of a doctor do not end with the delivery of care. I was obligated to fight for my patient to get him his prosthesis.

Mr. Menendez also taught me that some patients with a strong will to fight disease and live can overcome bad odds of survival.

33

The Texas Bowler

I HAD ONE PATIENT WHO HAD followed me and kept up with cards and letters over the years. He came to me in Texas as a young man who was trying to make a living as a professional bowler. He was skinny and had a red mustache and a mop of red hair. His medical conditions were working against him. Other men would have given up, but he was very persistent at wanting to be a professional bowler.

As a teenager Bobby had developed keratoconus. This is a disease in which the center of the cornea thins and bulges outward, distorting the spherical lens shape of the cornea and ruining the optics of the cornea. It bulges until it is somewhat cone-shaped, hence the name keratoconus (*kerato* meaning cornea, *conus* meaning cone-shaped). Early or mild cases are treated with contact lenses, which correct the front shape of the cornea and restore vision. If the cone bulges too high, the lens will ride on the peak of the cone. It is like a hubcap on a traffic cone.

Bobby had already had two corneal transplants, one in each eye. He came to me because he could not focus both eyes together to see the bowling pins in three dimensions and could not see what kind of split he had to convert. His transplants were both clear and in good position. One was slightly larger than the other, which should not make much difference.

When I tried to fit him with glasses, I learned that he was slightly nearsighted in one eye and very nearsighted in the other eye. Glasses for nearsightedness make objects look smaller: the stronger the lens, the smaller the object looks. Bobby's eyes were so different that the images through his glasses were very different in size. The brain is able to put slightly different-sized images together to make one image, and in so doing spreads the objects into three-dimensional space. When the images are too disparate they stay double, or the three-dimensional space becomes all cockeyed. That was Bobby's problem. One transplant was much too nearsighted.

I told him that I could possibly correct his problem by doing another transplant, but predicting the optical power of the transplant after surgery was very difficult. He told me that he was game for anything that might help him return to his first love of professional bowling. We scheduled him for a corneal transplant.

The transplant went well, and he could soon see with both eyes together. I fit him with glasses, and he went back home and began practicing his bowling. On his return visits, his mother brought a number of articles from the local papers and the bowling magazines that talked about his fight to be a professional bowler. They mentioned his eye problems, but he was also fighting a crippling rheumatoid arthritis. He had very large knuckles, and his fingers were starting to slant away from the thumb, which is typical of rheumatoid disease.

He managed to get back on the bowling circuit. He tried to get me to back him with ten thousand dollars so he could register for the tour. He assured me that I would get his first ten thousand dollars of prize money. I told him I would take care of his eyes, but that someone else would have to finance the bowling tour. He managed to find a wealthy oil man to back him.

Several years after the transplant, Bobby began having visual difficulties again. This time it was a cataract in the eye on which I had operated. The cataract had interrupted his stereo vision and ruined his bowling game again. He wanted it out. He had heard of intraocular lenses and wanted one, but at that time no one was allowed to put them into a patient under the age of sixty-five. He was in his early forties. I took out his cataract but made him use a contact lens rather than an implant lens to compensate for his missing crystalline lens. This worked for a while, but his rheumatoid disease was giving him dry eyes, so his soft contact lens became very uncomfortable. About that time they relaxed the ban on implant lenses in patients under sixty-five years old, so I relented and agreed to put in an anterior chamber intraocular lens.

When Bobby came for the surgery he had other problems. He had developed contractures of his right arm and the joints and tendons of his right hand, which were contorted. He was also complaining of not being able to eat. When he did eat he vomited immediately, and he could not keep anything in his stomach. He had lost about thirty pounds, which he did not need to lose. I put him in the hospital and began searching the faculty for a rheumatologist and a gastroenterologist. I finally found people who would work him up, but it was not easy on the University of Texas Medical Branch (UTMB) faculty. His workup led to a diagnosis of active rheumatoid disease with a rheumatoid stomach condition, which paralyzes the stomach walls, combined with rheumatoid contractures of the skeletal muscles. The physical therapy people worked on the contractures, and the gastroenterology people treated his stomach. After about three months he was ready for his implant surgery.

Placing an implant lens in front of the iris after a cataract has already been removed is a simple procedure. The anterior chamber implant lens sits in the angle between the cornea and the iris and must be exactly the right size. It was determined by anatomical studies years ago that adding 3/4 to 1 millimeter to the distance measured across the corneal from the white edge of sclera at three o'clock to the white edge at nine o'clock will give the right length.

The next day in the exam lane the lens was in perfect position. He could see with both eyes again. After his eye surgery, the hand surgeons at UTMB replaced six or seven knuckles on his right hand and his fingers were working well. The patient was theoretically rehabilitated.

About six months later, when Bobby came in to see me for a routine follow-up examination, he showed me his hands. Two knuckles had orange plastic sticks protruding from then. He told me that he had ordered several ten-pound bowling balls, the lightest allowed in pro bowling, and had them bored for him. He had been practicing with these ten-pound balls and his artificial joints had broken.

He had returned to see the doctor who had replaced his joints and discovered that the doctor had left the medical branch. The new doctor had told him he was stupid to have tried to bowl and threw him out of his office. I called the new doctor, but he said that the patient was too stupid for him to operate and he would not take the liability.

My secretary called one of the orthopedic secretaries and learned that the previous doctor had gone to Toledo to teach in the medical school there. She obtained his forwarding address, and we gave it to the patient.

The next time I saw Bobby his knuckles were fixed. I asked him how he managed to get them repaired, and he told me that he had called the doctor in Toledo. The doctor had agreed to fix the joints for free if the patient could pay the hospital bill. The patient went to one of his wealthy friends who had backed him on the bowling tour and got the backer to give him ten thousand dollars to pay for his expenses and the hospital. He had gone to Toledo and had his joints fixed.

About one year after he had his joints repaired, he came to see me for a routine visit. He told me that his ophthalmologist back home told him that the intraocular lens implant was moving in his eye. When I looked at him, it was located vertically from six to twelve, exactly where I had put it. We talked for a while and he asked me another question, which required me to look at his eye again to be able to answer him. When I looked again, the lens was turned horizontally. I put anesthetic in the eye and took a sterile, cotton-tipped applicator to press on the limbus near the foot of the lens. The lens moved away from the point of pressure. I could move it a full 180 degrees, which meant it was too loose and could move, or "propeller," within the eye. This could cause inflammation inside the eye, which was bad for the eye over the long term. We scheduled a removal of the original lens and replaced it with a longer lens. The new lens fit perfectly and did not move.

A year later, when I saw Bobby again he was very excited because he had just arranged to buy a bowling alley in his hometown. The people who had run it for years were planning to retire on New Year's Eve and sell him the bowling alley on New Year's Day. He could pay off the purchase price from the profits over the next umpteen years to support them in retirement. He thought he had died and gone to heaven. He could run the bowling alley, be with all of his bowling friends, and support himself at the same time.

I received a letter from Bobby in January telling me that he had been at the bowling alley for New Year's Eve and said goodbye to the owners as they closed up the place. That night the bowling alley caught fire and burned to the ground, so he had not been able to buy the bowling alley and was back working in his parent's business. The insurance money went to the previous owners because the deal had not been closed.

Shortly after I moved to Pittsburgh I received another letter from Bobby telling me that one of his transplants had rejected. I realized that he was as close to Dallas as he was to Galveston, so I told him that he should go see either Dr. James McCulley or Dr. Dwight Cavanaugh, friends of mine and corneal specialists at Baylor Southwestern Medical School.

Several months later he wrote back that he had been to see the doctors at Southwestern and they told him that the other transplant was failing, but that both corneas had thinned so much from his rheumatoid disease that he was inoperable. He wanted to come to Pittsburgh to see me. He went to see his backers and they gave him money to come to Pittsburgh.

When I saw him, I immediately knew why they had considered him inoperable. His own peripheral cornea, outside of the transplant, had thinned from the edge of the transplants to the sclera because of his rheumatoid arthritis. It was less than one-fifth of the original thickness. If I took out the old transplant, there would be nothing to sew into. The solution would be a small corneal transplant inside the old transplant, which did have enough thickness to hold a small new graft.

I took Bobby over to the Hospital House and got him registered. I told him how to get back and forth to the clinic by bus. In two days we obtained tissue and I did the transplant. I put a six-millimeter button of new cornea inside his old eight-millimeter transplant.

The next day the eye had a low pressure. I checked it for leaks and could not find one. I followed him for three weeks in Pittsburgh, and his pressure gradually rose to low normal. He was running out of money and needed to go home. I called Dr. McCulley, in Dallas, who agreed to take over his care in Texas. Bobby had an open return ticket, so he flew back to Texas and has been followed ever since by Dr. McCulley.

When I see Jim at meetings, he gives me an update on our patient. Every Christmas I get a card from Bobby telling me how he is and what he has been told about his eyes. He occasionally sends me a fancy, ballpoint pen or a beer mug with my name on it. It also says something like: "He Followed His Fathers Footsteps," or "You Are the Greatest Doctor Ever."

Bobby taught me that fixing a problem is never as simple as it appears to be. His repeat transplant led to the need for cataract surgery. This in turn led to the need for an intraocular lens because of his rheumatoid-induced dry eyes. The rheumatoid disease or the keratoconus allowed the cornea to stretch, loosening the intraocular lens.

Bobby also had terrible luck. First it was his eyes, then his fingers, and finally his opportunity to buy a bowling alley. Through it all he has continued to fight and keep his head up. If he had stayed in Pennsylvania, I would have nominated him for the "Courage to Come Back" award from St. Francis Medical Center. I am thankful that I did not have to face all of the obstacles that Bobby experienced.

34

<o>

The Lady with Arthritic Contractures

ONE DAY, IN 1974, I was called to the rehabilitation service of our hospital to see Judy, a seventy-plus-year-old lady who was reported to have a leaking corneal transplant. She had been in upstate Texas when she had a corneal transplant in her right eye. She had been kept in bed for almost three weeks to allow the transplant to heal without stress on the wound. This was very common practice at that time. Unfortunately, this lady had rather severe rheumatoid arthritis. While she lay in bed healing, she had developed muscle contractures of her legs. When she was finally allowed to stand and walk, she could do neither. Her knees were bent at right angles, and she could not straighten them. She was referred to the rehabilitation unit of our hospital to treat her contractures and get her walking again.

When I first saw her, her eye was soft to touch. My examination detected a very slow pinpoint leak from the incision of her corneal transplant. The leak was demonstrable only by putting concentrated fluorescein in her tears and observing the tear film with cobalt blue light. When the leak flows into the tear film layer, it dilutes the dye and changes the fluorescence under ultraviolet light to a bright apple green. The streaming of the green leaking fluid is easily seen against the dull orange of concentrated fluorescein.

Since the leak was so slow and her sutures were still in place, I applied a soft "bandage" contact lens to her eye. This slowed the leak flowing through the wound sufficiently to allow the tissue to heal the incision, stopping the leak completely.

I also noted on my examination that she had a very dense cataract in the lens of the same eye. She could not see very well even though her corneal transplant was optically clear and should have allowed good vision. She was rather bitter about having had surgery and still not being able to see from that eye, and she wanted us to remove the cataract at once. At that time it was unusual to combine corneal transplants simultaneously with cataract surgery. It was my opinion that operating on this eye that had just healed a leak would be asking for more leaks and other problems. Most corneal surgeons agree that it is best to wait at least three months, but better still six months, after corneal transplant surgery or subsequent wound problems before attempting other surgery on the eye. This is especially true in a patient with rheumatoid arthritis, where healing is delayed. I advised her to wait a minimum of three months, but preferably six months, before having cataract surgery.

Within a few weeks she was able to walk again and was discharged. She went home with her corneal wound healing and without any leak. We expected to see her again in about six months.

About one month after her discharge, the chief resident came to me saying that we had been "dumped on" from another teaching hospital that had sent us a patient with a retracted conjunctival flap and a melted cornea. She had run out of Medicare hospitalization days. We were the charity state hospital and obligated to take such patients. When she arrived, we recognized her immediately as our patient with the previously leaking corneal transplant.

Judy had become frustrated with her vision and presented herself at the other hospital demanding a cataract extraction. The residents accepted her and arranged for her cataract extraction. I do not know whether she told them about her wound leak, which was no longer active at that time, and the advice about the timing of her cataract surgery. The residents from the other hospital, in subsequent conversations, admitted to our residents that during the cataract extraction the corneal wound began to leak profusely from several locations. They completed the cataract extraction, but in the days after surgery the corneal continued to leak from several points along the corneal incision line.

Several days after surgery, her cornea began to melt away around the leakage sites. It is not unusual for patients with rheumatoid arthritis to develop melting of the cornea, especially along incisions or at points of trauma. When the melting spread along the incision and toward the edge of the cornea, they decided to cover the entire cornea with a flap of conjunctiva (the loose tissue covering the white part of the eyeball). This would bring a blood supply onto the area, which should then stop the melting. (The normal cornea does not have a blood supply, and serum from blood is known to inhibit the melting activity.) This type of flap will not adhere to the cornea if the cornea is leaking.

When we examined Judy, the flap had retracted, exposing the cornea. There were several small silk sutures hanging from the edge of the flap that had originally held the flap in place. There was extensive melting of the cornea, which spared only the center. The cornea had melted to about 10 percent of its original thickness for almost the entire circumference of the cornea, and this melting extended all the way to the edge of the cornea. She also had several areas of active leakage of aqueous humor from the eye through the old corneal incision and areas of melting.

The eye was on the edge of a disaster. This leaking from the eye, along with the corneal melting, was a setup for infection within the eye and called for immediate intervention. The usual intervention for corneal melting is a corneal transplant, but that was not possible because the peripheral cornea was involved in the melting all the way to the sclera. There was no cornea edge of normal thickness to which to suture a corneal transplant. If a transplant is too large and extends too close to the sclera and iris, the eye develops severe glaucoma. The graft often rejects immediately because of vessels growing into it from the sclera.

Fortunately, while I was doing my fellowship training, I had assisted Dr. Claes Dohlman on several occasions with a procedure that he called a corneal cap graft. I decided that the corneal cap graft would be the correct procedure for this patient.

When a cornea is harvested from the deceased donor, the eye is cut through the sclera about four millimeters beyond the edge of the cornea, entirely encircling the cornea. The cornea and surrounding white sclera is removed from the eye. The ciliary body, the iris, and the lens are removed from the back of the sclera. The cornea and ring of sclera are preserved in a vial of culture media until it is used. At the time of corneal transplant, the donor cornea is usually cut from this donor material using a very sharp round punch of the desired diameter. In doing the cap graft, the entire donor tissue is often used, including the scleral rim.

With Judy in the operating room, under anesthesia, the loose sutures were removed from the edges of the conjunctival flap, and the conjunctiva was pulled back from the sclera. The patient's entire cornea was removed to excise all of the melting tissue to the edge of the sclera, leaving the iris exposed to open air until the cornea-scleral donor tissue was placed over the opening. The outer edge of this cap of tissue was sutured to the surface of the sclera three millimeter past the edge of the corneal hole. Because this cap was about eighteen millimeters in diameter, it took thirty-two individual sutures around the edge of the graft to make the junction watertight. The conjunctival flap edges were advanced over the scleral part of the cap graft, where they were sutured.

At the end of the procedure, the eye looked remarkably normal. When viewed at the slit lamp in the clinic, the anterior chamber, behind the cornea, looked much deeper than normal. This was because the new cornea was attached on top of the old sclera, not sutured in an edge-to-edge manor with the old sclera.

The removal of the corneal tissue all the way to the edge of the cornea may severely damage the aqueous outflow channels. The trabecular meshwork, where aqueous escapes from the eye, is within the sclera near the edge of the cornea and is either damaged or removed when the entire cornea is removed. Damage to this area would usually lead to glaucoma, but in the case of a cap graft it often does not. Perhaps it is because the new cornea-scleral cap graft has an intact trabecular meshwork within it. Or perhaps escape channels develop between the donor sclera on top and the recipient sclera beneath, serving as a relief valve.

She did very well after the surgery and was pleased with her vision. The epithelium on the donor cornea survived the surgery, and the conjunctiva healed to the sclera around the cornea. The intraocular pressure remained normal, and after several days she was sent home. I followed her every week for about two months.

Later, when I returned from the American Academy of Ophthalmology meeting during the third month after her surgery, I learned that she had come into the clinic while I was out of town. She had developed a central corneal ulcer within her cap graft. She had gone to the coin laundry with her sister and had somehow gotten powdered soap in her eye. She washed it out thoroughly, but her vision became worse and worse over several days, so she returned to the clinic.

Judy had developed an ulcer that was reported to be very deep and threatened perforation of the cornea of the cap graft. The ophthalmologist who had stayed home from the meeting to cover the clinic had done an emergency corneal transplant to treat the ulcer. Because of her rheumatoid condition, and to promote rapid healing of the transplant, he used exposed 9-0 silk sutures to sew in the graft, instead of buried nylon sutures. The transplant did heal rapidly, with blood vessels growing into the cap graft, drawn by the silk sutures. Once the vessels reached the edge of the transplant, the transplant was rejected and became cloudy, and her vision was poor. This eye was stable and her other eye had good vision. The vessels that were now present in her cornea lowered the prognosis for a successful repeat corneal transplant, so she declined any further surgery. This was probably the right thing for her to do.

She was still able to walk and get around with the vision in her good eye. We will never know if things would have been different had she waited for six months before having her cataract removed. We can say only that statistics would favor a better outcome if she had waited.

The consequences of doing early surgery had been explained to her, but she apparently manipulated the surgeons at the other hospital to operate on her cataract. Whether the other surgeons knew the true time frame of the corneal transplant is unknown. Patients do not always take the advice given to them but decide that they know best. I suppose that I could have been more emphatic with my instructions to avoid any surgery for at least six months, but I am not sure she would have heeded more strident advice any better than she did.

This cap graft did remarkably well until the incident with the soap powder—they usually vascularized and became opaque, even without injury. The main reason for the cap graft was to close the eye and save the eye from perforation and possible loss of all vision in that eye. We actually succeeded in restoring useful vision to her eye for a short period of time. Her final outcome was a stable eye that, if needed in the future, could have a repeat corneal transplant to try to restore that eye to useful vision. Progress is being made toward preventing transplant rejection.

Her whole problem was induced by the first physician not caring for the whole patient by placing a very arthritic patient at total bed rest following her initial corneal transplant. This made her go into severe leg contractures and need rehabilitation treatments, which probably caused her wound to leak, starting the cascade of events. She needed passive rehabilitative care during the bed rest to prevent the contractures. It would have been less strenuous and less likely to cause a wound leak than the vigorous therapy that was necessary to straighten her legs so that she could walk again after the contractures.

Judy taught me the possible harmful outcome of prolonged bed rest. She also taught me how difficult it is to repair a cornea in a patient with rheumatoid disease. I also saw that all of my explanations to Judy had been thwarted by Judy's desire for immediate restoration of vision and the willingness of another doctor to do surgery under adverse conditions. Our unusually good final result in a cap graft had been destroyed by a random occurrence of soap in her eye at the Laundromat.

35

The Deer Hunter

SOME OF THE PEOPLE WHOM I have helped the most are the least appreciative of the help they have obtained. I take some of the blame for not being what my father called a "crepe hanger." He used to rile against some of the doctors in my hometown for being "crepe hangers." When I asked him what that meant, he explained that some doctors make sure that their patients appreciate them by making them feel that they are sicker than they are before the doctor miraculously cures them. A bad cold becomes "double compound pneumonia–near death." A case of angina becomes "a series of near fatal heart attacks just waiting for the 'Big One' to happen," and so on.

Shortly after I arrived in Galveston, Dr. Ferguson sent me a patient with corneal edema after cataract extraction. Elmer complained that he had "trash" in his eye all the time and could not see. He had undergone cataract extraction in that eye years ago. His cornea was thickened with folds on the posterior surface and a haze of edema on the front surface. His vision was about 20/400 (the big "E" on the eye chart) with his best spectacle correction. His other eye had been injured at a young age, so this eye with corneal edema was his best eye.

I told him that his cornea had failed and that he needed a corneal transplant. He agreed to have the transplant, but said that it would have to wait until after deer season. I asked him how he could shoot a deer with his vision. I was not sure that he could see a deer at twenty yards, much less shoot one at fifty yards. He said he had to take his daughter, who was in her forties, deer hunting with him.

After deer season, Elmer appeared in my office saying that he was ready for the transplant. I asked him if he got his deer, and he said that he did. I asked him how he managed to shoot one with his vision. He explained that he and his daughter went out to a deer blind and waited for a dear to come into the meadow. When they saw the deer, he held the gun to his shoulder while his daughter sighted the deer over his shoulder. When she got the deer in the sights, she told him to pull the trigger. It apparently worked, since he said he killed the deer.

Because he had undergone his cataract operation before intraocular lenses, he was aphakic, which means he had no lens in his eye. At that time, we were using pupil-supported intraocular lenses to replace the human lens when we took out the cataract. These lenses were like small hard contact lenses with two platinum wire loops protruding from the back side of the plastic lens. These two loops bent at a right angle to run parallel to the back surface of the lens. The loops were placed through the pupil to rest against the back of the iris. The lens was large enough that it would not (usually) go through the pupil from the front side, so the lens was held in front of the pupil.

Occasionally, the patient's pupil would dilate so large that the lens would fall into the space in front of the iris or back into the eye. It is a physiological fact that the pupil dilates during orgasm, so we expected to see dislocated lenses, especially in our younger patients. I do not recall any of the patients I saw with dislocated lenses admitting to having the lens dislocate during sexual activity.

While I had the eye open during the corneal transplant, I slipped one of these lenses through his pupil before sewing on the new cornea. This would give him much better vision than he would have had with a good cornea and no lens. There was very little added risk, since the eye was open for the corneal transplant anyway. In fact he saw very well after the cornea healed.

One drawback of the platinum loop intraocular lenses was that the platinum loops were very soft and malleable and had no memory or spring to the loops. The platinum also made the lens heavy. Apparently when I placed the lens through the pupil, I lifted up on the top of the lens and bent the loop backward about 30 degrees. When his pupil dilated in dim light, the lens would sit on the lower edge of the pupil, and the whole lens would drop down in the eye. As it dropped down, the upper posterior loop would ride against the back of the superior border of the pupil. Since the loop was bent backward, it allowed the lens to fall forward into the anterior eye. The loop never came all the way to the edge of the pupil, so the lens did not fall forward through the pupil. However, I was worried that the forward tilt would allow the lens to touch the back of the cornea, which would eventually ruin the corneal transplant if the lens did touch the cornea repeatedly.

This worried me so much that I proposed to the patient that I do a minor procedure and fix the problem. In the operating room, I made two small stab incisions through the limbus: one at three o'clock and one at nine o'clock. I introduced two stainless steel wire surgical spatulas through the two holes and fed one in front of the lens and one behind the superior loop. By squeezing the lens between the spatulas, I bent the loop into the proper position. The entire procedure lasted about two minutes. There was no need to suture the stab incisions since they were self-sealing.

After the surgery the lens stayed at the front surface of the iris, where it was supposed to be, and did not come near the cornea. The transplant stayed clear. I thought that he had a splendid result and told him so. He told me he was disappointed with his vision because he could see 20/20 only at distance; he could not see to read unless he wore his glasses. He thought that he would have some kind of "super" vision after he had the corneal transplant. I did not bother to explain to him that his corneal edema would have been causing him constant pain by this time if he had not had the transplant. His daughter told me that he was never satisfied with anything.

When I saw Elmer for the first time, he could see only the big "E" on the eye chart and complained of constant discomfort. After two procedures and a near perfect result of 20/20 vision at distance, Elmer complained about his near vision. I learned that no mater how much you help people, some will always complain—get used to it.

Elmer also taught me that even a blind man can shoot a deer.

36

<o>

The Eighty-Year-Old
Tennis Pro

SHORTLY AFTER WE MOVED TO Galveston, my wife and I were invited to the Galveston Artillery Club for dinner. This club was hidden behind a high, thick hedge of oleanders and was not visible from the streets that went past the club. The club dates back to the artillery battalion that helped win the Battle of Galveston during the Civil War. The flag from that battalion, with its several cannon shot holes, still hangs, in the entry to the club.

One of the things that impressed me about the club was that they had a tennis court, which doubled as a parking lot in the evenings. The club also had a swimming pool and a nice club house, but not much in the way of grounds. It was wedged into the space available.

A year or so later, before I belonged to the Artillery Club, an eighty-year-old man came to see me about the poor vision in his left eye. Wilber had been hit in that eye with a tennis ball several years before, and his vision had been gradually decreasing ever since.

When I examined him I found that he had a cataract in the eye that had been hit, but no cataract in his other eye. He told me that he thought that his poor vision in one eye was interfering with his tennis game. As the club's tennis professional, he was concerned that he could not play well against the better members anymore. It is not unusual to develop a cataract after being hit in the eye with a tennis ball, golf ball, racket ball, or anything else that strikes a blow to the eye.

A cataract in one eye does interfere with depth perception and could definitely interfere with his tennis game. A monocular cataract creates another problem; at least in 1975 it did. When the human lens containing the cataract is removed, the patient is left very farsighted. Glasses to correct for the farsightedness are very thick and magnify everything by about 30 percent. The brain can deal with small differences in image size between the two eyes to make one picture in three dimensions, but it cannot fuse two pictures that are 30 percent different in size.

If a contact lens is used to correct the farsightedness, it creates an image size disparity of about 5 percent. The brain can fuse two images of that difference in size and create a three-dimensional image. Therefore, in those days, a contact lens was used to correct farsightedness after removing one cataract. Since the advent of intraocular lenses in the mid to late seventies, this is no longer the case. Intraocular lenses do not magnify or minify, so there is no problem with removing just one cataract.

I explained the problem to the patient and asked him if he would be able to handle a contact lens and put it in his eye. He told me he had never handled a contact lens and did not know, but he didn't think it would be a problem. I emphasized that he could not use glasses after his surgery, except over his contact lens for reading. He said that he understood and wanted to have the cataract removed.

The surgery went well and he recovered rapidly. By six weeks after surgery, he was able to see 20/20 with his cataract lens prescription. I proceeded to fit him with a contact lens, and at eight weeks after surgery I delivered it to him and taught him how to put it in and take it out. I also showed his wife how to place and remove the lens.

About two weeks later, he returned for follow-up for his contact lens. He told me that he was disgusted with the contact lens and could not wear it. He wanted glasses to wear instead. I reminded him that I had explained to him why that would not work. He denied that I had ever told him that he would have to wear a contact lens. He had never heard of anyone having to wear a contact lens after cataract surgery. He demanded a pair of glasses. I told him that I would order him a pair of glasses, but that he would not like them. I explained that I could fit either eye, but not both together, because of the image size difference.

It had been known for many years that people will only tolerate a difference in lens power of three diopters between the two eyes. In this case, the difference was about eighteen diopters. I gave him the prescription and he left the office. When he returned several days later, he was carrying the glasses in his hand, not wearing them. This is always a bad sign.

He tore into me for ordering him a pair of glasses he could not wear. He said that when he put them on he got sick at his stomach and felt dizzy. He could hardly walk in the glasses, let alone play tennis. I took out one lens and let him see with only one eye to get rid of the distortion and dizziness. He could not see three dimensionally with only one lens, through either lens.

I finally told him that he could wear his old glasses for his nonoperated eye around the house, and that his operated eye would be too blurred to interfere with his nonoperated eye. I explained that when a cataract eventually developed in his right eye, he could have it removed, and then he could use cataract spectacles for both eyes and would quickly learn the image size difference and probably be able to return to tennis.

Wilber taught me that patients hear what they want to hear. Long explanations of what to expect are not heard or are not remembered when the problem happens later. When it was time to teach him about the contact lens, he showed a negative attitude about the contact. This probably led to his being unable to accept the contact lens and probably made him repress the preoperative warning further.

There have been many studies about whether the patient hears what is told to them or whether they imagine what was said and fit the facts to their situation. I think he retired from tennis shortly after this, accepting the fact that he was eighty years old and it was time to retire, especially since he could not see to play the game.

37

<o>

An Intraocular Lens for a
Handball Player

ABOUT TWO YEARS AFTER I arrived in Texas, Dr. Ed Ferguson decided that the Medical Branch Ophthalmology Department, to stay on the cutting edge, should start doing intraocular lens implants and phacoemulsification. Both phaco and implants were still very controversial at that time. Some ophthalmologists were putting in implant lenses without first doing phacoemulsification, and instead did routine intracapsular or extracapsular cataract surgery before inserting the implant.

Ed had researched this thoroughly and decided that we should go to Santa Monica, California, to take the course on these procedures. This was a three-day course, complete with practice on eyes of dead rabbits and cats. Many of the participants did not take advantage of all of the eyes furnished to each of us, so Ed and I went around the lab practicing on those that were left over. When we finished, there was not one eye that had not been used.

Even though we had practiced a lot, we decided that we needed more practice before we did phacoemulsification on a patient. So I set up a laboratory for practice sessions. Eventually, Ed and I did start putting anterior chamber and pupillary supported intraocular lenses in patients after intracapsular cataract surgery. We were early adopters of using intraocular lenses in cataract surgery.

One of the faculty members in the internal medicine department learned that we were doing lens implants and contacted me about his uncle. Uncle Alan lived on the east coast and had heard about implant lenses, but he could not find a local ophthalmologist who would take out his cataract and put in an intraocular lens. The nephew asked if I would consider a cataract extraction and an intraocular lens for his uncle. I agreed to see his uncle, who was planning a visit to Galveston, and said that I would consider doing the surgery. The appointment was arranged.

Alan had a significant cataract but no other problem. He said that he wanted an implant lens because he was an avid handball player who played several times each week. I discussed this with Ed, and we decided that Alan would not be a good candidate for a pupillary lens because these lenses moved forward and backward in the eye with physical activity and might dislocate within the eye. Instead, Ed thought that the patient would be a good candidate for a rigid, anterior chamber lens, which was anchored within the eye by being wedged between the iris and the cornea, resting on the angle structures. Once in the eye, this lens would not move except from severe trauma. We explained this to the patient, and told him that he would have to always wear his "combat glasses" when playing handball.

He agreed with this, so I performed routine intracapsular cataract surgery without any complications. The lens was slipped into the eye, and all four feet of the lens were placed in the angle between the iris and cornea. The surgery went very well, and he was kept in the hospital overnight as was usual. I checked him that afternoon and the eye looked great.

About 2:00AM, the eye resident in the hospital was called to see the patient, who was complaining that he was awakened by the sudden onset of pain in the eye and nausea. The resident checked the eye and found that the anterior chamber of the eye was full of blood, and that the intraocular pressure was elevated. He gave the patient Diamox to lower the pressure and replaced the patch on the eye.

When I saw the patient the next day on rounds, he still had some blood in the eye, but the lens could be seen in some areas and appeared to be well positioned. Usually, postoperative hyphema (blood in the anterior chamber) will clear spontaneously without any aftereffects, but I kept him in the hospital for observation.

The next night, the eye resident was again called at 2:00 AM for the same reason. He found a new hemorrhage in the eye and treated it the same way. This continued for the third night, always at about the same time. The blood in the eye in the morning was increasing each time this happened. This occurrence at 2:00 AM reminded me of a patient I had treated who had recurrent erosions (spontaneous tears of the corneal epithelium) at 2:00 AM that would awaken her with pain in the eye. She took Dalmane, a relative of Valium, as a sleeping pill, and it stopped the erosions.

Librium and Valium were among the drugs assigned to me at the Food and Drug Administration when I worked there after my internship. I knew that this group of drugs (Librium, Valium, Dalmane,) all decreased rapid eye movement (REM) sleep. REM sleep occurs during dreaming and is most common about 2:00 AM in most people.

I decided that REM sleep had something to do with these recurrent hemorrhages in this patient's eye. I started him on Valium, and he stopped having the hemorrhages. However, the amount of blood that had already accumulated was enough to fill the front of the eye, and it appeared to be clotted. I knew that it might take days to clear and could stain the cornea a rust-brown color. The stain could last for years. I discussed this with the patient, and he said he wanted to move on as quickly as possible, so he wanted me to remove the blood.

We opened the cataract wound and washed a large clot from the front of the eye. The lens was in place, but there was a large clot behind the lens. To remove the second clot from the eye, I had to remove the lens. When I delivered the lens, it was obvious that the clot was stuck to the iris next to where one of the feet of the intraocular lens had been, indicating the source of the bleeding. As soon as the lens was out of the eye, the clot rose into the anterior chamber. When I expressed the second clot, it was in the shape of a collar button, with two circular clots that were connected by a stem where the pupil had been. The vitreous was clear and free of hemorrhage. I closed the eye without replacing the lens because it might cause the bleeding to recur. I decided that he would have to wear contact lenses or have another implant lens inserted after everything healed. I examined the removed lens under the surgical microscope. I had seen reports of poorly made lenses with rough feet that caused bleeding, but the feet of this lens looked smooth.

He did well after the removal of the clots. After the eye had healed for about a week, I looked into the angle structures with a gonioscopic lens and saw that there was a large vessel crossing the angle at the position where one of the feet of the anterior chamber lens had been. This vessel was in an unusual place. The lens had been resting against the vessel. Apparently, when the eye moved rapidly during REM sleep, it would tear the vessel and cause the hemorrhage into the eye. The Valium had stopped the REM sleep and stopped the bleeding.

Alan went back home and called me about six weeks later to say he had been fit for contact lenses and that he saw 20/20. He was able to play handball in his contact lens, and he did not plan to have an implant.

I had been talked into using an implant lens, although the rationale was well thought out in advance. I was bending the rules a little by doing a new procedure on a patient from so far away and I got caught. I let my ego get the best of me.

He had a very rare situation wherein a blood vessel runs across the place where the foot of the lens rests, creating a source for hemorrhages. I also learned that REM sleep can cause intraocular hemorrhages under certain circumstances. This patient was not displeased with us for having the complication, because he had sought out a new and somewhat untried device.

Serendipity can be good or bad. In this case, it was a vessel in the wrong place.

38

◀◎▶

Paper-Thin Cornea

I HAD A PATIENT IN GALVESTON who had early corneal edema that interfered with his vision. I started him on sodium chloride (salt) eyedrops, and his vision cleared dramatically. He was so pleased that he brought his sister, Effie, from Louisiana to see me. When my resident brought Effie back to the exam room and introduced her to me, she turned to her brother and said, "He doesn't look like he can walk on water to me!" I knew I had my work cut out. It is hard to start with such high expectations.

I told Effie that I did not walk on water, but that I could try to help her. I could not give her any guarantee. That was before I examined her. She had been fighting the complications of trachoma since she contracted it as a child, when it was endemic in Louisiana. When I everted her eyelids, she had large scars of the conjunctiva on the back of both eyelids, which is typical of trachoma. This scaring on the back of the eyelids pulls the conjunctiva on the back of the eyelids and draws the lid margins onto the back surface of the eyelids. It also pulls the skin from the front of the eyelid over the lid margin, pulling the eyelashes with it. For years her eyelashes had been rubbing her corneas. Her vision was reduced to about 20/400 (the big "E" on the eye chart) in both eyes.

Chronic rubbing of the eyelashes on the cornea causes repeated epithelial abrasions, in which the epithelium is scraped off the underlying corneal stroma. The epithelial defect allows the collagenase enzymes made by the epithelial edges to dissolve the collagen, which constitutes the majority of the corneal stroma. Over the years, her cornea had melted to paper-thin over the entire cornea. It was basically Descemet's membrane with a layer of endothelial cells attached, a very thin layer of stroma with a few blood vessels, and an overlying epithelium. The epithelium, which was now supported by the vessels in the thin stroma, did not have abrasions. She needed a corneal transplant, but there was insufficient corneal thickness to which to sew the edge of the transplant.

I explained to Effie that she might benefit from a corneal transplant, but that her cornea was too thin to receive one. I would have to do a nonoptical corneal transplant over her present cornea to be able to do a second one through the first for visual purposes. She was so happy to hear that she might see again that she was willing to go through the first operation, which would not give her vision, so that she could be able to eventually have an operation that could restore her vision.

I obtained a donor cornea that was not suitable for a penetrating keratoplasty but was suitable for a lamellar, cornea-restoring, transplant. I trimmed the sclera from the edge of the donor cornea and peeled Descemet's membrane with the endothelium from the back surface of the graft tissue. Effie's cornea was scraped free of all epithelium so that the graft would fuse to her remaining cornea.

The conjunctiva was dissected from the sclera at the limbus and elevated from the sclera for several millimeters posterior from the limbus. The graft tissue was sewn to the sclera to hold it centered on the cornea. The conjunctiva was then drawn up to the edge of the graft by a purse string suture.

To spare the graft from more eyelid trauma, I split the eyelid along the scar and placed sutures in the eyelid to rotate the lid margin out to where it belonged. The sutures were tied over rubber tubing to evert the eyelid and left in place until the eye lid had healed in the everted position.

After the surgery, the patient complained that she did not see any better than before the surgery. I reminded her that this was not a vision-improving surgery; rather, she would have to wait for six months to a year before it healed sufficiently to allow the second operation, which would improve her vision. In the meantime, her lashes were not rubbing her cornea, which would allow her to be much more comfortable.

She loved to complain. Every time I saw her she wanted the surgery right away, and she complained when I told her that her eye was not ready. She said that she was broke and could not afford more trips to Galveston. Her brother asked her if the oil and gas wells on her farm had gone dry, and she assured him that they were still flowing. Her brother agreed that she liked to complain, but said that she could afford the trips to Galveston.

Six months after the first surgery, I removed the sutures. I tested the edges of the tectonic graft and found them well healed. We scheduled surgery for a corneal transplant and a cataract extraction in the eye we had prepared. The surgery went well, the tectonic graft stayed attached to the patient's cornea, the lens came out through the corneal opening for the transplant, and the graft did well after the surgery.

After about six weeks, I fit her for glasses, and she was amazed by how well she could see. As I recall, she could see about 20/30 with her glasses. I followed her for a year until I removed her corneal transplant sutures. The transplant stayed clear and did not try to reject. After her sutures were out, she told me that she wanted to be followed by her local ophthalmologist, because she could not afford the trips to Galveston. I realized that it took her three hours to drive from Louisiana to Galveston, so I sent her back to her prior ophthalmologist for observation.

She told me when she left that I came close to "walking on water" because she could see again for the first time in years. She really did appreciate what I had done for her.

Effie professed to have the patience needed to wait for the second surgery, but when she had to wait, she was very impatient. People expect immediate results or they lose patience. This made me think about having the patient sign a written explanation of what was expected that I could show the patient later when they complained. Some doctors do this, but I did not want to embarrass the patient by using such a tactic.

Her initial statement that I did not look like I "walked on water" let me know that she expected miracles from me. This made me extra conscientious in the informed consent process, and I always made sure that I gave the downside of everything. In the end, Effie did express her gratitude to me for restoring her long lost vision.

39

The Newsstand Operator

WHEN VITRECTOMY BECAME AVAILABLE, THERE was a large backlog of patients, mostly diabetic, who had lost all vision except light perception because of hemorrhages into the vitreous jelly that fills the eye. These hemorrhages organize into fibrous sheets that block light from reaching the retina. Many of these people had been blind for many years and did not return for eye care because they had been told that there was nothing doctors could do for them. One of these was a diabetic man who ran the newsstand at the Galveston County Courthouse. The Blind Commission for the State of Texas controlled the news concession in all of the county courthouses in Texas and placed blind people in them to give them employment.

Henry had been blind for many years and had run the newsstand for almost twenty years. He came to us because he had heard that we could restore vision in some diabetics. Examination indicated that he had membranes in his eyes from previous hemorrhages, so we offered him the chance for vision by having a vitrectomy to cut out the membranes.

During surgery, Henry was found to have several successive membranes between his pupil and his retina. We would cut through one membrane with the vitrector to discover another membrane just as dense. These membranes become dense and yellow and have been described as "French's Mustard Yellow membranes."

After we had cut large round holes in four different membranes, we could see the retina. It appeared relatively normal for someone with years of diabetic retinopathy and multiple hemorrhages from that diabetic retinopathy, so we were quite encouraged.

On the day after surgery, Henry could see well enough to read some of the letters on the vision chart. We followed him closely for the first two weeks, and he was doing fine. He could see 20/40 with glasses and was very pleased. We told him to come back in two weeks for a final fitting for glasses.

When he returned, he was upset because he had awakened that morning, unable to see anything with the operated eye. The intraocular pressure in his eye was very high. We dilated his pupil to look at his retina and discovered that the high intraocular pressure had completely occluded his central retinal artery, which had shut off all of the blood supply to his retina and killed the retina.

He had many little sparkling dots that swirled around in the eye. They appeared to rise in the back of the eye, where it is warm, and fall in the front of the eye, where it is cooler. These sparkling dots were broken red blood cells. He had hemorrhaged into the eye after we had seen him the last time. These red blood cells ruptured and lost their hemoglobin and became empty cell wall sacs called ghost cells. These sacs floated in the aqueous humor that filled the eye and eventually were carried to the outflow channels in the trabecular meshwork, where the aqueous escapes the eye. The cell wall vesicles plugged the outflow pathways and obstructed the flow of aqueous from the eye, thereby raising the intraocular pressure. His pressure when we saw him was 38 mm Hg and may have been much higher on previous days. It had obviously been high enough to cause the central retinal artery to close, blocking the supply of oxygen to the retina.

When we saw him there was nothing we could do to restore his vision in that eye. We told him that we could do the same operation on his other eye. We explained that we would follow him very closely for any postoperative hemorrhage and remove it as soon as it appeared so he would not lose his vision in the second eye. He thought about it for awhile and decided not to have surgery in his other eye.

Henry explained to me that he had been employed running the newsstand for twenty years and had been able to support his family. Since the operation, he had been contacted by the blind commission and told he would probably lose the newsstand because his vision had been restored. Now that he had lost the restored vision, he decided to remain blind so that he could keep his job, knowing that he could still have the operation at some time in the future if his circumstances changed.

The one thing that Henry taught me was that those of us who see well and are used to having good enough vision to take care of ourselves do not understand the world of the person who has become blind after seeing. We have not made the adaptation that the blind person has made to learn to be independent without vision. Sometimes this decision to remain blind is made through stubbornness, and sometimes it is made from careful reasoning about family responsibilities. I had to admire this patient for sacrificing his own happiness from renewed vision for the responsibility to care for his family.

40

<o>

Unusual Results from an Alkali Burn of the Eye

RANDY WAS REFERRED TO ME several days after he sustained a severe alkali burn to his left eye. He was a truck driver for a refinery. He was standing next to his tank truck while the hose men were filling it with alkali. When they swung the filler hose away from the truck, the hose leaked alkali as it was moving, since it had not drained completely. Some of this strong alkali hit Randy in the face, particularly his left eye.

He was rushed to the local emergency room, where his eye was flushed with water and saline for several minutes to remove the alkali. In spite of this care, he developed a severe chemical burn of the eye, with damage of the conjunctival blood vessels. He had total loss of the corneal epithelium and much of the conjunctival epithelium. Over the first twenty-four hours, the cornea became hazy and the intraocular pressure rose. At this point he was referred to me.

I treated this eye with antibiotics, steroids, a soft contact lens, and patching. After about ten days, I discharged Randy from the hospital to be followed as an outpatient. He explained to me that he could not drive a truck until both eyes had good vision. The refinery was paying all of his medical bills, but he was out of work and had no savings, so he had hired a lawyer to seek compensation from the refinery. He told me that he tended to hang out in bars in the evenings and would often talk the bartender into letting him sleep through the night in the bar after it closed.

It took several weeks for the epithelium to heal, and during that time the eye was kept covered with a firm patch. I was seeing him almost daily to instill eyedrops and replace the patch. Each time I saw him the tape edges on the patch were rolled and the patch was very dirty. Not having a regular place to stay, his hygiene had suffered. He was often unshaven, wore dirty clothes, and lacked oral hygiene. Occasionally he would appear in clean clothes, clean shaven and well groomed. I learned that this was when he had visited his sister who lived near Houston.

Once the epithelium had covered the surface of the cornea, the corneal stroma remained cloudy and thickened. It was apparent that the corneal endothelium had been damaged by the alkali and that he would need a corneal transplant to restore the vision in this eye. He was anxious to have the transplant. I explained to him that corneal transplants in alkali-burned eyes had the lowest prognosis of any disease for obtaining a clear, visually successful outcome— less than 50 percent. Many corneal specialists think that people with alkali burns should wait at least one year, if not several years, before attempting a corneal transplant. He was sure that the refinery would not pay for the surgery if he waited too long, so he wanted to go ahead immediately. He assured me he understood the added risk of failure.

I agreed to proceed with the transplant as soon as we could get tissue. In those days, tissue donation was somewhat rare, and patients had to wait for a cornea to be donated. I told Randy that we would put him on the list and call him when tissue became available. He told me he did not have a phone number or a regular address. Sometimes he slept at the labor hall, sometimes in bars, and sometimes, during the summer, under the stars. I asked him about contacting him through his sister. He said that she lived in an apartment, the location of which was the second door in a row of apartments one block from the Shell station, but he did not know the address or phone number, and besides, he felt that he had worn out his welcome with his sister. He finally agreed that he would take a room in a cheap hotel near downtown and call me with the payphone number.

A week later tissue became available. My secretary called the hotel, someone located Randy, and he came into the hospital. At that time, corneal tissue could only be kept for about twenty-four hours before surgery, so corneal transplants were an emergency, usually done at night. Randy's was no exception. The corneal transplant surgery was uneventful, and it ended at about eleven o'clock that night. As I wheeled Randy back to the hospital floor, I explained to him that he had to stay in bed that night, but I would allow him out of bed the next morning. He immediately told me that he had to go move his pickup truck that he had parked in the no parking zone on the circle in front of the hospital. I told him to stay in bed, and we called security to move his truck. They put it in the hospital parking garage.

Randy did well post operatively. At the time that this procedure was done, corneal transplant patients were kept in the hospital about five days. On the fifth day, I told Randy that he was ready for discharge. He panicked. He said that he had no place to go. His sister would not take him, and he had left the hotel that he was in before surgery without paying his bill. He begged me to keep him in the hospital until he could go back to driving a truck. I knew that driving would not be possible for at least six weeks, possibly a year. I kept him in the hospital, courtesy of the State of Texas, and called social services to find him a place to live.

It took over a week to make those arrangements. I finally discharged Randy, but my office received a call immediately. It was from the parking garage. Randy had no money to pay for the two weeks of parking and could not get his pickup truck back. A call to social services solved that problem too, so he got his truck.

I continued to follow Randy's progress as an outpatient. He did well and did not have the complications that often occur after transplants for alkali burns. Eventually he arranged to live at the union hall near Houston, and he visited his sister often. With my assistance, he was seen by an ophthalmologist I knew and trusted in that area, but he still came to see me about once a month. Once the sutures were removed and he was fit with spectacles, I asked him to return to see me about once a month.

He told me that his lawyer had obtained a settlement of six thousand dollars from the refinery for his pain and suffering. When I asked him what he intended to do with the money, he told me that the lawyer had claimed half and that he had spent the rest on whiskey and women for a "really great weekend in Seaside, Texas."

Randy returned to driving a truck and did not keep his appointments with me. I did not see him again until about two years later. He walked into my office, wanting to see me immediately. His eye was reddened, and he could not stand to be out in the sunlight. I examined him and determined that his immune system was trying to reject his corneal transplant. I found sample bottles of steroids and antibiotics in the clinic and told him to put a drop of each one in his eye every hour during the day and every two hours at night. He was given an appointment to see me the next day. I was not sure whether he would keep that appointment, but the next morning he arrived on time in his red Bermuda shorts, beer T-shirt, and cowboy boots.

His eye had responded well to the steroids, and the eye was much improved. I told him that the treatment was working and that he should continue to put a drop of each medication in the eye every two hours and return in three days. I did not see him again for another two years.

Two years later he walked into the office, again with a red eye. A quick exam showed that he was again trying to reject his graft, but that the grafted cornea was in remarkably good condition. I gave him fresh samples and told him to use them every hour and come back to see me in the morning. I explained to the resident, who was working with me, that this had worked two years before and that Randy had returned the next day. The next day came and went without Randy returning. My resident at the time, who was a long distance runner and jogged the seawall every morning, told me a week after that last visit that he had seen Randy sitting on a planter box on the seawall that morning. He was leaning against a palm tree holding a jug of wine. The resident did not stop to check his eye. I assumed that he was doing well since he had always come in when he had a problem.

About a year later, Randy walked into the office, wanting to be seen. He said that his truck driver's license had expired and that he needed new glasses to pass the test to get it renewed. I examined him and was amazed at the beautiful condition of his corneal transplant. It hardly showed any damage from the two rejection attacks. With new glasses he could see 20/20 with his good eye, and 20/25 with his transplant eye—certainly good enough to pass the truck license test.

Randy taught me that the old saying that "God looks after drunks and fools" is true, because Randy certainly did not look after himself. Randy had a corneal transplant in a disease that causes failure of the transplant more than 50 percent of the time. He did not take care of his graft unless it was causing pain or poor vision. His lifestyle was not conducive to avoiding rejection, and he did not have a good diet. After the way he abused his health and the care of his transplant, it is remarkable that he did not destroy his transplant when the body tried to reject it. I had told him to come see me as soon as he noticed his eye being red or sensitive to light. He did this every time, and it saved his graft.

Several years after the driver's license problem I left Texas, so I do not know if he had any more rejections or if he is still driving a truck. I do know that he is a very lucky man.

41

<o>

The Big Thicket Thorn

THERE IS A REGION OF Texas along the southeastern border with Louisiana that is characterized by extremely dense underbrush and trees. The undergrowth is so dense that it is difficult for a man to walk through it. This region is known as the "Big Thicket." For some reason, hunters are drawn to the Big Thicket to hunt, and many get lost. It is the native land of the Alabama-Coushatta Indians, who are said to know how to go through the Big Thicket without getting lost or injured.

A young black man came into the clinic one day complaining of severe pain in his left eye. Bill had been hunting with a friend in the Big Thicket. He told us that he had been following his friend through thorn bushes. They had to hold back the branches of the thorn bushes as they walked past to keep from snagging them. He had gotten too close to his friend, and when his friend let loose of the branch, it snapped back and hit Bill in the eye. He had to pull the thorn out of his eye. He had brought one of the thorns with him to show us what hit him. The thorn was about seven inches long and about one-fourth of an inch in diameter at the base. It tapered continuously over the seven-inch length to a very small sharp point.

When I examined the patient, he had a small hole in the center of his cornea, directly over the pupil. This hole had sealed and did not leak, even when slight pressure was made on his eye. I could see that the thorn had penetrated his lens, and it appeared to have passed all the way through the lens. The lens was clear except for the tract left by the thorn. His vision was still about 20/40, but there was an inflammatory response in the eye. The inflammation could be caused by infection, or by a reaction to something left by the thorn, or perhaps by protein leaking from the lens where the thorn had perforated the capsule of the lens.

Since the hole in the cornea had closed and sealed, we elected to treat him with antibiotics, steroids, and watchful waiting. He returned to the clinic every few days for us to see the progress of the therapy. His pain quickly went away, and the reaction within the eye subsided. His lens remained clear, which was unusual after a perforation of the lens capsule. Usually the lens will turn white within days.

About one month after his injury, I noticed that blood vessels were growing from the edge of his pupil into the lens. There were four or five tiny vessels growing toward the center of the lens. This told me that he was developing an immune response to his lens material as it leaked into the aqueous humor. The only way to stop this was to remove the lens so the body would stop trying to eliminate it.

He was about thirty-five years old, and the iris was attached to the lens by the blood vessels. Usually, at this age, the back surface of the lens is attached firmly to the front surface of the vitreous jelly so the capsule cannot be removed. The reaction is usually directed to the lens core, not the capsule. Therefore we planned an extracapsular cataract extraction to remove the core. The capsule bag is opened, and the soft lens substance is aspirated from the eye. The capsule is left in the eye, attached to the vitreous, and in this case the iris.

The operation went smoothly, and we felt that we removed almost all of the soft cortical part of the lens (some always remains at the equator of the lens). We did not put an implant lens in this eye because of the vessels from the pupil and the possibility of a preexisting infection in the eye.

He did well for about six weeks and then began having a little reaction, with white blood cells and protein in his eye. This slowly became worse and made him sensitive to light. He wore sunglasses, but direct sun still bothered him. We started treatment with topical steroids, with good results. Fortunately, he was not one of the people who get glaucoma from the steroid eyedrops after two weeks. His eye was always slightly red, which bothered his wife but not him.

I followed him for several years until he did get inflammatory secondary glaucoma, which was difficult to control with medications. I finally sent him to a glaucoma specialist in Houston, who did a filtering procedure to treat his glaucoma. He transferred his care to the glaucoma specialist, and I did not see him again.

He was an even-tempered young man who blamed himself for his problem and did everything we asked him to do to treat his problem. He did go blind in that eye from his glaucoma about five years after the injury, but he probably adapted to the loss as it occurred.

I learned that an apparently minor injury could not be saved due to long-term consequences. I also learned that patients do appreciate being able to maintain vision in the injured eye as long as possible and will go to great lengths to do so.

42

Man-o-War Sting

WHILE IN GALVESTON, I WAS called upon to treat a number of eye injuries that I did not learn about in my residency in Richmond, Virginia, or my fellowship in Boston. On one such occasion, I was called at the office by a resident who was working at the U.S. Public Health Hospital in Galveston. He was seeing a patient who had been swimming in the Gulf of Mexico at a Galveston beach and had swum into the tentacles of a Portuguese Man-o-War. He had been swimming with his eyes open and complained of pain in his forehead, cheek, and eye.

The resident said that he had a vertical red streak that ran down his forehead, his eyelid, and his cheek in a straight line. When the resident stained the cornea with fluorescein, there was a vertical streak of missing epithelium across the center of the cornea.

The standard treatment of Man-o-War stings is well-known in Galveston: flood the skin with alcohol to stabilize the stings so that they would not discharge. Then sprinkle Adolf's Meat Tenderizer on the area to dissolve the stings. They had treated the skin but wanted to know from me whether they should put the alcohol and meat tenderizer on the eye.

Meat tenderizer is dried papain from papaya juice. This enzyme dissolves collagen, a component of meat fibers. The cornea is made almost entirely of collagen fibers, so I decided that it would not be wise to put an enzyme on the cornea, which might damage or dissolve it, causing it to perforate. Alcohol can be used to remove the corneal epithelium, which in this case we wanted to heal as quickly

180

as possible. Therefore, using the alcohol was not a good idea either. I told them to use some topical anesthetic and irrigate the cornea to see if the stings would wash off. The resident told me several days later that they had irrigated the cornea for several minutes and the patient still had pain for several hours. By the third day the epithelial defect had healed with good vision, but the patient still had the red streak on his face.

Later the resident on this case approached me with the idea for a research project. His father ran a Chinese restaurant, and he knew that there were large boxes of meat tenderizer in the restaurant store room. He wanted to see if meat tenderizer was safe on the cornea.

Since the outcome of enzyme activity is dependent on living tissue and we could not experiment on people, we decided to use laboratory rabbits for the research. I ordered the rabbits, and he brought in a shaker of meat tenderizer without spices. We drew up a protocol for the experiment. He would anesthetize the rabbit's eye and scrape a streak of epithelium from the cornea, similar to what happens in a Man-o-War sting. He would then sprinkle meat tenderizer on the cornea and leave it there for twenty seconds before washing it off with saline solution. We did this to ten rabbits: five treated with meat tenderizer, and five with scraped corneas and no tenderizer.

We treated the corneas every day with antibiotics and checked them every day for melting or other problems. The rabbit corneas treated with meat tenderizer ulcerated, and by the fifth day all of the tenderized corneas had melted through and perforated. The animals were put to sleep when the cornea perforated. The rabbits that did not get the meat tenderizer all healed the cornea within four days.

That year the resident presented the findings to the annual alumni meeting to advise ophthalmologists on the Gulf Coast not to put meat tenderizer on the cornea. Several of the attendees told us that they had wondered whether it was safe to use the meat tenderizer on the cornea and were glad that we had done the study.

This resident had seen a patient who generated a significant question about the treatment of Man-o-War stings. No one knew the answer to the question, so a study was designed to learn the effects of meat tenderizer on the corneal abrasion caused by the

43

◄○►

Daddy Is Going to Die

ONE MORNING THE RESIDENTS PRESENTED a patient to me who had come into the hospital through the emergency room the night before. He was a retired carpenter in his late eighties. He had suddenly developed severe pain in his left eye, so his daughter had brought him to the ER.

Many years before, he had undergone a series of silver injections from a doctor who had told him that they would prevent polio. He did not get polio, but the silver caused his skin to turn a dusky blue-grey. When the nurses in the emergency room saw his skin color, they assumed that he was cyanotic from an acute heart or respiratory problem and started a "code blue" routine on him. This alarmed his daughter, who demanded to know why they were treating him as a heart patient when his problem was pain in the eye. She explained to the nurses that he was always blue.

The eye resident was called to the emergency room and quickly determined that he had a dense cataract in his left eye. The cataract had swollen and pushed forward against his iris, blocking the pupil and precipitating an angle closure glaucoma attack. The pressure had risen to a painful level and the eye felt rock hard. The resident started the routine treatment for an angle closure attack by trying to dilate the pupil and giving him oral Diamox to stop aqueous production in the eye.

When I saw him the following morning, his pressure was still elevated and he said that it continued to be painful. In an attempt to lower the pressure, he was given intravenous Manitol to shrink his vitreous body. The medications or his high intraocular pressure caused him to become nauseated, and he had several episodes of vomiting.

The intravenous Manitol did lower his pressure and relieve his pain, but the effect was only temporary. Within six hours, the pressure went up to painful levels and he began vomiting again. It was obvious that the swollen lens continued to block the flow of fluid in the eye, and we could not break the attack physically to permanently stop the pressure and the pain it caused.

After two days of medical therapy with eyedrops and intravenous Manitol, we were getting nowhere, and he was developing an electrolyte imbalance because of the Manitol and the vomiting caused by his obstructed eye. I explained to the patient and his daughter that we would have to remove the swollen cataract in order to break the glaucoma attack. His daughter exclaimed, "If you take out the cataract, daddy is going to die!" She explained that several years ago he had successfully undergone removal of the cataract from his right eye. After the operation, his family doctor had told him not to have his other cataract removed, because the operation would kill him.

She was adamant that we could not remove his cataract. He was getting weak and risked death from the electrolyte imbalance, so we had to do something. We were trying to manage his electrolytes, but the sporadic vomiting made this difficult. The daughter finally consented to our doing a peripheral iridotomy. This is a surgical procedure to cut a small hole in the peripheral iris to allow the fluid trapped behind the lens and iris to escape into the anterior part of the eye, where it can possibly escape from the eye, lowering the pressure. This would only work if the iris would fall back from the cornea.

Under local block anesthesia, a small hole was cut through the peripheral iris. This was in the days before the laser was used to burn a hole in the iris. The eye was entered with a scratch incision at the edge of the cornea. The iris was allowed to herniate from the eye, and a small, full thickness piece of the iris was excised near the base. The cut edges were milked back into the eye, and the wound was closed with one stitch. Unfortunately, the surgery did not overcome the blockage created by the swollen lens. The iris did not fall back from the cornea, and the pressure returned to high levels, because the swollen lens held the iris against the cornea.

Even though the patient was in his late eighties, he was in good health and maintained good mental faculties. I knew that he had very little risk of dying from cataract surgery, but the statement from the trusted, old family physician was set in the daughter's mind. I explained to her that the risk that the electrolyte imbalance and the constant pain would trigger an episode of cardiac arrhythmia or a hypertensive stroke was greater than the risk of his dying from a cataract operation. She finally relented and convinced her father that he needed the cataract extraction.

To safely perform the cataract extraction, the pressure in the eye had to be at a low level, which would require a significant dose of Manitol at the beginning of the surgery. Manitol causes a large urine output that would fill the patient's bladder to an uncomfortable level at the critical point in the operation.

To avoid his having to use a bedpan in the middle of the surgery, it was elected to insert a urinary catheter into the patient before surgery, which was done by the resident in the operating room. The resident had difficulty getting the catheter through this old man's large prostate, which resulted in the retention balloon of the catheter being inflated within the prostate, rather than the bladder, on the first attempt. This caused significant pain to the patient. After the catheter was repositioned and the balloon inflated within the proper place, the cataract extraction was uneventful.

The daughter was greatly relieved when her father was returned to the room in no pain and talking with anyone who would listen. She saw that the surgery did not kill him and had hardly seemed to faze him, except that he was now free of the pain from the high pressure in his eye.

At about 10:00 PM, I received a call at home from my resident. He had been called in to see the patient, because the patient had developed a fever of 103 degrees and his blood pressure was dropping, putting him into shock. I remembered that the catheter balloon had been inflated in his prostate and assumed that he had developed sepsis, bacteria in the blood stream, from bacteria forced out of the prostate. I told the resident to start antibiotics and steroids to combat the sepsis and shock. The resident told me that he had called in the medicine resident on call, who was afraid that the patient had thrown an embolus to his lung and who wanted to X-ray the patient's chest. I approved the X-ray, but only after the intravenous antibiotics and steroids had been started. The X-ray turned out to be negative.

The patient's fever and low blood pressure responded quickly to the antibiotics and steroids. It was clear that the patient needed to be on a hospital floor with nurses who were familiar with treating sick patients. The nurses on the ophthalmology floor were accustomed to relatively well postoperative patients. To transfer him to a medical floor, I needed the permission of his medical doctor. The patient still considered the family doctor who had advised him not to have his cataract removed to be his medical doctor, even though the doctor had semiretired several years prior to this time. This doctor had been a prominent physician at the medical branch, but had entered early senility. Nevertheless, I had to have his permission to transfer the patient to a covered service (with residents present).

By this time it was one o'clock in the morning, but I called the doctor at home. His wife answered the phone, and I explained the situation to her. She agreed to awaken her husband, but warned me that it might take awhile before he could talk coherently.

I introduced myself to the doctor and told him I was a friend of his son, who was also a physician. I reminded him of his blue patient and explained the situation before I asked him if I had his permission to transfer the patient to the internal medicine service in the hospital. He said one word, yes, and hung up. I probably could have successfully faked his permission, but that would not have been ethical.

The next day on rounds, the patient's fever was gone, his blood pressure was normal, and he felt fine. He could see my fingers well enough to count them, which was good, since he did not have an intraocular lens in those days. His electrolytes were beginning to return to normal, but it was elected to keep him in the hospital until they were normal.

On the third day after the cataract surgery, he broke out with a rash all over his face, inside his mouth, and all over his tongue. The rash burned and itched and made him miserable. We had the dermatologists look at him, and they diagnosed it as an eruption of herpes simplex. The herpes would run its course in about one week and go away.

I discharged him to home before his rash disappeared completely. His cataract healed on the usual schedule, and his vision was very good with both eyes after he was fit with his cataract glasses. He told me when we refracted him for glasses that he was very anxious to get back to his workbench. He had several projects that had been put on hold because of his eye problems.

Six weeks later when I saw him, he complained that he could not work at his workbench very well because the things he needed to see were always out of focus. This was before aspheric "4-drop" cataract spectacle lenses, or implant lenses, so his cataract glasses were the usual bifocal lenses. His problem was that he needed to see at distance, at near (14 inches), and in between (20 to 30 inches). This required trifocals. Progressive lenses had not been invented, but I called our optician to see if he could make the patient some cataract trifocals. It took the technician about a week to find an optical laboratory that would make the trifocals.

The patient loved the trifocals. He was able to work again like he had before he retired. His daughter told me that he had already lined every closet in the house with cedar. All of the walls in the house were wood paneled, and the stair banisters were beautifully carved wood. He had also made most of the wooden furniture in the house.

The prophesy "Daddy is going to die if you take out his cataract" seemed pretty ludicrous before the surgery, but we kept having episodes of real doubt that he might die when he developed sepsis and a possible pulmonary embolism.

Once his three-dimensional vision returned after the second cataract was removed, he was better able to work at his workbench and keep busy. This was very important to him as he neared the age of ninety.

The last time I heard of this patient was an article in the Galveston newspaper about his being the grand marshal for the Labor Day parade. He was the oldest living labor union member in the county and still going strong, and he was still known as the "blue man" from Galveston.

"Daddy" taught me not to brush aside the concerns of the patient or his family. He could have died after his cataract operation, just as his daughter had said repeatedly. He also taught me that a ninety-

44

<o>

Bushy Eyebrows

P RACTICING MEDICINE IS NEVER DULL because of the unusual problems that people develop, often as a result of the treatment of other diseases. A man who looked much older than his stated age of sixty came in to see me because he felt something scratching his right eye all of the time.

Zeke was an interesting little man who had obviously had a hard life. He was usually unkempt, the nurses complained to me that he smelled bad, he was typically unshaven, his hair never saw a comb, and he had the look of a burned-out chronic alcoholic, but I felt a spirit of fight in him that made me want to help him.

Zeke had been treated for a malignant parotid gland tumor by surgical removal of the parotid gland, the salivary gland behind the angle of the jaw, just below the ear. The facial nerve, which supplies the muscles of the face, comes out of the skull near the ear and goes through the middle of the parotid gland, and removal of the gland for malignancy requires removing part of the facial nerve. Surgeons often try to do a nerve graft to restore the facial nerve, but it takes several months for the cut end of the nerve to grow back through the graft and reach the end of the nerve, if the graft is successful.

Once the facial nerve is cut, the muscles on that side of the face do not respond and go flaccid. The corner of the mouth droops, the lower eyelid droops, and the whole side of the face sags. Additionally, the patient cannot smile on that side of the face and has difficulty closing the eye on that side.

Zeke had a full right facial palsy: his mouth sagged, his lower eyelid hung down, and he could not close his eye. He was very uncomfortable because of the constant exposure and drying of the eye.

When the lower eyelid sags away from the eye, the tears run out onto the cheek. Usually they are held in a pool along the eyelid where it contacts the eye. The upper eyelid pulls them across the front of the eye with every blink, keeping the eye moist. Because this mechanism was not working in Zeke, his lower lid was sagging and he could not blink, and thus his eye dried out and felt scratchy, giving the sensation that he had dust or hair in his eye.

I performed a procedure on his lower eyelid to pull it up to position it against the eyeball and narrow the eyelid fissure so that there was less gap between the eyelids for the tear film to spread across. This gave him some relief, and with artificial tears in the eye every hour or so, he could remain comfortable.

When I saw him back about two months after the surgery, he was complaining that his eye was scratchy all of the time. His face had sagged some more since I had last seen him. He was drooling tobacco juice from the corner of his mouth, his eyelid had begun to sag again, and his forehead had relaxed so much that his eyebrow slid down over his upper eyelid. He had long, bushy eyebrows that hung down and scratched his cornea. I had never seen a facial palsy so severe that the eyebrows actually scratched the corneas.

He had a habit of shaving about once a week and had never trimmed his eyebrows. I trimmed his eyebrows to get them out of his eyes, but in about two weeks he was back telling me that his eyebrows still scratched his eye. The skin had relaxed so much that the shorter eyebrows were still scratching his eye.

I took him back to the operating room to tighten his lower eyelid again and raise his eyebrow. This time I did an elliptical excision of the skin above his eyebrow and lifted his eyebrow about one and one half centimeters, which got his eyebrows out of his eye. Zeke remained comfortable for several months after the second surgery. I never saw any evidence of regeneration of the facial nerve through the nerve graft, so the facial palsy would not have repaired itself.

About six months after the second surgery, Zeke began having symptoms from the metastasis of the tumor, and he never came back to see me again. I suspect that he died soon after I last saw him. I hope that his eye remained comfortable until he died.

I could have written him off as being a terminal patient who did not need to have further surgery just to make him comfortable, but I thought he needed to be free of any pain that could be prevented. He certainly did appreciate the pain relief that he obtained from the surgery I performed, and I received satisfaction from doing what I could for him. It may have made his other pain from the cancer more tolerable.

45

A Stubborn Keratoconus Patient

SHORTLY AFTER I MOVED TO Galveston, a patient came to see me, having been sent by Dr. Ferguson. She had a disease that fell within my specialty expertise. She had known for many years that she had keratoconus. She had been wearing contact lenses for years, but recently she had been having discomfort from her contacts, especially after wearing them for several hours.

I examined her and verified that she had keratoconus. Her contacts did not fit very well and did not correct her vision better than about 20/100 in either eye. She did not have the visual acuity she needed to drive an automobile, but claimed to drive just fine. I told her that I could change her contact lenses to improve her vision and to get rid of her discomfort.

She let me know that I was not to touch her contact lenses. They had been fitted by the leading ophthalmologist in Galveston twenty years ago and were fit perfectly. The patient had been told by this ophthalmologist to never let anyone change her lenses. They were perfect! The doctor had learned to fit contacts in Europe and was the only one in Galveston who was qualified to fit contact lenses at that time.

These lenses had been fit the old trial and error way in which she had been through a number of trials that had caused pain and possible injury to her eyes. They had finally "gotten it right," and she was not ever to change the lenses.

This lady was well-known in town and very outspoken. I did not want to alienate her, so I played along. I told her that her vision was not good enough to drive, but she did not believe me. She said she could read very well with bright light and that no changes were necessary.

Other than her keratoconus and ill-fitting contact lenses, her eyes were quite normal. I continued to follow her with yearly checkups and to offer to change her lenses, an offer that she always refused. I became acquainted with the patient and her husband socially, and she became a close friend of my wife's.

One day I received a call from her. She was in panic. She was getting ready to leave on a vacation and had decided to treat her house for fleas before she left. (Because of the warm weather, it was a common practice in Galveston to fumigate before leaving for vacation. Everyone who had pets had fleas in the house unless they constantly flea-bombed the house.) She had bent over a flea bomb to latch the nozzle and had set off the flea bomb into her eyes. She had immediately removed her contacts and washed out her eyes with water. When she put the contacts back in her eye, everything was foggy. Since she did not see well without the lenses anyway, she was worried that she had damaged her eyes. I told her to come in right away so that I could check her eyes.

When she arrived, she had her contact lenses in her eyes. One look told me what was wrong. Her eyes were not red from chemical injury, but her lenses were speckled with white spots that were almost confluent. I removed the lenses and tried to clean them with standard cleaning solutions. They were permanently etched by the flea spray. I told her that I could not repair her lenses, but I could make a rush order for some new lenses from the optician who made all of the lenses for the clinic. I could probably get them the next day so she could see on her vacation. She really had no choice, since the previous doctor had died before I first saw her and the records were not available.

I took keratometry readings of her keratoconus and refracted her over some keratoconus trial lenses that I kept in the office. I explained the situation to the optician, and he delivered the contacts the next day when he came to teach in the residency program. I delivered the lenses to her that afternoon and was surprised to see that her vision was 20/25 without any adjustments and that the fit was much better than she was used to. She went off on her vacation.

When she returned, she made an appointment to see me. I thought that she was going to complain about her lenses, which might be giving her problems after the changes that I had made. Instead, when she arrived, she was beaming. She said she had thoroughly enjoyed her trip and had been seeing better than she had seen for years. Not only that, she could wear her lenses all day without discomfort. She wanted a backup pair of lenses made. Her only question was why I had not insisted on changing them before. I did not remind her of her intransigence, but told her that I was very happy that we did not have to adjust them further after the change in fit and glad that I had done it right the first time.

I still wonder if I should have insisted on changing her lenses when I first saw her or whether my patient approach was best. She was forced to change lenses and afterward was glad that she did. Refitting contact lenses can open a can of worms because the patient always compares the new lenses to the old ones and sometimes prefers the old ones. In this case the old ones were ruined, so she could not compare and criticize. In a way, she had punished herself by refusing to allow me to change her contact lenses.

46

<o>

The Rock Musician

ROCKY WAS TWENTY-TWO YEARS OLD when he presented to the emergency room with shaking chills, fever, and weakness. The emergency room doctors suspected sepsis and drew blood cultures. While waiting in the emergency room, Rocky started feeling better, slipped out of the emergency room, and disappeared.

About ten days later, Rocky came to the emergency room again, this time complaining of pain and redness in the right eye, with decreased vision in that eye. He also had photophobia (sensitivity to light) and a low-grade fever.

Examination of his eye showed that he had a white "cotton ball" mass floating in his vitreous just above the retina. This is the most typical presentation of fungus growing in the eye when it has been seeded by the blood stream. We checked on the cultures that had been done in the emergency room, and the blood cultures had grown out *Candida albicans*, a common fungus, which was probably what was growing in his eye.

It is uncommon for a young person to develop spontaneous fungal sepsis, so we asked him some pointed questions. We learned that he was performing in town with a rock band. The band was staying in a hotel where they played, and he and the other band members routinely used intravenous drugs.

The next day, one of his fellow band members admitted that he had been using Rocky's intravenous drugs. To keep Rocky from finding out, he had drawn water from the water bowl of the band's pet dog and injected it into the vial of drugs. Rocky had then injected himself with water from the dog's bowl without knowing it. We concluded that the fungus got into his blood stream from the dog's bowl.

We started him on intravenous antifungal medication. Most kinds of fungus are slow to respond to antifungal medications, so he was in the hospital for about ten days before the fluff ball above his retina disappeared. He needed another week of intravenous medications to be sure that the infection did not recur.

After two weeks of intravenous antifungal medications, Rocky must have learned that the band was leaving town because he signed out against medical advice and disappeared. The two weeks of intravenous antifungal medication that he received had probably killed the fungus, and his body had probably cleaned up the reaction to the fungus. Without further medications, he would likely recover from the infection and return to fairly normal vision.

I learned that people on drugs can do some stupid things that have consequences to other people. Ricky did not know that his drugs had been contaminated and could not tell us where the fungus originated. In a sober moment, his fellow band member realized that what he had done caused the problem. I knew that intravenous drug users gave each other hepatitis and HIV, but it is rare to see fungal transmission by this route.

47

<o>

The Golf Pro

ONE DAY SHORTLY AFTER THE new cataract procedure, phacoemulsification, became popular, a little white-haired gentleman was led into my office. Arnold was a retired golf professional who made some money repairing broken golf clubs and putting new grips on them. It was obvious that he had great difficulty seeing, and he wore a visor and covered his eyes as though the light was painful to him. He told me that he had undergone cataract surgery on both eyes about a week apart. It had been about ten weeks since the surgery and he still could not see, so he was seeking a second opinion.

Arnold told me that the first surgery had not gone well and that he could hardly see after the procedure. The doctor told him that it would take awhile for his vision to clear and that they should proceed immediately with the second eye. From his standpoint, the second procedure went slightly better in that he could see forms, but everything was still very hazy.

He saw the doctor every week, but his vision slowly became worse. At one point he started seeing bright flashes and fireworks in his right eye. The doctor told him not to worry because they would soon go away. He said the doctor was correct, the flashes had all gone away, but so had the remainder of his vision in that eye. When I saw him he could not see light at all with that eye.

Arnold said that vision in the left eye had become a steady blur, with white "lace curtains" over everything. He told me that he was having pain in both eyes, what he described as sand in his eyes. He told me that what he really wanted was some relief from the pain.

When I examined him, I found that both of his corneas were white and had swollen to almost twice the normal thickness. He had edema of the corneal surface in both eyes, as well as blisters, which were the cause of his pain. By narrowing the beam of the slit lamp, I was able to see the capsules left from his cataract surgery in each eye. Both were torn, and there was damage to the iris in both eyes. I was unable to see the retina in either eye through the white thickened corneas. I was able to determine by ultrasound that the retina in the right eye was totally detached and contracted into a ball in the center of the eye. The left retina was in its normal position. He could see light and identify colors with that eye, which indicated that the damage was probably limited to the front of this eye.

I am assuming that Arnold had been one of the first patients on whom this surgeon had performed phacoemulsification. The capsule had ruptured, and some of the cataract had probably fallen into the back of the right eye. The capsule was torn, and the iris and cornea were damaged. Repair of the damage had been ignored. Instead of referring the patient to a retina specialist for removal of the lens fragment, the surgeon proceeded with the cataract surgery in the left eye, tearing the capsule and iris, and severely damaging the cornea. These are the marks of a beginning phacoemulsification cataract surgeon with little practice and poor judgment. He still did not refer the patient to a specialist but ignored, or tried to cover up, the consequences. When the patient reported the flashes and fireworks, the doctor should have recognized the signs of retinal detachment. Maybe he decided that the cornea was too thick to see through to repair the retina. Maybe he did not want anyone to see his mistakes. The patient had finally lost patience and sought a second opinion.

I told this patient that he would need a corneal transplant in his better eye to restore his vision, but explained that since I could not see his retina, I could not promise that his vision would return completely. I put a soft contact lens in his both eyes to stop the pain from the corneal edema and scheduled a cornea transplant for his left eye.

The transplant should have been routine, but I had never done one on a cornea that was twice the normal thickness. I placed the sutures very deep and tight on both sides of the wound, even though the patient side of the wound was twice as thick as the donor side.

I hoped that the new cornea would soon dehydrate his remaining cornea where they joined, so that they would soon be almost the same thickness. There was a large hole in the lens capsule with vitreous gel coming through it, so we performed a vitrectomy to keep the vitreous from rubbing the new cornea and damaging the endothelium.

He did well after the transplant and was soon seeing 20/40 with that eye. He told me that he was able to repair golf clubs again to supplement his social security. His right eye stayed comfortable with the soft contact lens, although the vision would never return.

His wife was a very pleasant person who dressed in a very sporting manner, in tweeds and scarves. She was very attentive to him, and she made sure that he received his eyedrops on time and did not overexert himself. She was very grateful that he could see again to take care of himself and have some independence.

After I removed the sutures, about a year after the surgery, I told him that I was very happy that he was seeing about 20/40 after all of the problems he had experienced. He told me that he was rather disappointed in the outcome. He had to wear cataract glasses to read, and they gave him some distortion. He was also disappointed that I had not been able to restore the vision in his other eye.

He bore no animosity to the doctor who botched his two cataract surgeries, because the doctor had predicted that the flashes in his right eye would go away and, indeed, they had gone away. He did not understand that the doctor should have referred him to a retina specialist before the retina detached and that he should not have operated on the second eye with the first eye still in jeopardy. However, I did not feel that it would help matters if I explained the situation to him; it would have been considered self-serving for me to place the blame where it was due, on the other doctor. I hope that he still has Arnold on his conscience. I learned that a patient who was brought back from near blindness to useful vision, but who fixated on some irritation or minor flaw in vision, can harbor great dissatisfaction with the care they received. For some reason, the blame for the less-than-perfect outcome is placed on the last doctor seen.

I learned that patients hope for miracles.

48

A Corneal Transplant
Patient Who Did Drugs

IN MEDICAL PRACTICE, DOCTORS LEARN to spot warning signs.
Sometimes, however, it is too late to take action, and complications
ensue. I had a patient, from about one hundred miles away, who came
to me with an old scar on his cornea from an "infection" some years
ago. Larry was a well-dressed, fifty-something gentleman who was in
good health except for a corneal scar blocking his vision. He wanted
to have a corneal transplant to restore his vision. On examination,
he did not have any other problem with his eye to prevent a corneal
transplant from being successful, so I agreed to do the transplant.
The surgery went well, and everything looked satisfactory when I saw
him in the clinic the next day.

At that time, we were only keeping the corneal transplants in the
hospital overnight after the surgery. As I was writing the discharge
orders, the patient's wife reminded him to ask me a question. Larry
asked, "How soon can I go back to smoking pot?" Bingo! A warning
sign—a relative contraindication to corneal transplant. Too late! The
surgery had been done.

Because of his age and appearance, I was surprised by the
question. I could not recall any studies of the effects of marijuana
smoking on corneal transplants. I was, however, well aware of the
consequences of trauma to corneal transplants, so I told him that
he should not smoke pot or have more than one highball or beer
per day for at least three weeks. He said that he only smoked pot at

home, but he could live without it and limit himself to one drink per day.

He kept his appointments and used his medications as directed, and his transplant did very well. His vision improved rapidly, and he appeared to be the model patient. Therefore, I was surprised when I received a call, about five months after his surgery, from the resident on call in the emergency room saying that this patient was there with a rupture of his corneal transplant incision site. He had told the ER ophthalmologist that he had been drinking heavily before going to bed and that somehow he had fallen out of bed and struck his head on the night table. He experienced immediate pain and visual blurring in his eye. He had told his wife to bring him immediately to Galveston to the emergency room.

The circular wound was split open, and the injury had torn out the suture for 180 degrees from twelve to six o'clock. The other half of the wound was intact. We took him to the operating room, resutured the wound, and inflated the eye with saline. Within three weeks, his vision was back to 20/25. I removed all of the sutures at one year after the original surgery, and he did well with good vision for several years until he was lost to follow-up. He was yet more proof of the old adage that "God looks after drunks and fools."

Although I did not learn of his drug use until after the surgery, I am not sure whether I would have refused to do the surgery. I would have at least had a long talk with Larry and elicited a promise to quit using drugs, at least until the sutures were removed. That might not have made any difference concerning his drug usage, but I might have felt better about doing the surgery. The resident said that Larry admitted drinking before the injury, but he suspected that Larry had also used drugs at the same time. I learned that being well dressed, fifty, and polite is no assurance of good behavior. I already knew that people on drugs and alcohol make promises they do not keep.

49

Disingenuous Patient with a Melanoma

O NE OF MY RESIDENTS CAME to me saying that he had a patient in the clinic with a traumatic ruptured lens that he wanted to surgically remove immediately. He wanted me to come quickly to see this patient.

Dan was in his early forties, wearing a Coors T-shirt. He stated that he had been working in a refinery about a week before and was struck in the left eye by a heavy electric welding cable. He had been sent to see the company nurse, who told him that the eye looked fine and that he did not need to see a doctor. He had stayed home from work since then because of severe pain, and finally, when the pain became too much, he came to the emergency room. They took a quick look at his eye and sent him to the eye clinic.

On examination, Dan had a steamy cornea behind which the anterior chamber was normally formed. He had a dilated pupil with something snow-white filling it. Through the cloudy cornea, the white surface appeared split and irregular, with red lines along the splits. Although the hazy cornea limited the view, I thought this was a ruptured lens that had become a cataract and had swollen. The red lines appeared to be streaks of blood layered on the lens material within the splits in the lens capsule. His intraocular pressure was about 45 mm Hg (normal is 10 to 21 mm). The corneal swelling interfered with an accurate pressure measurement. Elevated pressure can be caused by acute traumatic cataract formation, a blocked pupil, and/or by hemorrhage into the eye, all of which he appeared to have at this time. The appropriate treatment of this situation is removal of the cataract.

I immediately scheduled the operating room for the purpose of removing the ruptured lens and thereby relieving the pressure in the eye. Our technique for removal of a ruptured lens in someone under the age of fifty was to open the anterior capsule of the lens and aspirate the swollen lens material using a suction cutter. The suction cutter was a special needle introduced into the eye through the limbus (the junction between the cornea and sclera).

Once the suction cutter was in the eye, an attempt was made to aspirate the white material in the pupil. The material did not aspirate as it usually would, so the cutter part of the suction cutter was used to nibble into the material, which was firm and "rubbery." It started to bleed. There are no blood vessels in the crystalline lens of the eye, and the lens should have been soft and fluffy and easy to aspirate.

I immediately decided that this was not the lens, but some other tissue. The patient had said that he had not had any prior surgery to the eye, so the lens should have been in the pupil. The tissue did not look, or respond, like retina tissue, and I could not think of any solid tissue, like a tumor, that could form in this location within one week. The patient had told us that a nurse said that his eye looked normal one week before.

I proceeded to cut a hole through the center of the tissue and eventually cut through the tissue at a depth of approximately two millimeters, until I could see the red reflection from the retina (like the red pupil one sees in flash photographs). Our suction cutter was of the design that employed manual suction with a large syringe to pull fluid and small particles from the eye. The fluid removed this way was replaced by a constant flow from a tube into the eye from an IV bottle. This maintained the shape of the eye and controlled the intraocular pressure. I had the scrub nurse save all of the fluid removed from the eye. By the end of the procedure, this amounted to about two hundred milliliters of cloudy fluid. After the surgery I personally took the two specimen cups of fluid to the pathology laboratory to ask the pathologist in charge of ocular pathology to spin down (centrifuge) the fluid and make a tissue block of the solid material and tell me what it was. (The suction cutter nibbles the tissue into pinhead-sized pieces that are too small for the pathologist to manage, but large enough to see what the source is once they are processed as a clump of tissue.)

Two days later, the pathologist reported that the tissue was from an amelanotic melanoma, a malignant tumor that probably came from the ciliary body or iris within the eye. Melanomas are usually black or brown-black, but some do not contain the black pigment and thus are white (amelanotic). They contain many blood vessels, which explained the rubbery consistency of the mass and the bleeding during surgery.

I discussed this finding with Dan. I told him that I was concerned that the tumor had been there for several years and that the surgery might have caused the tumor to spread to the tissue around the eyeball. At his age, the usual advice is to remove the eye and hope that the tumor has not metastasized to other parts of the body, especially the liver. I told him that, because the eye had been opened to obtain access to the mass in the pupil, the eye socket might have been contaminated with tumor during the operation. Since there was the possibility that there was tumor in the tissue surrounding the eye, the eye socket should be completely emptied of all tissue at the same time the eyeball was removed.

Dan finally decided to level with me and told me that he had been having trouble with the eye for two years. He had made up the story about the welding cable so that the refinery would pay for his medical care. He had seen an ophthalmologist in his home town two years ago and was found to have elevated intraocular pressure in his left eye only. He had been started on several different eyedrops for glaucoma, but did not respond, so he quit seeing that doctor.

About one year before seeing me he had consulted another ophthalmologist, who again tried the glaucoma drops with unsatisfactory results. When the drops did not work, the doctor had elected to do surgery for glaucoma to relieve the pressure. The ophthalmologist performed a filtering procedure on the involved eye to drain fluid out of the eye into the eye socket. The other eye remained normal. After the surgery, his pressure was still high, so he left that doctor. When the pain in the eye became too much, he came to our emergency room with his story.

I contacted both ophthalmologists. The first told me that the last entry in the patient's chart was the registered letter that he had sent to the patient asking him to return to the office because the unresponsive glaucoma in only one eye made him think that the patient might have a ciliary body melanoma. The letter had been returned, unopened, marked refused by addressee.

The second ophthalmologist confirmed that the patient had undergone a filtering procedure for glaucoma that did not relieve the pressure. This doctor also had sent a registered letter to the patient that had been refused and was now in the patient's chart.

The history of a glaucoma filtering procedure meant that fluid from the eye, possibly containing particles of a malignant tumor, had been draining into the eye socket for about one year. This greatly increased the possibility of local spread of tumor to the eye socket and to the lungs or liver. We did scans of the chest and abdomen to determine if there were any metastases large enough to be detected. The scans did not show any metastasis, so the patient elected to proceed with surgery to remove the eye and all of the contents of the orbit. He told me that he wanted to look as normal as possible after the procedure.

The procedure we devised was done to preserve the skin and muscles of both the upper and lower eyelids. The plane of dissection separated the skin and muscles from the back half of the eyelids and extended behind the eyelids to the rim of the socket. Everything within the periosteum (the tissue covering the boney walls of the socket) was removed back to the apex (posterior end) of the socket, leaving only bare bone behind the eyelids. The eye socket was filled with glass spheres and plastic conformers to decrease dead space. The eye lids were positioned on top of the orbit fillers and sewn together.

He was checked every three days as the orbit filled with granulation tissue. The orbit filled with tissue but became infected during the second week. Because of the infection we had to remove the glass and plastic objects from the orbit and fill the socket with gauze to permit the orbit to fill with granulation tissue.

The pathologists examined the eye and orbital contents, which showed a malignant melanoma involving the entire ciliary body (behind the iris or pupil) for 360 degrees. Samples from throughout the removed tissue did not find any visible local metastases, but it was too early to tell if there had been microscopic seeding or distant metastases.

Dan was referred to an oncologist to discuss the possibilities of spread of the cancer and ways to reduce the chances of growing metastases. Because of the history of prolonged drainage from the eye into the orbit, the oncologist recommended a course of chemotherapy. However, the first dose caused nausea and vomiting, so Dan refused further chemotherapy.

Once the orbit had filled about 90 percent with granulation tissue, we proceeded with the second stage of the reconstruction. I whittled a block of silicone into a flattened oval pattern the size of the pocket I wanted to form behind the eyelids and had it sterilized. In the operating room, we removed a superficial skin graft from the inside of his left upper arm where there was no hair. This graft was wrapped around the silicone block, with the outer skin surface against the block, raw side out. The skin was then sewn together to cover the block. The skin on the block was then inserted behind the lids onto the granulation surface. The edges of the eyelids were sewn together over the skin-covered block. A pressure dressing was kept on the area over the block for one week.

After a week the sutures were removed from the eyelids, and the lids were separated with a scalpel, carrying the incision deep enough to incise the skin over the block. This allowed the block to be removed. Over 90 percent of the grafted skin had "taken," leaving a skin-lined pocket. The pocket was packed with gauze to hold the graft in place for another week and to allow the small gaps to fill with skin growing from the graft.

One month after the skin graft, the pocket behind the eyelids was well formed. I sent the patient to the best prosthesis person in the area at M. D. Anderson Hospital to have a prosthesis made for the skin pocket to restore his appearance.

He returned several weeks later without a prosthesis, wearing a black eye patch. He told me that he had asked the prosthesis designer if he could guarantee him, under penalty of lawsuit if it failed, that the prosthesis would never, ever, fall out under any circumstances. The prosthesis maker could not make that kind of promise, so the patient had decided to just wear a black patch.

I continued to follow him for several months. He refused chemotherapy although it was often recommended. When I would see him in the office, I noticed that he was developing an abdominal protuberance (pot belly). He was refusing to see any physicians about the possibility of metastases, so I did not examine his abdomen to check his liver. I suppose I was also put off by the fact that he usually wore T-shirts with beer trademarks on them; I hoped that possibly his protuberance was just a beer belly.

The refinery did pay all of his medical bills, even when they received the diagnosis of a long-standing ocular tumor. I had occasion to talk with the medical advisor for the company, who told me that the company decided to pay the bills, because it would be cheaper than a lawsuit from the patient.

This patient apparently allowed the cost of his care to interfere with obtaining the proper treatment for his problem. He quit seeing both of his first two doctors because he thought he had received a dunning letter in the mail from them. He had not paid them. The doctors were actually doing the proper thing by informing him that his diagnosis was uncertain and that he needed to have further workup. Neither doctor had mentioned anything about payment to the patient. He finally did figure out a way to have his care paid for by the refinery.

His failure to follow up with the first ophthalmologist led to not diagnosing his life-threatening melanoma. The second ophthalmologist, starting from scratch, treated him as a glaucoma patient and did a surgical procedure to treat the glaucoma. The tumor was probably hidden behind the iris at that time. When that procedure did not work, he too thought of the possibility of a melanoma and sent a letter advising the patient to return. The letter, perceived as a dunning letter, caused the patient to stop seeing the second doctor and delay seeking more treatment until the tumor had advanced significantly.

The nature of ocular malignant melanomas, especially in the front of the eye, where this one was located, is to metastasize to the liver and become apparent there ten to twenty years later; I will never know if he had metastases, since he was lost to follow-up. I do not think he understood how much concern went into his care by all three of his attending physicians, nor did he understand the gravity of his situation.

From this patient I learned that an apparently sincere patient could lie to his physician about the disease for which he was seeking care and that this same patient would jeopardize his own medical care because he did not want to pay for the medical care that he had received. He was not poor. I was told by people who knew him that he and his wife had a nice house, and he drove a recent model Cadillac. I also learned that if you threaten a lawsuit, some companies will pay big money to avoid that situation even though they know they could win.

50

<o>

A City League Baseball Player

L IVING ON THE GULF COAST of Texas, with all of the refineries and oil rigs, I saw many patients with thermal and chemical burns of the eye. These are extremely challenging to treat and often have poor outcomes.

We were contacted one afternoon and told that Life Flight was bringing in a young man with a severe chemical burn to both eyes. They were irrigating his eyes with saline on the helicopter on the way down from Lufkin, Texas. Casey had been flushing a pipeline in a pulp mill with caustic. When he turned the valve on the pipe, the valve disintegrated and sprayed caustic in his face. He was not wearing his safety goggles when this happened. Once this accident happened, the company was seeing that he had good medical care and doing everything possible to keep his wife happy so she would not complain to OSHA (Occupational Safety and Health Administration) or file a lawsuit.

When this twenty-two-year-old white man arrived at the hospital, they rushed him to the clinic, where we examined his eyes. His eyes were very red, but the corneas were hazy. The burn was worse in the left eye than the right eye, and I started him on multiple antibiotics and topical steroids.

By the next day Casey's corneas were very hazy, and there was no epithelium left covering the left cornea. His conjunctival epithelium had been burned from the edge of the cornea posteriorly for four to six millimeters all the way around the cornea in his left eye and in the inferior nasal quadrant of his right eye.

The epithelium began to grow back over the burned area of his right eye, and the cornea became clear. After about thirty days, it was apparent that the epithelium was not going to grow back over the burned area on the left eye very soon. I elected to do a conjunctival graft from the undisturbed area of his right eye to cover the cornea and denuded scleral area of his left eye.

Because of the recent chemical burn to his right eye, we would have preferred to use the mucous membrane from the back of his lower lip to get tissue to cover the burned area. However, when we checked his lip for a possible graft donor site, we found that it had linear scars all over the area we wanted to use. He admitted that he dipped snuff and had been dipping for several years. The inside of his cheek was also scarred, since he often carried his dip in his cheek. The scars were old, blocked blood vessels in the mucosa caused by the nicotine and indicated that the tissue would not have a good enough blood supply to use as a graft.

Consequently, a large conjunctiva graft was obtained from the superior temporal surface of the right eye. This was sewn to viable conjunctival tissue all around the sclera in his left eye. The tissue covered the cornea completely. A semi-pressure dressing was placed over the eye to hold the graft in place so that it would stick to the cornea.

After three days, I removed the pressure dressing, and the graft looked very good. It had a good blood supply and was flat against the cornea. I left the patch off to get more oxygen to the graft, and I asked him to return the next day for me to look at the graft.

He returned the next day with the center of the graft bulging forward between his eyelids. When I examined him with the slit lamp, the edges of the graft were still firmly attached, but the graft was now floating about a millimeter above the cornea. I realized that the corneal endothelium on the back of the cornea had been severely damaged by the alkali and was allowing aqueous humor to leak though the cornea. This fluid came out of the front surface of the cornea and was trapped behind the new graft, ballooning it forward.

I put a pressure dressing over the eye and left it there for one week. When I removed it, the graft stayed very flat and did not separate from the cornea again. I soon arranged for him to be followed by a local ophthalmologist in his hometown, so that he would not have to make so many trips to Galveston.

Because of the burn and subsequent glaucoma, he had lost all vision in his left eye, but it was comfortable. It took some time for him to get used to not having depth perception, which he lost because he had only one functional eye. He told me that the thing he missed the most since the accident was that he had been playing baseball in a city league. He was the star batter, with a three hundred plus average, and he played center field. Because he lost his depth perception, he could no longer hit a fastball or judge pop flies into center field, so he had to quit playing baseball. He became a father shortly after his accident and had a lot to keep him busy, but he still missed baseball.

Throughout his hospitalization, the company where he worked made a driver available to his wife at any time, day or night. She was pregnant with their first child, and having her husband over one hundred miles away was very difficult for her. The driver would bring her to Galveston and would take her shopping or to the doctor. The company even rented an apartment in Galveston for her while her husband was in the hospital. I do not think that Casey ever filed a lawsuit against the company.

When he was healed enough to return to work, the company appointed him the safety inspector. His job was to be sure that everyone wore their goggles and safety equipment and to make sure that OSHA regulations were met. The first thing he did was to evaluate all of the equipment to see if it furnished the protection that was needed and if it was comfortable to wear. Most people did not wear the goggles because they were too hot in East Texas in the summer. He told me that they changed from goggles to a hood that was open at the bottom and was not uncomfortable to wear.

I followed Casey for several years. After two years he came in to see me, greeting me with "Guess what? I am back playing baseball, batting .300, and playing center field." He had not regained vision in his left eye, but he had learned some form of depth perception that allowed him to hit fast balls and judge pop flies. Science cannot explain this phenomenon, but I have seen it many times. His little girl could now watch him play baseball.

Casey taught me another reason not to dip snuff. He also showed me that alkali burns to the cornea can cause it to leak fluid, which makes grafting a surface onto the cornea difficult. I was glad to learn that there are still people who take responsibility for their own actions. He realized that he lost the vision in his left eye because he was not wearing his safety glasses and that it was not the company's fault. He taught the resident who was working with me that people can regain some three-dimensional vision after losing an eye.

51

The Bottle of Jack Daniels

OCCASIONALLY A PATIENT COMES TO you with no, or low, expectations and you find that you can really help them. They often respond disproportionately to what you do for them. One such patient was a businessman from Beaumont, Texas. Leon was sent to me because he was getting a cataract in his only good eye. Many ophthalmologists do not like to operate on cataracts on one-eyed patients because of the risk of making them go blind if surgery does not go well. They send these patients to "experts."

Leon had experienced an attack of angle closure glaucoma about ten years before and had undergone surgery to treat the attack. The surgeon who treated the attack had used a procedure, iridenclysis, which was no longer in common use. To perform an iridenclysis, an incision is made into the eye at the edge of the cornea, just in front of the iris. The iris is then cut radially, from the base at the incision to the pupil. Some surgeons pull one cut edge of the iris into the incision and wedge it into the end of the incision; other surgeons pull both edges, wedging them into both ends of the incision. This holds the incision open to allow the aqueous humor to leak from the eye. The conjunctiva is then pulled over the open incision, allowing the fluid to leak out under the conjunctiva to relieve the eye pressure from the glaucoma.

Leon had both edges of the iris incarcerated in the incision. This had lowered the pressure so much immediately after the surgery that it left the front of his eye collapsed, with the lens and iris against his cornea. The lens in this eye was now a cataract, and the cornea was swollen. He said that he had been unable to see with the eye since the glaucoma attack and surgery. The records he brought with him showed that his vision was recorded in that eye as "no light perception" for the past ten years. He now had an early cataract in his other eye that reduced his vision to 20/40, the vision he needed to pass the driver's license test in Texas.

We trained our residents to always check the patients vision themselves. When my resident checked Leon before I saw him, he found that he could actually see with his bad eye. Leon could see light and tell what color it was. This indicated some visual function in the eye, much better than no light perception.

In further review of his history, he told us that there had been only one glaucoma attack and that he had been operated on immediately. The doctor had been happy with the immediate lowering of the pressure. He also told us that his doctor never personally checked his vision, but the nurse checked it and wrote it in the chart for the doctor. Actually they only checked his good eye, because they "knew" that he was blind in his other eye.

I told him that he could see with his bad eye and that he might see fairly well once the cataract was removed and his swollen cornea was replaced with a good one. I explained that it was better to operate on his bad eye and let him depend on his better eye during recovery than to risk his good eye since it still saw fairly well. If he did not get good vision from the first operation, we could always do the good eye. Leon thought that operating on his bad eye first was a good idea.

We scheduled him for a corneal transplant and cataract extraction as a combined procedure. We did not use an intraocular implant lens because of his prior glaucoma surgery. The surgery went well, with removal of the cataract through the round eight-millimeter hole in his cornea that was made for the corneal transplant. I left the iridenclysis procedure alone since his ocular pressure was now normal.

When I took the patches off his eye the day after surgery, he could see well enough to count my fingers and see my blurry face. Within a few weeks, he could see 20/40 with a cataract spectacle lens in front of the eye. He was very pleased.

Once the patient could see better, he started having difficulty making his follow-up appointments. He constantly called to reschedule and missed a number of appointments. He continued to do well, so it was not a problem, but he explained that once he could see, he was prevailed upon to be chairman of the United Fund campaign in his hometown, so he was kept very busy with meetings for the campaign.

Leon's brother happened to be the chief administrator at the University of Texas Medical Branch. Word got around that I had operated on his brother's eye and restored his vision from totally blind to 20/40. My reputation at the university went up dramatically. I ran into people all over the hospital that had heard of the "miraculous" operation I had performed. I had to decide whether to tell the long story, explaining that he had not been totally blind, or just shrug and say that it wasn't that spectacular, depending on the situation I was in at the time and the person to whom I was speaking.

The operation was done in October, and the results were very good by December. I was surprised one day to walk into my office to find a two-liter bottle of Jack Daniels on my desk. There was a card thanking me for the spectacular operation I had performed on the whiskey donor's father. The son was a dentist who was very grateful for his father's rehabilitation.

The patient eventually found it difficult to come the hundred miles for follow-up visits, so I turned him over to a hometown ophthalmologist to watch for rejection or other problems. I knew he continued to do well because every holiday season the two-liter bottle of Jack Daniels would show up on my desk with a short note from his son. This continued for several years until I left Galveston.

This patient taught my resident the value of checking the patient's vision himself. I enjoyed seeing this patient return to active involvement in society. I was also impressed by the tremendous boost in my status at the university by performing a routine procedure on the right person. I also learned that there are unexpected benefits for being successful, like a bottle of Jack Daniels.

52

The Fixed Cornea Episode

THERE IS DANGER IN ASSUMING anything in medicine. We had a patient who had corneal dystrophy, glaucoma, and an early cataract. Bess had taken pilocarpine for her glaucoma for many years. The cataract was minimal, so we decided to do a corneal transplant without a cataract extraction. Dr. Fred Feaster was the resident on the case and very interested in corneal transplants. He later did a fellowship with me to specialize in the field of cornea and external diseases.

Fred had done other cornea transplants, so I let him handle the case, with my assistance. We started surgery at about midnight and were proceeding nicely with the corneal transplant. Fred made a circular hole in the cornea and removed a button of central cornea. The donor tissue was checked and removed from the bottle, and the donor name and time of death were recorded from the slip taped to the bottle. We punched the donor button from the donor cornea and started suturing it into the recipient cornea.

When Fred was placing the first sutures into the donor cornea, he bent the tiny needle several times. This is a time in the procedure when everything is very delicate because the donor tissue is loose and free to move around, and movement could possibly damage the donor endothelium, which would then jeopardize the success of the transplant. I was concerned and asked Fred why he was having trouble with the suturing. He replied that the donor cornea was very tough. The cornea looked completely normal, but he was having difficulty getting the needle through the tissue. He had tried

216

both needles on opposite ends of the suture, so it was not a rare bad needle that was causing the problem.

I thought that he was probably using poor technique, so I told him to let me put a suture in the cornea. When I tried, I discovered that the tissue was, indeed, very tough. I had never experienced a cornea this tough.

I asked to see the bottle in which the cornea had been stored. The slip of paper with the donor's name, age, and time of death was still taped around the bottle. The nurse removed the tape and the donor identity slip of paper to show me the bottle. It did not have the familiar MK Medium label, but had a thin, paper label taped to the bottle. The label said "lens fixative." This bottle had been full of osmium tetroxide and gluteraldehyde, a fixative for electron microscopy.

We did not have any other tissue available. The patient's own cornea had been damaged during its removal, so we could not sew it back into the cornea. Our only way to proceed was to sew this button into the eye to maintain the integrity of the eye until we could get better tissue.

As soon as the surgery was complete, Fred left the operating room to determine what had happened. He called the resident who had harvested the corneas from the deceased patient. She said that she had done as she had been taught and had put the corneas in the bottle of solution in the laboratory refrigerator. Fred went to the lab and found that there was a box of MK Medium on the shelf of the refrigerator. Next to the box was a row of bottles marked lens fixative. These were bottles that Dr. Ray, our PhD physiology researcher, used to prepare frog lenses for electron microscopy for his research on cataract formation.

Fred called the Eyes of Texas Eye Bank in Houston at about 2:00AM. The technician on call said that there were three corneas available, but that he could not deliver any of them because he had to harvest several corneas in Houston. Fred left immediately for the fifty-mile drive to Houston.

At 8.00 AM that morning we brought Bess back to the operating room to exchange the damaged cornea for a new cornea, which had been properly stored in MK Medium.

She did well during the postoperative period. The only problem she had was that the pupil would not dilate, or constrict. This may have been from taking pilocarpine for many years or because the donor cornea had leaked fixative into the eye. This gave new meaning to the phrase "fixed pupil," which usually means that it is paralyzed or stuck to underlying tissue. We were concerned that the fixation chemicals had affected the pupillary muscles. We were also concerned that the fixative would cause the cataract to progress or cause damage to the retina.

We performed an electroretinogram on this eye and determined that there was no immediate toxic effect on the retina. Her vision quickly improved to 20/40, which was a big improvement from her preoperative vision, and her glaucoma did not progress. We thought that her vision was consistent with the extent of her cataract. We followed her for several years, doing annual electroretinograms and cataract evaluations. Neither her cataract nor her vision changed over the next two years.

We had assumed that the resident who retrieved the corneas and preserved them had used the right solution and that the bottle had the right label under the patient identification slip. Fortunately, this misadventure did no harm to the patient, except for the extra operating room time. She was rather amused by the situation when we told her what had happened, after the first surgery. From that day on I always personally checked the label on the bottle, under the patient name label, before removing the tissue. I learned to never assume that correct procedures have been followed and to always check and double check these things myself.

53

◄◦►

The Vision Needs of a Preacher

ONE OF THE INTERESTING PROBLEMS I solved for a patient involved a black itinerant preacher with glaucoma and cataracts. Walter was over seventy years old and was still active as a minister. He actually served several small churches and had to preach six or seven sermons every Sunday. He also preached evening services several times each week to cover his territory.

Walter was a big man, about six feet two inches tall, and at least two hundred and fifty pounds. He was impeccably dressed in a black pinstriped suit, with pocket handkerchief. He was accompanied by two matronly black ladies who were also very nicely dressed, including mid-sized heels and big colorful straw hats. They fussed over him constantly and told me what a good minister he was and how hard he worked to care for his flock.

When I first saw him, he had lost all of the vision in his left eye from glaucoma, which had gone undiagnosed until it was too late to save the vision. The glaucoma in his right eye had lagged behind that in his left eye, and he was on medications for it. His "good" eye had vision of 20/50, which was not good enough to drive a car in Texas. He explained that the two women with him took him everywhere he needed to go. He had already developed peripheral field loss in his good eye from the glaucoma, which was poorly controlled on medications.

Walter had an early posterior subcapsular cataract, right in the middle of his pupil in his right eye. His optic nerve was cupped, showing that the glaucoma was starting to cause him to lose peripheral vision. He was already on maximum medical therapy and had been treated with laser surgery to open the outflow tracts in that eye, so knife surgery was now indicated.

At the university, we had studied the results of various surgical procedures for glaucoma and had determined that most black patients responded differently to various types of glaucoma surgery. The most successful surgical procedure in black patients was the cyclodialysis procedure. Knowing what worked best on black patients, I chose the cyclodialysis procedure for Walter. This is a simple procedure to separate the white sclera from the underlying dark choroidal tissue to allow the fluid in the eye to leak under the choroid, where it is absorbed, lowering the intraocular pressure.

One of the reasons this procedure works to control glaucoma is the connection of the zonules between the ciliary body and the lens in the eye. The tension of the zonules holds the ciliary body away from the sclera, maintaining the cleft.

The procedure worked very well, and he had good pressure control, with no medications. I followed him for several months to be sure that the glaucoma had not returned. The two ladies always accompanied him to each appointment. About two years after his glaucoma surgery, one of the ladies told me that he was having difficulty reading the scripture during church services. He was developing cataracts in both eyes, but only the one in his seeing eye was critical. I had been waiting until he developed problems reading before raising the possibility of cataract surgery.

One of the things that will cause a successful cyclodialysis to fail is the removal of a cataract from the eye. When the cataract is removed, the tension of the zonules is decreased or removed all together, allowing the cleft to close and the glaucoma to recur.

The cataract extraction was to be done by the extracapsular technique in order to preserve the lens capsule and the zonules. This procedure results in some relaxation of the zonules. To avoid the problems of the old-style cataract glasses, Walter would receive an intraocular lens implant to replace the optical power of the removed cataract. This intraocular lens is usually placed in the remains of the cataract capsule bag to hold it in place. The usual orientation of the lens places the spring loops of the lens at six and twelve o'clock in the eye and tends to stretch the bag toward these directions. The cyclodialysis cleft was at twelve o'clock, so a lens in this position would relax the zonules the most in the area of the cleft. This was an undesired effect of the cataract surgery. Therefore, the lens was placed in the capsule bag and rotated so that the spring loops pointed to three and nine o'clock, actually adding tension to the zonules at six and twelve o'clock.

This position of the lens worked well, and his glaucoma continued to be under good control. The intraocular lens power was calculated to focus the eye at about two feet in front of the eye, and the final result was just as calculated.

About six weeks after surgery, when it was time to fit him with glasses for distance, with a bifocal for reading, he reported that he did not need glasses. He did not drive, because the two ladies drove him wherever he needed to go. Walter loved to preach holding the Bible, in his left hand, open to the text of the sermon, while he walked back and forth on the chancel and gestured with his right hand. He did not need glasses to do this.

The ladies told me that he was a better preacher since his surgery and thanked me for helping him to serve the Lord and his churches in a better way. This was gratifying, but I know that most ophthalmologists would have done much the same as I did and obtained the same results.

Walter had a difficult set of problems to manage. By carefully selecting the procedures, I was able to manage his glaucoma without medications and then remove his cataract and place the lens in an atypical position to maintain the glaucoma control. The lens I chose for the implant gave him vision at just the right distance to be able to preach without glasses. His particular situation, with the two ladies who took him wherever he needed to go, allowed him to function without additional glasses.

The lesson here is that not everyone fits the same mold. By having a number of ways to treat each of his diseases, I was able to tailor a set of procedures to fit his needs. Learning only one way to treat each disease makes this approach very difficult.

54

The Ungrateful Expulsive
Hemorrhage Patient

I WAS APPROACHED BY ONE OF the division chairmen at the university who asked about complications his mother had after cataract extraction with an implant lens. I agreed to see her for an evaluation, and he brought her to Galveston to see me.

She had been operated for a cataract, with placement of an implant lens about six months before, and was now experiencing recurrent pain and blurred vision in the operated eye. She had a cataract in the other eye, but was afraid to have it operated because of the result of the first surgery. She had corneal edema, which had progressed to the corneal clouding stage, as well as epithelial blisters, which would break when she blinked, and were very painful. The edema made the cornea rough and cloudy, interfering with her vision, and she wanted it fixed.

I explained that the only way to remove the pain and restore her vision was a corneal transplant, which she agreed to have done. I also explained that it might be necessary to replace the implant lens if it did not stay in position during the surgery. She wanted to proceed, sooner rather than later.

We had prepared the donor button, removed the edematous cornea, and started placing the new cornea over the open corneal hole. We were progressing nicely, when suddenly she coughed, which partially dislocated the implant lens and caused vitreous to be expelled from the eye through the hole in the cornea. The lens would have to be repositioned in the eye or replaced with another type of lens, once the extruded vitreous was removed.

We opened the suction cutter that we had readied in the operating room in case there was a need to remove the vitreous from the anterior part of the eye. After we removed the instrument from its case and assembled it, which took about thirty seconds, we discovered that the motor was frozen, so we sent for the other vitrector, which was kept in the instrument room on the floor below. Before the second vitrector could arrive, she had another episode of violent coughing. The first cough of this series completely expelled the implant lens from the eye, and much of the vitreous jelly followed. I placed my thumb over the open hole in the cornea to keep her from expelling all of the vitreous or the retina. Her coughing quickly subsided, so we could resume the operation.

When the second vitrectomy machine was set up and ready, I removed my thumb and saw that the normal bright reflection from the retina had turned dark, which was a sign of hemorrhage behind the retina. I removed enough vitreous from the front of the eye to be able to sew in the corneal button with eight sutures to close the front of the eye. I then lifted a conjunctival flap to expose the sclera and made an incision through the sclera. The blood from beneath the retina and choroid drained through this incision. The blood drained copiously for several minutes and then stopped, indicating that the broken vessel had clotted. I left the scleral incision open in case the bleeding recurred, but closed the conjunctival flap.

Now that the hemorrhage had stopped, I used the suction cutter to fill the eye with saline and clean up the remaining vitreous that continued to come forward. I decided to not replace the intraocular lens because I had removed the vitreous and I was not sure that the hemorrhage would not start again. I then finished suturing the new cornea into the corneal rim and made sure that the eye was watertight.

The following day, the cornea was still hazy, so we did an ultrasound to determine the position of the retina and the presence or absence of blood behind the retina. The ultrasound showed that the retina was in the normal position and that there was no elevation of the retina by underlying blood. The cornea healed nicely and became clear. The vitreous was replaced by the watery fluid that usually fills the front of the eye. Her vision gradually improved to about 20/40, which is OK vision for a corneal transplant, but a fantastic outcome for an expulsive choroidal hemorrhage, which usually causes total blindness. Unfortunately, the patient let me know how disappointed she was with her vision when I fit her glasses to give her the 20/40 vision at six months after the surgery. She told me that her son had promised her that I would make her vision perfect. I am sure that she did not know how close she came to being completely blind in that eye.

I worried about whether I should have done this procedure under general anesthesia so she could not have coughed. I went to the literature to review expulsive choroidal hemorrhages and learned that several reviewers had decided that these hemorrhages were just as common under general anesthesia as under local blocks. They attribute this to the habit of anesthesiologists to carry patients under as little anesthesia as possible. When anesthesia becomes too light, they buck on the endotracheal tube, and the strain causes the hemorrhage within the eye. The tiny vessels that enter the eye around the optic nerve are very susceptible to damage, particularly after arteriosclerosis. They rupture as they enter the choroid and, hemorrhage into the choroid and beneath the retina, pushing the retina forward. This can lead to retinal detachment and total loss of vision.

The lesson learned from this episode is that we physicians are held to the expectations of our patients, even when we do not create these expectations or they are the expectations of others. If she had not coughed during the procedure, her expectations might have been met. Her vision after the hemorrhage was far above my expectations, but not hers.

55

<o>

Vision after Twenty Years of Blindness

WHEN THE VITREOUS SUCTION CUTTERS were invented, we had the opportunity to restore vision to people who had not seen for many years. One such patient came in for routine examination for glaucoma and diabetic eye problems. Alvin had experienced hemorrhages from his diabetic retinopathy about twenty years before and, since that time, could only see light and tell what color it was. The hemorrhages had organized into membranes of blood and fibrous tissue within the vitreous body and had significantly blocked the path of light coming into his eyes.

I had been looking for patients who would benefit from having vitreous membranes removed, so one of the residents called me to see this patient. We could see the anterior most membrane behind the lens of the eye, but we could not tell how many other membranes might be behind the one we could see. The membrane was pale yellow and did not have any blood vessels visible within the membrane. Visible vessels would indicate that the membrane was an inoperable, permanently detached retina rather than organized hemorrhage.

I explained the surgery to the patient and told him of the risks involved. He felt he had almost nothing to lose. I explained that in some cases, diabetic retinopathy had destroyed the retina behind these membranes and that removing these curtains could reveal a dead retina. In addition to his diabetes, he also had high blood pressure, which was well controlled by the drug Aldomet.

The suction cutter is about the size of a ballpoint pen refill and has a rotary cutter inside a small aspiration port. The tissue is gently sucked into the port, and the cutter slices off that part that is within the port. It can nibble along an edge and expand a small hole into a larger one. I performed a vitrectomy that cut through at least four layers of membranes before we could see the retina. I focused the operating microscope in on the retina and found that it looked essentially normal. We then proceeded to open large holes in the membranes to increase the subsequent field of vision.

The next day we brought him down to the clinic from the hospital floor to remove his bandages. When I removed the eye patch, he looked around and started to cry. He told me that he could see me and see his wife. He had not seen his wife in twenty years. He was overwhelmed with joy. He started calling it a miracle and saying that I could perform miracles, but I reminded him that it was just an operation that had been successful.

I saw him back two days later. When he came into the exam room, he threw his arms around me and hugged me very tightly for about two minutes. When he let go, he was in tears again. He thanked me and told me that he had seen his daughter for the first time in twenty years, and that he had also seen her two-year-old daughter, whom he had never seen. He told me that he had walked around the house simply looking at things.

Three months later we did his other eye so that he could have some depth perception to help him get around. Unassisted walking was something he had not been able to do for a long time, and he was afraid of falling because he had no sense of distances and could not judge steps or pour coffee into a cup.

The procedure on his second eye went well, but during the recovery period he was hospitalized for profound anemia. He almost died from heart failure caused by anemia. I went to check on him in the hospital and learned that he had developed a hemolytic anemia. They eventually traced the anemia to a rare reaction to the Aldomet that he was taking for his high blood pressure. After they stopped the Aldomet, they discovered that his blood pressure was normal without any medication. Everything seemed to be going his way at last; he could see again, and he no longer had high blood pressure.

I followed him for several years and his vision stayed good. His retina did not show signs of diabetic retinopathy after the vitrectomy, and he did not need laser photo coagulation to treat his retina, as many diabetics often do after vitrectomy. He is one of the patients who I feel I have helped the most during my career in ophthalmology, and I benefited greatly by seeing his reaction to the restoration of his vision.

If there was a miracle here it was the invention of the vitrectomy instrument that enabled the surgery to remove the vitreous membranes, allowing him to see again. This patient experienced the return of his vision because new technology was developed to treat his disease. Research and application of new technology must proceed to provide new treatment modalities for old diseases. When I started my training, these cases were untreatable. Ten years later I had adopted the technology to help this patient. Doctors must keep up with new technology to be able to give the patients the care they deserve.

56

The Myopic Librarian

SEVERAL YEARS AFTER MOVING TO Galveston, I was consulted by the librarian of the medical branch library, who could not see well with his present spectacles. Arthur was wearing lenses that were very thick at the edges and thin in the middle, indicating that he was very nearsighted. He told me that he had been nearsighted as a child and had learned to love books because he could not see well enough to participate in sports or other outdoor activities. Recently, he had been having trouble seeing with his glasses and had to hold books up close to his face to read them.

I examined Arthur and discovered that he needed even stronger glasses. The cause of his increased myopia was early, nuclear sclerotic cataracts. As the lens becomes cloudy, the refractive index of the human lens changes, causing the light to be bent more as it passes through the lens. This results in increasing nearsightedness. Unfortunately, the spectacle lenses used to refocus the light onto the retina also cause diminution of the image size on the retina. This makes the image look smaller to the patient. At the power he needed, the image was very small.

I changed the librarian's glasses, and he could see almost 20/20 and was happy with that for a while. Several months later he came to see me again, complaining of the same symptoms as before. In the interim, he had become more nearsighted because of progression of his cataracts. This time, when I tried to improve his vision, the images were so small that he could see only 20/40. He was desperate for better vision, but corrective lenses were not enough. He needed cataract surgery.

By the time he needed surgery, I was replacing the cataracts with intraocular lenses. These little lenses, which ophthalmologists suspend in the eye, are made of special plastic that the eye tolerates very well, and are manufactured in a range of powers, which allows us to correct for near or farsightedness. By placing the appropriate power lens in the eye when we remove the human lens, we replace the need for glasses.

We did the measurements of the eye to determine the lens power needed to correct his myopia. I did the right eye first because it was his dominant eye. After surgery, he could use it without interference from the poor vision in his nonoperated eye. Correcting his vision with the implant lens rather than spectacles would make his image size much more normal.

About two weeks after the surgery, the university president called me to tell me that he had received a letter from the librarian praising me and claiming that I had performed a miracle. He told the president that he had never seen as well as he saw after the surgery. The patient had proposed that I be promoted to full professor immediately. The president did not promote me, but the call did wonders for my ego.

Three months later, I took out the other cataract and inserted the appropriate intraocular lens to correct for the myopia in that eye. With both eyes corrected to better vision than he could remember through his "coke bottle" glasses, Arthur was ecstatic. He went around campus telling everyone who would listen that I was a miracle worker. It was as if I had my own public relations person on campus.

About a year after the surgery, he came to me to tell me that his improved vision had prompted him to pursue his interest in antique medical books. At the University of Texas Medical Branch, he was the librarian for a large collection of rare medical books, and he had been accepted to do a sabbatical to study old medical books at the Sorbonne in Paris, France.

Near the end of that sabbatical period, the dean announced that the library had just conducted an audit of the books in the library and discovered that many of the rare books had vanished from the shelves. Most of the missing books were the library's second and third copies of very rare books. The FBI was called in, and they soon determined that this librarian had stolen the books and had taken them, a few at a time, to Paris as he traveled back and forth to his sabbatical. He had financed his travel and studies by selling the rare books from the library. The last I heard of him, he had been convicted of theft and was spending time in prison, where he had lots of time to read.

I sometimes wonder if I had facilitated his turn to a life of crime. Perhaps he would have stolen the books just as easily as a highly myopic librarian, but he probably would not have enjoyed Paris as much through his thick glasses. I was sorry to lose such a staunch supporter on campus, although his reliability suffered with his conviction for theft.

Arthur taught me that a person who had been handicapped all his life by extreme nearsightedness would be very grateful for having his retinal image size improved by cataract surgery, but this would not make him a better person. I was embarrassed when one of my staunchest supporters at the medical school turned out to be a thief.

57

◄○►

A Nun with a Sexually
Transmitted Disease

I FIRST MET SISTER MARY ANN when she was working as a floor
nurse, taking care of my father-in-law during his hospitalization
for intractable pain from metastatic prostate cancer. She was a very
efficient, attractive, no-nonsense young nurse who swore like a
trooper if an IV infiltrated or some piece of equipment would not
function properly. I did not know, at that time, that she was also a
nun. She was usually dressed in scrubs, with no name tag, nurse's
cap, or habit. She was not the picture of solemnity that I associated
with nuns.

She came to the room one day to say good-bye to my father-in-
law, saying that she would be leaving the medical floor for another
position. She explained that she was specialty trained as an obstetrics/
gynecology nurse and had been transferred to that service to be the
head nurse of the delivery suite. The nun who had supervised that
service for forty years had finally retired.

Several years later Sister Ann came to see me professionally
because of a chronic pink eye. She had been seen by a local
ophthalmologist, who had treated her with various topical antibiotics
and topical steroids. The pink eye continued unabated, so she was
sent to see me.

I examined her and found significant follicular reaction in the
conjunctiva in a distribution, which told me that this was chlamydia
conjunctivitis rather than a bacterial infection. Unfortunately,

treatment of chlamydia with topical steroids tends to nullify the antibiotics and modifies the infection so that it takes about twice as long as usual to clear completely after the correct treatment is instituted for the chlamydia. I explained all of this to Sister Ann and started her on the combination of sulfacetamide eyedrops in each eye and oral tetracycline capsules. I asked her to return in three weeks for me to check her progress, but explained that her eyes would probably take six weeks or longer to clear since she had been on the steroids.

The following day, I received a phone call from the mother superior of the convent. She was very upset with me and wanted to know how I could possibly diagnose a sexually transmitted disease (chlamydia) in one of her nuns. I started to explain that chlamydia could be spread by finger-to-eye contact when I remembered that Sister Ann was in charge of the maternity suite of the Catholic hospital. I asked the mother superior if Sister Ann was still in charge of the delivery suite. She replied that she was indeed in charge of the obstetrics unit. I then explained to her that Sister Ann was repeatedly checking women in labor and could have easily contracted the disease by careless handling of the surgical gloves or other contact with the women in labor. I also explained to the mother superior that I had never suspected that Sister Ann had experienced any heterosexual contact in contracting this disease.

The mother superior thanked me profusely for explaining this to her and ended the conversation by saying that she would have to immediately tell the other nuns in the convent what I had said. Apparently the word about Sister Ann had spread throughout the convent. She was an attractive, younger nun with a rather free spirit, and I guess the other sisters were not too hesitant to believe in the possibility of Sister Ann contracting chlamydia in another manner.

It did take eight weeks for Sister Ann's conjunctivitis to clear up completely, and she had no further recurrences in the subsequent years that I continued to follow her. She probably was more careful with her sterile technique after this. I certainly learned from her that all nuns are not alike. My acquaintance with Sister Ann occurred before I spent twelve years working at St. Francis Medical Center with nuns, where I learned that nuns are normal people with a religious profession.

58

A Small Epidemic

EPIDEMIOLOGY IS THE STUDY OF the spread of epidemics, or infectious diseases. Occasionally, even an individual practitioner had occasion to do some epidemiological investigation. For example, while I was in Texas, we had an unusual epidemic in the clinic involving the combination of two diseases.

I arrived at morning rounds to be greeted by one of the residents, who wanted me to review a bacteria slide with him after rounds. He told me that he had been called to the emergency room the night before to see a man with a red eye. The emergency room doctors told the resident that they had already diagnosed the man's urethral discharge as gonorrhea. They wanted to know if he had the same disease in his eye.

The resident had taken conjunctival scrapings and done stains for bacteria in our lab. He told me that he saw red (Gram stain negative), diplococci (round bacteria in pairs), in polymorphoneuclear lymphocytes (a form of white blood cell called polys) on the smear and wanted me to verify his findings. When I looked at the slide, I could not find many polys, and I found none with Gram-negative diplococci. I did see many lymphocytes, another type of white blood cell that is typical of viral conjunctivitis.

The emergency room physicians had started the patient on penicillin, which would also cover his eye infection if it was gonorrhea. The resident had asked the patient to return to the clinic that day so that one of the attending physicians could look at him. When he arrived at the clinic, I looked at his eyes and decided that he had adenovirus conjunctivitis. He did not have the hyper purulent, very nasty looking red eye that is typical of gonorrhea. Instead, he had a red watery eye without pus, but with conjunctival follicles, which is typical of adenovirus. There is no specific treatment for adenovirus. It runs its course and goes away, but it is highly contagious. It may spread from one eye to the other and often goes through entire families. The incubation period is ten to fifteen days from exposure, until the disease becomes apparent, so it is often spread before the original patient knows he or she has the disease.

During the next week, we saw six more men who were sent from the emergency room with a diagnosis of gonorrheal urethritis and a red eye. All had adenovirus of the right eye. On further checking, we learned that they came from different parts of town, but all had the same diseases and, strangely, the same eye involved.

At the end of the week, a woman was sent from the emergency room with a diagnosis of gonorrhea and a red right eye. Bells rang! By now everyone in the ophthalmology clinic knew about the seven cases of gonorrhea in men with adenovirus. Since gonorrhea is a sexually transmitted disease, it was not hard to put together the seven men with the source of the epidemic. The resident who saw the woman determined through her history that she was a prostitute who was working in a local motel. The resident who saw the first case knew that his patient was the manager of that motel. Eventually, we learned that the other men were all customers of the prostitute.

In a probably unrelated happening, the motel manager, our initial case, was shot and killed in a bar brawl within two weeks of our having seen him in the clinic. His adenovirus had not even cleared. We never learned the cause of the bar brawl, but we did learn that the prostitute was not paying cash for the motel room in which she stayed and apparently had a working arrangement.

It is seldom that an epidemic presents in such a confined space and is so clearly traceable to its source. The size of the town and the convenience and anonymity of the university hospital emergency room probably concentrated the cases. I informed the local ophthalmologists to suspect adenovirus patients of also having gonorrhea so that they could be treated, but I did not receive any feedback from them about additional cases. We do not know if any others were treated privately for either disease by physicians outside of the emergency room. We may not have seen all of the cases, but we had enough to verify the source. She was treated for the gonorrhea, but we had no treatment for the adenovirus conjunctivitis that had to run its course. Without the second disease, adenovirus is too ubiquitous to be able to track to a source. I guess the fact that this involved a sexually transmitted disease made the effort to trace the disease more interesting and the solution more satisfying.

I learned that a patient can have two different diseases at the same time that are transmitted together. I also learned that the concentration of these cases in our clinic allowed us to find the source of this epidemic and treat her. Had these patients all gone to private doctors who each saw one case, the fact that it was an epidemic might not have been discovered, and the source might not have been treated.

59

◄○►

The Recreational Vehicle Driver

IT IS SELDOM THAT AN ophthalmologist can save a marriage, but I can remember once when I may have done just that. A patient came to see me one day complaining that he had "curtains" in his good eye. Herman explained that he had some infection in one eye when he was a small child, which had caused him to lose all of the useful vision in that eye, though he did have some peripheral vision in that eye. He had learned to adapt to his monocular vision and had not given it much thought for many years. Recently, however, he had developed a curtain in his good eye that radically interfered with his vision.

He told me that this veil, or curtain, interfered with his ability to drive. He had learned that if he shook his head from side to side, the curtain would swing up and out of the way for five to ten seconds and he could see very well. However, the curtain came back down and blocked his vision to the point that he could not see the large letters on my eye chart. He also told me that he and his wife had purchased a forty-foot long, self-contained motor home so that they could tour around the country after he retired in about a year.

I examined Herman and discovered that he had a large, long-standing scar in the macula, the center of the retina and center of vision, in his left eye. Everything was normal in his right eye, except for an area of the vitreous gel that had formed a lacy opacity, which was attached to the retina at the top of the eye at the front edge of the retina. The vitreous gel is very mobile but has attachments around the inside of the front of the eye. When he moved his head, the veil moved with the sloshing of the gel, but it would eventually come to rest in the same place, blocking his vision.

When he laid back and looked up to the ceiling, the veil would hang back and clear the visual axis, and he could see very well. However, when he sat upright, the veil hung down over his pupil, blocking the visual axis and markedly reducing his vision.

I told him that I could remove the veil, using the suction cutter. This was a very risky procedure, because the veil was attached to the retina at the edge of the retina. If the membrane exerted traction on this point of attachment during the operation and was not nibbled cleanly, the retina could tear or pull loose, creating a retinal detachment. This type of detachment is difficult to repair once it occurs.

Since this was his only good eye, he said he wanted time to think about whether he wanted to risk his vision and would call me after he had a chance to think about it. He called about two weeks later to say that he did not want to take the risk. I told him that I understood his situation, but if he changed his mind to give me a call. I often wondered how he got along driving his RV around the country after he retired.

About two years later he called me to say he wanted to see me again. When he came in, his wife was with him. He told me that he had retired on schedule and had tried to drive the RV. He had some near misses while driving it, so he parked the RV in his driveway. His wife refused to learn to drive the RV and was afraid of it, so it sat in the driveway, and he sat around home. He told me that both he and his wife had become sick and tired of sitting around the house, getting on each other's nerves, which he thought might lead to a divorce. After much consideration, he had decided to go for it.

Dr. Michael Nesbit had just joined our faculty as a retina specialist, and we agreed to do the surgery together. As soon as the vitreous was removed, Mike would do a complete examination of the retina through the dilated pupil. We did a standard vitrectomy through the sclera and part of the ciliary body into the back of the eye. It was obvious once we started that the posterior surface of the vitreous body was detached from the posterior retina and had shifted forward in the eye. The curtain he was seeing was the back surface of the vitreous, which now hung from the top of the eye. Since the vitreous was not attached to the back of the eye, it was easily removed from the center of the eye. As we were removing some of the last peripheral attachments of the vitreous, we noted a wisp of blood in the water that filled the eye. It had swirled forward through the pupil.

Mike and I looked at each other, and Mike asked for the indirect ophthalmoscope to be placed on his head so that he could examine the retina. The indirect ophthalmoscope uses a virtual image system to be able to look at the peripheral retina through the dilated pupil. It allows the examiner to see all the way forward inside the eye to the attachment of the retina at its anterior edge. Sure enough, there was a tear in the retina that coincided with the anterior attachment of the vitreous veils. It extended about one clock hour of the ring insertion of the vitreous and appeared as a red line on the retina.

Mike marked the location of the hole, and we proceeded to apply a circling band and a buckle over the hole, and we treated the area with cryotherapy to cause the retina to stick to the choroid over the area of the buckle. This cryotherapy closes the hole and prevents a retinal detachment. We had done the procedure we came to do and had experienced the most frequent complication of that operation. We had diagnosed the complication on the table and had already repaired the complication before the patient was awakened from anesthesia.

We followed Herman for several weeks until we considered him to be out of danger from the retinal tear. He had good vision from almost the day after surgery and was very happy with the result. He did not return for another check up until more than a year after his surgery. When he did return, he told us that he had been gone for a year, driving his recreational vehicle all over the United States. He and his wife had visited most of the national forests, parks, and monuments. They had been having a great time together in the RV and were about to depart on another trip. There had been no recurrence of the curtain, and his vision had remained at almost 20/20 in the operated eye. His vision in the eye that was damaged when he was young was no better or worse. Herman told us that, in hindsight, he wished that he had undergone the vitrectomy surgery when he retired, but he understood our reluctance to recommend it to him.

This case reinforced my reluctance to push patients toward surgery. This patient did have the most common complication of vitrectomy surgery, that of developing a hole in the retina during surgery. Fortunately, our awareness of this complication allowed us to repair it on the table before it became a vision-loss problem. The fact that it worked out made him wish he had had the surgery a year earlier. Once he got on the road, he and his wife quit quarreling and had a great time.

60

A Dislocated Lens in a Myasthenia Patient

F OR SOME PATIENTS, LOSS OF vision is only a small problem compared with the problems they face every day to stay alive. One such patient came to me one day, saying that his vision in one eye came and went, but it was never very good. This had been going on for several years, ever since he was involved in a labor demonstration on the wharves and was hit on the side of the head with a two-by-four.

When I examined Sam, I discovered that the lens in his right eye was resting in front of the iris, instead of behind the iris where it is supposed to be. It was being held there by the iris because the hole of the pupil was smaller than the lens it was holding. The blow to the head had probably dislocated his lens and knocked it loose from the threads that typically hold it in the pupil. The lens was grey-white throughout and completely blocked the pupil. His vision was light perception with projection, which meant that he could tell the direction from which a light was coming when the lens was in his pupil. With no lens in the pupil, he was so out of focus that his vision was not much better, but he could see better to his right side.

It is not good for the lens to sit against the back of the cornea, so I put pupil dilating drops in the eye to see if the lens would drop back into the eye. After about half an hour, the lens did drop back through the pupil and disappeared into the back of the eye. When I looked into the back of the eye with the indirect ophthalmoscope, the lens was lying on the retina, right over the macula. The patient was lying on his back, looking at the ceiling so the lowest part of his eye was his macula, so the lens settled there. If the lens came forward and was trapped by the pupil, it could cause an acute attack of glaucoma and would also damage the cornea.

I told him that we should remove the lens because the majority of patients with dislocated lenses develop chronic glaucoma. He agreed to the surgery, but told us that he would have to take medicine every three hours before, during, and after the surgery so that he would not die.

It had been determined several years before that he had myasthenia gravis, a neuromuscular transmitter disease that causes weakness of the muscles, including the respiratory muscles. Without his medications, he would stop breathing and die. He had to set his alarm clock for every three hours to be sure that he awakened enough to take his medicine so that he would not stop breathing during sleep.

Removing a dislocated lens requires a plan. Since the lens floats around in the eye, it is hard to get it to a position where it can be removed. The best way is to trap it in the front of the eye. To do this, weak dilating drops are used to dilate the pupil. The patient is asked to lie on his or her stomach, face down, which allows the lens to sink down into the anterior chamber. Once the lens is seen in the anterior chamber, looking from below, pilocarpine drops at maximum strength are squirted into the eye. Pilocarpine constricts the pupil, holding the lens against the cornea. The patient is then rolled onto his back, and the operation proceeds. One or more needles are sometimes placed behind the lens to hold it in the front of the eye just in case the anesthetic block dilates the pupil by overriding the pilocarpine.

We did this in our patient and managed to remove the cataract uneventfully. Several days after the surgery, I was able to look into the eye and discovered that there was a large macular scar, right in the center of his vision. It had been hidden by the lens when I looked into the eye before surgery. This scar may have been caused by the lens repeatedly resting on the retina when the patient lay on his back, or it could have been from the original blow to the head with the two-by-four. He had definite improvement of his lateral vision where the retina was not damaged, and we had also removed the possibility of a glaucoma attack from the lens being caught in the pupil.

I saw him for several years after that, but I learned later that he died from complications of his myasthenia gravis.

I had great admiration for this patient, who faithfully took his medication every three hours, regardless of the situation he was in at the time it was due. I had known that trauma could cause a dislocated lens, but I had never seen a lens dislocated by a blow to the back of the head with a two-by-four. If the scar in the back of the eye was caused at the same time that the lens was dislocated, he was probably hit directly in the eye, but did not remember it after the blow to the back of his head. I wondered at the time if whatever he was demonstrating about on the wharf was worth the loss of vision in one eye.

61

The Lions Club President

THE LIONS CLUB HAS HAD eye care as a major activity for many years. They have run eye banks and contributed to eye care nationally and internationally, with an emphasis on corneal transplants and the eye banking that supports that activity. I have been invited to talk to them about corneal transplants and related topics on many occasions.

Shortly after one of these talks, the president of the local Lions Club came to see me because he was having trouble with his vision. I examined him and found that he had early cataracts in both eyes as well as Fuchs' corneal dystrophy. As I have stated earlier, Fuchs' dystrophy, a hereditary disease of the cornea, causes the inner lining (the endothelium) to leak fluid from the inside of the eye into the cornea, allowing it to swell. Fluid eventually accumulates beneath the surface layer (the epithelium), causing blisters on the cornea. These blisters enlarge and break, causing pain and the feeling of something scratchy in the eye.

His corneal disease was minimal, and his cataracts did not interfere significantly with his vision. I fit him with a new pair of glasses to compensate for the near-sightedness caused by his cataracts, which enabled him to perform all of his business tasks for several years. Eventually, the vision in his left eye became worse from the cataract and the progression of his corneal dystrophy. I recommended a combined corneal transplant and cataract extraction, with an implant lens. The surgery was uneventful, and he regained good vision in that eye.

I always follow the patient until the wound appears healed before removing the sutures from the cornea. The best sign of healing is the appearance of white tissue in the corneal wound. By fifteen months after surgery, there was a faint white line in the wound, and my patient was anxious to have the sutures removed. I put him off for three more months, waiting for more healing. Corneal transplant patients use steroid eyedrops to prevent rejection of the transplanted tissue, and steroids delay the healing of the corneal wound, a common side effect.

When he returned for follow-up, eighteen months after his surgery, he still had a faint white line in the incision. I decided that it was time for the sutures to come out, so they were removed that afternoon. He did well after suture removal and healed the epithelium quickly.

About three months after the sutures were removed he came to see me as an emergency. He had bumped his head on the car door as he was leaving a taxi and noted pain in his eye, with a sensation of something in his eye.

When I examined him I found that the wound had separated from twelve o'clock to three o'clock on his cornea. The central button had shifted forward about half of the thickness of the cornea. The eye was not leaking, so I placed a soft contact lens to hold the cornea down and permit it to heal. The soft lens also stopped the foreign body sensation.

I saw him every few days to watch for possible leakage from the wound or other complications. The next time I saw him the edges of the wound were starting to enzymatically degrade, or melt away, and the wound had begun to leak aqueous humor through the hole. I covered the leaking hole with tissue glue to stop the leak and replaced the bandage lens. Two days later he returned, complaining of severe pain and light sensitivity in the eye.

Examination showed that the glue had come off and the eye was leaking profusely, resulting in a soft eye. The melting had extended into the peripheral cornea and also into the graft. The only treatment was a larger corneal transplant to get rid of the leaking tissue. I put a patch on the eye after placing a soft contact lens on the cornea to try to retard the leakage. I called the eye bank, and tissue was available. They dispatched a cornea from Houston, and we sent the patient to the operating room holding area to prepare him for surgery. When I arrived in the operating room, I learned that the anesthesiologist was holding the patient in the preoperative area because he had excessively high blood pressure caused by his severe pain. They gave him Clonidine to lower his blood pressure, and he responded in about half an hour. They then brought him to the operating room and put him under anesthesia.

When I removed the eye patch, there was blood on the eyelids. Opening the eye revealed more blood behind the eyelids and within the eye itself. His high blood pressure had caused him to have an expulsive hemorrhage within the eye. The eye had a hole in the cornea, and blood continued to leak from this hole. I needed to stop the bleeding and close the eye.

I dissected the conjunctiva from the eye and made several holes in the sclera so that the hemorrhage could drain from the eye. When the bleeding stopped, the eye was positioned for a transplant, and a large corneal transplant was performed. While the eye was open for the transplant, the blood within the front of the eye was removed.

When we examined the eye the next day, the cornea was intact and the anterior part of the eye appeared normal. There was blood in the vitreous jelly in the back of the eye, so we could not see the retina. We performed an ultrasound on the eye, which showed that the retina was in the proper position. As the hemorrhage cleared from the vitreous over the next few weeks, his vision gradually cleared to about 20/80—useful vision, but not back to where it was before suture removal.

One year and nine months was the longest that I known for a wound to split open after the sutures were removed. I feel that the bump he received getting out of the taxi played a major role in the wound rupture. In retrospect I should have re-sutured the wound when it first split open, but I had seen several eyes do well with just the soft bandage lens. I also witnessed the fact that eye pain can cause high blood pressure, which in turn can cause an expulsive hemorrhage in a soft eye.

Because of the long time from suture removal to the wound rupture and the role of trauma in the wound problem, the patient did not blame me for the complications. He remained friendly and even invited me back to speak again to the Lions Club. His operated eye stayed the same, and his other eye did not need cataract extraction or a corneal transplant while I was in Galveston.

At the cornea fellows meeting that year I asked many of my colleagues how long they left nylon sutures in their corneal transplant patients. No one had heard of a spontaneous wound rupture after removing sutures at eighteen months. Most of them removed the sutures twelve months after surgery.

Because of my activity with the Lions Club, this patient had become a friend and had great trust in me. I had insisted on waiting to remove the sutures, so he did not blame me for the breakdown of the wound. I concluded that the cause of his wound rupture was the trauma of hitting the car door. Part of his goodwill toward me was because we had a long-term, very open relationship, so he trusted me.

62

<o>

A Strange Reaction after Cataract Surgery

I WAS CALLED TO THE PRIVATE patient examination area of the clinic on a Monday morning to see a sixty-plus-year-old woman with an emergency eye problem. Virginia was complaining of extreme pain in her left eye. She had undergone cataract surgery by a private ophthalmologist on the previous Thursday.

She had returned to the office of the surgeon on the first postoperative day, complaining of discomfort in the eye. She was examined and told that some discomfort was common after eye surgery. She was started on the usual steroids and antibiotics and told to come back in one week.

The pain progressed, so on Saturday she called the ophthalmologist on call for the practice. He told her that the office was closed and that she did not need to be seen, but to continue with her eyedrops and take Tylenol if the pain got worse. If the pain persisted, she was to come into the office on Monday morning to be seen. Virginia was not happy with this reply. The pain did increase, so on Monday morning she appeared in my office, rather than his.

She was obviously in pain and was very sensitive to light, making the examination difficult. Topical anesthetic did not help the light sensitivity. When I did get a look at her eye, the conjunctiva was very red and she was tearing. Her iris was very remarkable. Her iris surface was pale grey, but the usually invisible vessels in the iris were easily visible and were dilated and tortuous, looking like corkscrews.

The aqueous humor between the cornea and the iris contained many white blood cells and was in a gelled state. This indicated that there was a pronounced inflammatory reaction, which could mean infection or a toxic response to something used during surgery. The eyelid was not swollen, and there was no layer of white blood cells between the cornea and iris, which made me think her eye problem was probably inflammatory rather than infectious.

I covered both bases by putting her on hourly drops of tobramycin (an antibiotic) and fortified prednisilone acetate (steroids). Because of her anxiety, I asked her to return the next day to evaluate her progress. Later that day, around five o'clock, she called to tell me that her eye was feeling much better.

When I saw her the next day, the conjunctival redness had decreased. The tearing was less, and the dilation, tortuosity, and diameter of the iris vessels had lessened. I told her to cut back the eyedrops to every two hours while awake and come back on Friday.

On Friday she was much better and greatly relieved, but still mad at the surgeon whom she thought had been unresponsive. She pulled a video cassette from her purse and handed it to me. She told me that her surgery had been videotaped as part of the cataract extraction package and the video was presented to her at the end of surgery as a memento.

This was done by many of the cataract surgeons at that time as a marketing tool. The surgeons also sent roses to their successfully operated patients and invited them to parties to which they invited patients who they felt needed to have cataract surgery but were afraid of doing so.

She said that she wanted me to watch the tape to see what the surgeon had done wrong and what had caused her eye to respond so violently. While reviewing the tape of her cataract extraction, I noticed there was a gap in the recording during the placement of the intraocular lens; however, everything else during the surgery appeared perfectly normal—a smooth cataract extraction. The iris did not prolapse and was not treated roughly on the tape. There was no difficulty in the part of the lens placement, which showed on the tape. I returned the tape to the patient and told her that there was nothing unusual about the operation, unless something happened during the gap.

As she recovered from the severe reaction, the gel of the aqueous humor retracted from the cornea and shrank to become a membrane, which covered the pupil. As this membrane matured, it became translucent. The posterior capsule holding the intraocular lens also became opaque over the first few weeks after the surgery. These two membranes reduced her vision to 20/400 in that eye. I told her that we could open the membranes using the YAG/Neodymium laser once the eye had recovered from the inflammation. The laser is used to pop holes in these membranes. By placing the holes close together to connect them, a large hole can be made.

About six weeks after her surgery, I took her to the laser room and used the YAG/Neodymium laser to open the membrane at the pupil and the opaque posterior capsule. This was done with a minimum of laser shots and was otherwise uncomplicated. Her vision improved remarkably after the laser procedure, and she went home very happy.

The next day she called to say that her vision had become cloudy and her eye had started to ache. I had her come into the office immediately. She came in that afternoon with a very red eye and pronounced inflammation. She again formed gelled aqueous and cork screw vessels in her iris. The laser procedure had recreated the original situation. The only time I had seen this reaction to the laser was when I had performed a laser capsulotomy on a capsule with bulls-eye shaped deposits on the intraocular lens and capsule.

I learned at a microsurgery conference several years before that these bull's-eye deposits are the glycoid slime laid down by the bacteria, micrococcus. In the process of opening the capsule and membrane, the laser had disrupted the slime encapsulation of the micrococcus bacteria, releasing the bacteria to scatter through the eye and cause inflammation. When micrococcus enters the eye during surgery, it is not very virulent and usually causes a very low grade inflammation. It eventually encapsulates in its own glycoid slime, and the eye stays quiet unless something disrupts the slime releasing the bacteria. The slime forms rings, or bull's-eye deposits, on surfaces.

In retrospect, the probable cause of the first episode was a large contamination of the eye with micrococcus bacteria that prompted an immediate inflammatory response. The bacteria responded to the high levels of antibiotics that I had added by withdrawing into the glycoid slime, which it secretes for protection. The eye recovered until the slime was disrupted by the laser.

The course of the inflammation from the laser treatment followed the same course as the inflammation following the cataract operation. The aqueous clot retracted to form a new membrane in the pupil. The posterior capsule opening was also covered by a new membrane. This was essentially the situation that existed in the eye before the laser treatment. The micrococcus was probably still present in the eye, sequestered in the glycoid slime.

The only antibiotic that has good ocular penetration and is effective against micrococcus is clindamycin. Several years before this case, several old, infirm, or weakened patients died of mucous diarrhea caused by taking clindamycin, and the drug was almost taken off of the market. This patient was about sixty years old, employed, and in good health.

The cause of the mucous diarrhea had not been determined at the time I saw this patient. It was later learned that the cause of the diarrhea problem was Clostridia bacteria residing in the gall bladder. The Clostridia grew out of the gall bladder and spread through the gastrointestinal tract when antibiotics killed the other bacteria. It was also learned later that the spread of Clostridia could be avoided by treating the patient with Flagyl whenever clindamycin is given. We did not know about the Flagyl treatment at the time of this patient.

I explained the problem to the patient. We had to eliminate the micrococcus from the eye so that it would not be released by the laser every time the membranes were opened. I explained the problem with clindamycin and the possibility of diarrhea and even death. She agreed to take the clindamycin for ten days to internally sterilize the eye so that we could open the membranes with the laser without having another flare up.

The afternoon after I explained all of this to the patient, her sister, a nurse, called to accuse me of trying to kill her sister by giving her clindamycin. I explained the situation to the sister and then called the patient. The patient said that she understood the risk and was willing to take the medication and told me to ignore her sister.

Two weeks later the patient returned, having taken the clindamycin for ten days and reporting that she was fine. She had experienced only mild diarrhea. Several weeks later I used the laser to open the membrane again. This time there was no reaction to the laser treatment and no recurrence of the membranes. Although the micrococcus bacteria were never cultured from this eye, I feel that the most likely explanation for the events was an infection with these micrococcus bacteria.

Virginia continued to do well with that eye. A year later she was developing a cataract in the other eye. When I told her I was leaving Galveston, she said that she would come to Pittsburgh to have me do her cataract there. I convinced her that there were other cataract surgeons in southeast Texas who could do an excellent cataract extraction for her without her needing to travel.

She called me in Pittsburgh two years later to tell me that she had found a cataract surgeon in Texas and that her cataract extraction had gone very well, with nothing happening like on her first eye. I told her that the reaction in the first eye was so unusual that I would have been surprised if it had happened in her second cataract surgery. I had not seen the same reaction before, but it was very rewarding to me to be able to figure out the cause and cure.

I learned that my initial impression that this patient had inflammation rather than infection was not entirely correct. She had a low-grade infection from a minor organism. The presentation that I heard several years before, about micrococcus bacteria hiding in the eye, proved instrumental in treating this patient. Information that seems to be of little value at the time may prove to be the key to solving a future problem.

I also learned about the danger of recording surgery and giving the tape to the patient. I think that Virginia would have sued the cataract surgeon if I had found any error in the surgery.

63

<o>

An Unusual Steroid Complication

S OME MEDICATIONS THAT SEEM TO be miraculous in their effects on disease may have side effects that could manifest in medical or social ways. I was sent a patient who had a severe case of shingles. The shingles were unusual in that they continued to erupt every few days. Usually the lesions appear, mature to vesicles, the vesicles rupture, scab over, and go away in about one week. Often the pain continues for months; sometimes it subsides shortly after the outbreak, only to return after the lesions have healed.

Fred had involvement of the first division of his fifth cranial nerve on the left, which means his shingles involved the forehead on his left side and extended from the corner of his eye up to the top of his head. About once a week, he would have a new crop of lesions appear on his forehead. Instead of taking a week to mature and disappear, these matured and disappeared in three days.

Fred also had involvement of his cornea on the same side. The epithelium had sloughed from his cornea and would not grow back to cover the underlying stroma. Although the cornea becomes numb in shingles, he had constant irritation and occasional pain from his corneal involvement. I trimmed the epithelial edges; I gave him carbachol drops to stimulate the epithelium; I fit him with a soft contact lens to protect the epithelium; and I covered him with antibiotics: but still the epithelium would not grow to cover the cornea.

Eventually, after about three months, the epithelium did finally close the defect and created a ridge across the center of his pupil, with a faint scar in the middle of his cornea. This ridge and scar severely distorted his vision, making it necessary for him to have a corneal transplant to restore his vision, unless the epithelial ridge remodeled itself and became smooth again while the scar faded. It was best to wait until the disease had been inactive for at least one year before doing the corneal transplant, so there was time to wait for his vision to improve.

At about the time Fred's corneal defect closed, his internist decided to put him on systemic steroids to stop the continuing recurrence of new crops of shingles lesions. We did not have the acyclovir-like drugs to control herpetic diseases at that time, so the patient was given large doses of oral steroids.

Since he had been off work for several months, he decided to try to go back to work at his job as vice president of a local bank. He was talking with his boss shortly after he returned to work, and something the boss said threw him into a rage. He yelled and screamed and called the boss a number of unflattering names. The boss responded by firing Fred on the spot. Later, when the patient realized what he had done, he approached the boss and asked for forgiveness, but the boss was steadfast and said that no one could work for him who had said the things that the patient had said to him.

Such behavior is a little known side effect of steroid therapy, known as steroid rage. A small number of patients who take high doses of steroids will become paranoid and are easily provoked into a rage. Although little was known about this when this incident took place more than twenty years ago, it is now a well-recognized reaction to steroids. This potential reaction can even be pretreated with antipsychotic medications if there is a history of this reaction and the steroids are needed to save a life or control a serious disease.

In this case, his physician went to the boss and tried to explain that it was the medication speaking rather than the patient, but the boss said that the medication would not use such language, and he would not reconsider his firing of the patient. Shortly after this incident, I received a call from the patient asking for a referral to a cornea specialist in another city and a transfer of his medical records to that physician.

I lost track of this patient when he left Galveston and would like to have known what happened to him. I had one other patient, years later, who had recurrent shingles. She was placed on acyclovir to stop her recurrences, but she felt that the medication caused her hair to fall out. She said that every time she combed her hair, her comb was full of hair that had come out. She was a very attractive lady, with blond hair, who could not bear the thought of going bald and wearing a wig, so she stopped the medication, saying that she would rather put up with the shingles than go bald.

The acute phase of all of the many other cases of shingles that I treated over those years resolved in two weeks. Many had post-herpetic pain that went on for months to years. The herpes zoster virus damages the nerves, causing them to fire spontaneously. If it is a pain nerve, it causes the perception of pain, while a heat-sensing nerve will cause a burning sensation, and so forth. Drugs that stabilize nerves have some effect in controlling the pain.

Herpes zoster is the virus that causes shingles. It is also the virus that causes chickenpox. It is said that you cannot get shingles unless you have had chicken pox. There is a difference between the way the body responds to the virus on the first exposure and the way the body reacts when herpes comes back. There is an old joke about the difference between true love and herpes is that … herpes lasts forever.

Herpetic viruses hide in the DNA within the nerves of the body and become activated by some trigger mechanism, causing them to emerge as a new episode of the disease. They usually manifest along the same nerve each time. It is poorly understood why we do not acquire immunity to recurrent shingles like we do for measles or small pox and even chicken pox. Herpes simplex can recur many times, usually in the same part of the body as fever blisters, corneal ulcers, or genital herpes. We now have some drugs that work well on controlling some strains of herpes. Control of the virus often prevents the need for steroids and the subsequent steroid rage.

A new herpes zoster vaccination has just come onto the market. People who have had chicken pox but have not had shingles can reduce the possibility of developing shingles by taking the vaccine. It is strongly recommended that people over sixty years old who have had chicken pox but not shingles have the vaccination.

I learned about steroid rage from Fred. I also learned that medication can cause serious personal problems, but this cause may not be accepted as a valid excuse for the actions it causes. This was the first of several unusual manifestations of herpes zoster that I would see during my career.

64

<o>

Radial Keratotomy with Complications

A WOMAN, ABOUT SIXTY YEARS OLD, came into my office complaining of severe stabbing pain in her eyes that had become intolerable. Della told me that she had undergone cataract extraction in both eyes about two years ago. After the cataract extractions her vision became cloudy in one eye, and she was told that her cornea had failed and that she needed a corneal transplant. The corneal transplant was "successful," but she could not see without very strong glasses. The same surgeon had then done radial keratotomy in that eye to correct nearsightedness and warping of the transplant. Months after all of this, she began having severe, sharp pain in that eye, especially when she awoke in the morning. Blinking could also cause the pain.

Della kept telling me how happy she was that she had gone to this particular surgeon because he could do all of the procedures himself, apparently not relating her current condition to the surgery or the surgeon. She had come to see me because she had moved and found it too difficult to return to her original hometown for follow-up.

When I examined her I saw that she had an implant lens after cataract surgery. She had a circular scar of a corneal transplant and about ten radial incision scars, with a Ruiz modification to correct astigmatism. The Ruiz procedure is a series of cuts parallel to the edge of the cornea that is made between two radial cuts. The cuts parallel to the edge of the cornea should not intersect the radial cuts. Unfortunately, the cuts of this Ruiz procedure intersected forming corners, and the corners had pulled open like a three-corner tear. Several of the radial cuts were also spread open, and the epithelium was hanging loosely from the edges of the cuts. The reason for the gapping of the radial cuts was not immediately apparent, but was possibly from the ingrowth of corneal epithelium spreading the walls of the cuts apart. The threads of corneal epithelium that were loose and falling from the cuts were the obvious cause of her pain. The way to stop the pain was for the epithelium to be physically removed or squeezed out of the cuts by the wound healing from the bottom of the cut.

I removed the shreds of epithelium that were hanging from the cuts, and in the process the epithelium in the cuts often came with the shreds hanging out of the cut. I put her on antibiotics, steroids, and hypertonic salt tears to encourage the wounds to heal and to avoid infection. This helped some during the next several weeks, but she continued to have severe pain several times a day.

I had not attempted to measure the pressure in the eye because of the corneal distortion and not wanting to use topical anesthetics, which retard healing. The distortion made the instruments we use for checking pressure very inaccurate. One day she came in when I was not in the clinic, so one of my colleagues saw her; he checked her pressure and found it to be elevated in the range of 35 to 40 mm Hg. Normal is between 10 and 21 mm Hg. This elevated intraocular pressure was the probable cause for the gapping of the radial cuts. We started her on timolol to lower the pressure. This not only lowered her intraocular pressure but also decreased her pain, but the pain still recurred several times a week.

She came in demanding that I do something to stop the pain. The pain was still being caused by epithelium tearing loose from the cuts. The only solution I could think of was to scrape the epithelium from the cuts, replace most of the damaged cornea with a new corneal transplant, and suture the remaining peripheral parts of the cuts together.

In the operating room, I reopened and scraped the sides of the cuts with a scalpel blade to remove the epithelium. I then sutured the cuts to close the peripheral part of each cut that would remain after the corneal transplant. I trephined the cornea and removed the central portion. The donor button was then sutured to the edge of the peripheral cornea, placing the sutures in good cornea between the cuts. This recreated a smooth central cornea, but also reproduced the myopia from the first transplant, in which the cuts had been made to correct her astigmatism and myopia.

After the surgery, she was completely free of pain, but she complained about being nearsighted and told me over and over about how well she saw after the other doctor had operated on her. I guess she had forgotten her pain and the fact that when she first saw me that she could not see the chart with her painful eye.

She kept telling me how wonderful Dr. R. was. I guess that she did not realize that he had caused her corneal edema when he removed the cataract. Removal of the cataract, in turn, caused her to need a corneal transplant, which should not have led to so much myopia and astigmatism that she needed the radial keratotomy and Ruiz procedure. The radial keratotomy and Ruiz procedure, in turn, caused the epithelial erosions that caused her pain. Dr. R. also had missed the fact that she had glaucoma, which was a contraindication to the radial keratotomy and Ruiz procedure. I do not like to criticize the work of other physicians to a patient, so I did not explain all of this to her, thinking that she would eventually figure it out.

It is a common occurrence that the last doctor gets the blame for everything, even though the last doctor may only be repairing the damage done by the prior doctors. This was a common situation in which I found myself, being at the referral center where unsuccessful results tend to gravitate.

65

<o>

Spontaneous Transplant Rejection Reversal

S OME RULES IN MEDICINE ARE close to 100 percent true. I was taught
that once a corneal transplant rejects completely, there is nothing
that can be done to bring it back to clarity, but if a corneal rejection
is caught early, it is possible to bring it back if the endothelium has
not been severely attacked.

I had a patient who was a black lady from southern Louisiana
who came to me because of corneal edema. I determined that the
cause of her edema was Fuchs' dystrophy in both eyes. Her vision
had deteriorated to less than 20/200 in both eyes, and I told her that
she needed a corneal transplant to restore her vision.

She underwent a routine corneal transplant and did well for
several months after the surgery. She was from the Lafayette,
Louisiana, area, so I asked her if she knew one of my favorite artists
from there, Francis Pavy, named the "Picasso of Zydeco" by *Rolling
Stone*. I had just returned from his show in New Orleans, where I had
purchased one of his paintings. He was showing a group of paintings
from his "Drinking Muddy Water" series. She asked me if I knew
what the expression "Drinking Muddy Water" meant. She explained
that if you acted mentally off balance in southern Louisiana, people
would say that you had been drinking muddy water. That explained
a lot about Francis Pavy's paintings

About one year after her transplant she came to see me, telling
me that her vision had been blurred for several weeks. When I

looked at her, the corneal transplant button was totally white. It had swollen to almost twice the normal thickness and had edema on the surface. Since it had been rejecting for several weeks and was so edematous, I was sure that the graft was rejected and could never return to clarity. So, I told her I thought that her graft had rejected and that she should have come in when it first bothered her, as I had told her right after the surgery.

I explained to her that the only way to correct her vision was through another corneal transplant. She would have to have another operation. She said that she wanted to think it over and get back to me.

About a year later, she came back to see me. When I looked at her eye, I could not believe that her graft was crystal clear, the eye was quiet, and there was no anterior chamber reaction. There was no evidence of a graft rejection at all.

I asked her if she had undergone a subsequent operation to replace her transplant. She denied having anything done to her eye to restore her graft. She also denied any changes in medications or diet and believed that the cornea just cleared by itself. I had never seen a graft that had rejected completely come back to be so clear and compact. We were taught in medical school to never say never when it comes to illness or therapy. Nothing is 100 percent in medicine.

66

Medication Confusion

OUR NURSES ON THE EYE floor in Galveston were very good. They knew what to expect after eye trauma and eye surgery and did an excellent job working with the patients. When a patient was discharged from the hospital (yes, we used to put cataracts and other eye surgery, eye infections, and traumatized-eye patients in the hospital), the nurses would take all of the eyedrops from the patient's drawer in the medicine cabinet to the patient's room and go over the medicines and the dosage schedule with the patient.

One day we told Travis, a cataract surgery patient, that he would be discharged that morning. He was anxious to leave, so he went to the nurse's station and asked for his medications. The nurse got out his medications and explained to him the purpose of each medicine and when to take it, and then placed his medications on the counter of the nursing station in front of him. The nurse then answered the phone next to her and left the patient. He gathered up the medications and left with his wife.

When he returned the next week for his follow-up visit his eye looked all right, but it was slightly red. The resident who had done the surgery asked him how he was doing with his eyedrops and asked if he needed any refills. The patient replied that he had plenty of eyedrops and that he had not missed a dose. Then he mentioned to the resident that the drop that he put in with the brush really burned his eye for several minutes after he put it in. Since there were no eyedrops that were instilled with a brush, the resident asked him which drop he was talking about. His wife produced a bag containing the medications, and the patient quickly produced a bottle of Wite-Out typewriter correction fluid from the bag. When asked where he got the bottle, he said that the nurse had given it to him when he left the hospital.

After talking with the charge nurse on the floor, we determined that she had not actually given him the Wite-Out. The unit clerk had been using it and had it on the counter. Apparently it had been close to the patient's eyedrops, and he had gathered it in with his drops as he left the counter. The clerk remembered that her Wite-Out had disappeared on the same day that the patient had been discharged.

Needless to say, we told the patient to discontinue the drops with the brush, as the patient no longer needed them. The patient did very well after that. Fortunately, this was not a life-threatening or even a vision-threatening medication error. We took steps to assure that the clerk did not leave her Wite-Out on the counter and cautioned the nurses to be sure that the patients received only their discharge medications when they went home.

The large number of medication errors that are reported in the press and used by politicians to punish the medical profession are actually such errors as being more than ten minutes early or late in dispensing medication to patients. More serious errors occur when the nurse or pharmacist cannot read the doctor's hand writing. A doctor's writing did not cause this error with the Wite-Out. Computerized orders would not have prevented this mistake either. Perhaps the patient's own impatience may have contributed to the error, because the explanation was made at the nursing station rather than in the patient's room. Was the error caused by the nurse, or the patient, or the floor clerk? What formal procedures could have prevented this and will safeguard against a similar happening in the future?

Most corrective actions would be considered silly by those involved. Lock up the Wite-Out? Ban Wite-Out on the floors? Have the nurse check the medications as the patient gets on the elevator to leave the floor? Send instructions with photographs of the bottles with the patient? (What if the pharmacy changes suppliers, with different colored bottles?) How about educating the patient that typewriter correction fluid is not an eyedrop that you put in with a brush? Fortunately, it did no harm to the eye of the patient, so the first law of medicine, "First, do no harm," was not violated.

Actually, we had taken the precaution of having the nurse on the floor dispense the medications to the patient and explain how each was to be taken. This was to be done as the patient prepared to leave the floor so that they would not be mixed with other medications. I learned from this patient that even good precautions can be circumvented by random acts, like a clerk leaving her Wite-Out near where medications are explained.

67

◄o►

Herpes Simplex after Cardiac Catheterization

I WAS CALLED FROM MY OFFICE one day to see a woman in the clinic in consultation while she was in the hospital for cardiac catheterization. She had broken out with herpes simplex all over her face two days after having the catheterization. She had spiked a temperature about four hours after the procedure, but all of the blood cultures were negative, and the spike occurred before the usual interval of eight to twelve hours after the procedure, when it is caused by bacterial sepsis.

The woman, who was in her fifties, had a vesicular rash, mostly on the right side of her face, including the eyelids. Her right eye was inflamed, and she had a small herpetic lesion on the edge of her right cornea. The vision from that eye was reduced to about 20/50. We instituted treatment for herpes simplex with antiviral eyedrops.

We followed her for several days until the skin rash and all eye changes had disappeared. At about two weeks, she returned saying that she could not see at all from her right eye. The resident summoned me to the clinic to see if I could explain the lost vision. Her right eye was slightly red, but the dendrite was completely healed, leaving the cornea normal. There was no cellular response in the eye, the lens was clear, and the retina and optic nerve were completely normal. While we were examining her, she told us that she was mad at the hospital because of her fever and the herpes outbreak, which she blamed on the catheter procedure. They had not offered to pay her hospital bill or give her compensation. Now she claimed that the procedure had left her blind in the right eye. This linkage of injury and compensation within the same sentence usually suggests malingering.

Routine tests for malingering are difficult to use when one eye sees perfectly and the patient claims blindness in the other eye. Patients will not stumble over objects placed in their way. Threats like pretending to slap or hit the patient cannot be used unless they claim total blindness in both eyes. Opto-kinetic nystagmus is a jerky eye movement caused by movement of a row of objects in front of or past the eye. The brain attempts to track the first object, then jumps to the second object. This is involuntary if the person looks at the objects and can see them move. A person watching a train pass by at close range will have this jerking eye movement. Using a rocking mirror to simulate movement or stripes on a moving drum to induce opto-kinetic nystagmus in a seeing eye does not work unless the patient cooperates. If one eye sees the moving objects, it will cause the movement in both eyes.

Therefore we used a polarized projection slide to make the letters on the eye chart and put polarized lenses in the phoropter (refraction lens holder). One eye sees some letters, while the other eye sees different letters, and both eyes open can see all of the letters. To read the whole line, the patient must use both eyes. The patient does not know which eye is open through the phoroptor.

The equipment was set up for this test, and the 20/40 line was projected on the screen. She quickly read across the entire line without a mistake. We changed to the 20/30 line and asked her to read it. She started to read, but stopped and held up her hand in front of each eye. Realizing that she had just been tricked into reading with her right eye, she began to scream that we had tricked her, that we were supposed to be on her side if we were good doctors. We were to help her prove that she could not see with her right eye. She pushed the phoropter aside and ran from the clinic screaming that she would never come back.

She kept her promise and never returned. Instead, she went to another ophthalmologist, who recorded her vision as 20/400 in her right eye and 20/20 in her left eye. He did not record anything in the examination record to explain the poor vision in her right eye. I explained the importance of this to her lawyer when he deposed me, but he feigned lack of comprehension of this detail and would not accept the fact that she was malingering.

She did sue the hospital for her alleged blindness. Although we had several witnesses to her malingering, disproving her claim of blindness, the hospital settled the case. They settled because they had reused the catheter they used in her procedure. The febrile response from reused catheters had just been reported, and most hospitals still reused catheters at that time. The university did not want it known that they had reused catheters, so they paid her to keep quiet.

I was disappointed that this lady used malingering of vision loss to gain a settlement with the hospital. We knew that she was lying, which should have trumped her possibly legitimate claim from the reuse of the catheter, which had been standard practice until very recently. I never learned how much the hospital paid for this malingering.

68

<o>

The Danger of DMSO

ONE OF THE BENEFITS OF being affiliated with a major medical center is the number and variety of patients who are referred for subspecialty care. One of these patients was a hospital administrator from a nearby city who came to me because he was developing cataracts.

I examined Harry and found that he had very early cataracts. He had both nuclear sclerotic cataracts, which had made him nearsighted, and posterior subcapsular cataracts, which were small and did not yet interfere with his vision. He also had mild dry eyes, which went along with his arthritis and allergies to pampas grass, a South American grass often used for ornament.

I changed his glasses to compensate for his cataract changes and tried to give him a prescription for anti-allergy eyedrops. Harry was very talkative and a real "Texas Type" who was proud of his ability to get around regulations. He told me that he did not need a prescription, that all he needed was the name of the drug, the dosage, and the number of times per day he should take it. He would get the medication free from the hospital pharmacist. I gave him the prescription and told him to give it to the pharmacist to make sure that he got the right medication and dose. It made no difference to me whether he paid for it or got it free.

He continued to come to see me every few months, especially during the late summer and fall, when the pampas grass was blooming all along the Texas highways, courtesy of Lady Byrd Johnson's wildflower campaign. She did beautify the highways of Texas with blue bonnets, Indian paintbrushes, and other wild flowers, including pampas grass.

About a year after I first saw him, Harry complained that his vision had started to fail, especially when he read anything. I looked at his eye and saw that his posterior subcapsular cataracts had progressed to the extent that they covered his pupil when he looked up close. (The pupil constricts on near gaze.) The progression was greater than I expected in his right eye, where his vision was bad at both distance and near. His left eye could still see well enough to drive a car when his pupil dilated at distance, but dropped to 20/70 at near.

I told Harry that it was time to consider cataract surgery on his right eye. During the explanation of surgery and complications, I told him that I was surprised that he had progressed so rapidly. He wanted to know if it was something he had done that caused it to progress. I told him that we really did not understand why cataracts developed, but that we knew that some chemicals could cause cataracts. To illustrate, I explained that, while I was at the U.S. Food and Drug Administration, in the '60s, DMSO, dimethyl sulfoxide, was banned from drug preparations in the United States because it caused posterior subcapsular cataracts. You could still get DMSO to treat your horse's arthritis and pulled muscles, but it was banned for human use because of the cataracts it caused. DMSO is an anti-inflammatory that can penetrate the skin very easily. It goes directly to the muscles, where it is adsorbed quickly into the blood stream.

Harry told me that he went to Mexico once or twice each year, and while he was there he always bought a bottle of DMSO to rub on his shoulders and knees whenever his arthritis flared up. He said he had been using it almost daily for the past several months. I was not surprised that he could buy DMSO in Mexico, because I saw it for sale on the Indian reservations in Arizona, when I visited my parents there.

He agreed to stop taking the DMSO immediately, because I felt that it would only make his cataracts worse. I did not know if the cataract effect was reversible, but I told him we should wait a few months to see if the cataracts would shrink once the DMSO was stopped.

Harry returned to me about three months later. I was amazed to learn that he could read much better. The cataract in his right eye had shrunk to the point that he could see around it when his pupil was small. The cataract in the left eye had almost disappeared. He was very happy with his vision, but told me that his arthritis was really bothering him. Aspirin was not enough to control his pain, so he was on Darvon compound, and Darvon compound with codeine when he could get it. I told him that he should stop treating himself since he was not a doctor, and that he ought to go see his internist or a rheumatologist to get something specific for his arthritis.

I was surprised that the cataracts shrank so dramatically and did not return immediately. For the several years I followed him, the cataracts did not return, and he swore to me that he did not use a drop of DMSO after I told him that it could cause cataracts. I left Texas before Harry needed cataract surgery, so I do not know the ultimate outcome of his cataracts.

There is a saying in medicine that a doctor who treats himself has a fool for a patient. I think it is even worse when a nonphysician treats himself. There are laws to prevent that, but some people find ways around those laws. Harry's use of DMSO would not have been allowed by a physician, but the availability of the drug made it easy for him to self-medicate without knowing anything about the medicine, except that it helped his arthritis. He was smart enough to have figured out that there was a reason why he could not buy DMSO in Texas.

69

◄○►

A Grateful Patient Turned Benefactor

I WAS IN MY FACULTY OFFICE one day when I received a call from Dr. Ferguson. He told me he had a patient in his office that he wanted me to see right away. He was an important businessman and a member of the Presidents Advisory Council for the medical branch. He warned me that I should be careful about what I said in front of the patient because he might sue. I had Ed send him right over to my clinical office.

Mr. C. was recovering from his second cataract surgery done in Houston about six weeks before. The other cataract had been removed previously without problems. When he returned to the surgeon's office about one week after this surgery, he was experiencing a lot of pain and his vision was becoming more blurred. He was told that the eye was inflamed and was given an injection next to the eye. By the time he returned home that night, the eye was feeling much better and his vision was clearing. Over the next week the pain and blurring returned, and he received another injection next to the eye. This continued for five weeks. By the time he returned to his home after the shot on the sixth week, he experienced more pain and further decrease in his vision. At that point he called Dr. Blocker, the president of the medical branch, for advice. Dr. Blocker sent him to Dr. Ferguson, who lateraled him to me.

Mr. C. had vision of less than 20/200 in the recently operated eye. Examination of the eye showed white blood cells floating in the anterior chamber of the eye and a very hazy vitreous body filling the back of the eye. The time sequence for the inflammation was not right for an acute bacterial infection, but the vitreous was far too cloudy for simple postoperative inflammation. I thought that it could be a fungal infection or a low-grade infection from a "non pathogen" such as a micrococcus, which was smoldering in the eye.

I decided that the best course would be to remove the cloudy vitreous and start him on high-dose antibiotics. Antibiotics alone do not work well since there is no blood supply to the vitreous body to bring the antibiotics to the bacteria. We had recently obtained a vitreous suction cutter, and I had done several vitrectomies with it. Vitrectomies were done under general anesthesia and, therefore, required that the patient be hospitalized after surgery.

I called the admissions office to have him admitted. The clerk for admissions told me that there were no beds available and that there probably would not be for several days. I told the admissions clerk that the patient was a VIP and served on the Presidents Advisory Council. She said that there still were no beds. I called Dr. Ferguson for advice, and he told me to call Dr. Blocker, who could use his clout to get a bed. When I talked to Dr. Blocker, he told me that he did not think he would have any more luck getting a bed than I had experienced. I convinced him to call anyway. About three minutes later he called back to ask if a private room in the private pavilion would be all right. Mr. C. had a hospital bed. We started intravenous antibiotics and scheduled surgery for the next morning.

At surgery, I began removing the cloudy vitreous by nibbling it from the eye. The removal was moving right along, when a big white blob rose out of the cloud. The vitrector nibbled the blob and quickly removed it from the eye. I had the scrub nurse save all of the material that we had removed from the eye. We put some on culture plates and took the rest to the pathology laboratory to spin down, to make a pathology specimen. Some of the specimen was processed for light microscopy, and the rest was retained for possible electron microscopy.

The day after surgery Mr. C. was without pain for the first time in several weeks. I placed a plus-ten lens and a pin hole in front of his eye as a substitute for cataract glasses, and he could read 20/25 with the operated eye.

He was very happy and wanted to know more about the fancy machine I had used to make this happen. I called the operating room and learned that the machine had been cleaned but not sterilized. The operating room was in the next building to our clinic area, so I ran over to the operating room and picked up the vitrector.

When I showed it to Mr. C., he wanted to know how many we had and how much it cost. I explained to him that we had only one instrument because it cost $14,000. He asked why we did not have a backup unit in case something happened to the one we had. I explained that money was scarce in the department and that we would probably buy several other needed pieces of equipment before we got the second vitrector. He asked what we did if the instrument malfunctioned. I told him that a malfunction had not happened, but that the company in Chicago that made the instrument promised a twenty-four-hour turnaround on all repairs. He told me he did not think that was good enough if he needed another surgery and we had a problem.

Since he may have had an infection, I saw him at least twice a day. I saw him in the clinic in the morning and stopped by his room in the afternoon to see if everything was all right.

Mr. C., (his wife referred to him as "Big Daddy"), told me he could see his forty-foot fishing yacht from the window of his room. The marina was only about two blocks from the hospital. He asked me for a hospital pass so he could sit on the back deck of his boat to have a martini in the evening. I told him that I would have to go with him to supervise his move and make sure the drinks were not too strong. Somehow, it never happened. I did get to know his wife, who was a friend of one of my medical school classmates—small world.

The pathology report came back with a diagnosis of amorphous debris and inflammation, but no bacteria. The cultures did not grow anything either. The pathology department declined to do electron microscopy, saying that they probably would not know what they were looking for in the vitreous.

Dr. Jim Ray, a PhD physiologist, was working in the ophthalmology department trying to determine the cause of cataracts. He routinely did electron microscopy on the frog lenses that he used for electrophysiology studies. He agreed to fix and section the remaining material and look at it with his electron microscope.

The electron microscopy photographs were very interesting. They were filled with large, white blood cells, some containing chunks of black parallel lines. Some of the lines were straight and some were curved. There were large pieces of this material outside of the white blood cells. We determined, by the similarity to the frog lenses that Jim looked at with the electron microscope, that these were lens fragments from a piece of crystalline lens that had been dropped into the back of the eye during phacoemulsification of the cataract. The eye reacted to this "foreign" material with an inflammatory response. The steroid injections that he had received had been able to suppress small amounts of inflammation, but were not sufficient when the reaction increased with time.

During the early months of using phacoemulsification to remove cataracts, many pieces of cataract were dropped into the back of the eye when the capsule bag inadvertently ruptured. When this happened, the patient was usually referred to a retina specialist to perform a vitrectomy to remove the pieces. In this case, the fragment had been left in the eye and produced a significant inflammatory response.

When Mr. C. returned to see me one week after his hospital discharge, he reached into his pocket as he walked into the room. He took out an envelope and handed it me and said, "Half of this is from me, half of it is from Uncle Sam. Use it to get another one of those machines." I opened the envelope to find a check for $15,000.00. He said if I had money left over I should buy some spare parts.

Mr. C. happened to own the local newspaper, the *Galveston Daily News*. He alerted the editor that he had donated the money for the new vitrector. The editor wanted coverage for this donation to honor his boss. A reporter came to my office to interview me about the use of this instrument and then sent a photographer to take a picture of the instrument when it arrived. This picture and the article that she wrote appeared on the front page of the Sunday edition a week later.

Several days after the article appeared, I received a call from Dr. Blocker. He told me he was calling in his official capacity of ethics director for the Galveston County Medical Society. He had received a complaint that I had violated the ethical standards for advertising because of this article. He told me he was forwarding a copy of the standards for me to read and to reply to the charge that we had violated the standards.

The standards, which had been drawn up to prohibit the medical branch from overly publicizing their procedures, stated that no one could claim to have invented something that they had not invented and could not claim that they were the only one in the area to have a procedure or piece of equipment unless they were actually the only one. Fortunately, the article in the paper clearly credited Dr. Nicolas Douvas with the invention of the vitrector. It also mentioned that there was a vitrector in use in Houston. We were the only people in Galveston County who had a vitrector, but that was not claimed in the article. I wrote this up for Dr. Blocker and sent it to him. He called me a few days later to say that the complaint had been dropped.

I continued to follow Mr. C. to fit him with contact lenses to correct his vision. This was before intraocular lenses were popular, so contact lenses were the best way to correct vision after cataract extraction. After I fit the contacts, he complained of being unable to read. I explained that the contacts did not focus in and out, so he would need to wear reading glasses to see anything close. I told him that he could use +2.50 reading glasses from the drug store at a cost of ten dollars for each pair (it was in the early '70s), or he could buy a custom-made pair for over one hundred dollars. He tried the drug store glasses and liked them so much that he got a pair for his boat, a pair for his plane, one for each car, his reading table, the bedroom, and the kitchen. He said he was still saving money from what it would cost to carry around one custom pair of glasses.

He went away to Florida for the winter, so I did not see him for a while. When he returned in the spring, he had an intraocular lens implant in each eye. They had been put in by a well-known ophthalmologist in Florida. He had also had two knees replaced while he was in Florida. He joked with me about being the "bionic man." Then he asked me if I had any research proposals that needed to be funded. He was creating a medical research foundation as a tax-lowering device and was looking for research to fund.

The funding had just ended on my National Institutes of Health (NIH) grant to develop a corneal prosthesis, an artificial cornea. I told him that I had been awarded fifty thousand dollars per year for four years for this purpose, but that the four years had just ended. He said that my project would be perfect, because he wanted to give about fifty thousand dollars a year to four or five researchers at the medical branch. He told me to write up the project in words he could understand in two, but not more than three, pages and send it to the director of his research foundation. This was much easier than the eighty-page grant request to the NIH/National Eye Institute.

He funded my prosthesis research for several years until I left Galveston. The dean did not like the foundation grants as well as the NIH funding because it did not pay "indirect costs" to the university. Government grants often pay more money to the university than they pay for the actual research. This is supposed to be overhead money for the university, to pay for such things as heat, lights, A/C, administrative costs, etc., but sometimes includes deans' trips to Japan, health club memberships for faculty, lavish parties, and other such questionable expenses. The foundation did not pay any indirect costs.

The other "perk" that I received from caring for Mr. C. was an invitation to his eightieth birthday party. This was a party for about three hundred of his closest friends at the Remington Hotel in Houston. It started with cocktails and hot hors d'oeuvres in a small ballroom. This was followed by a five-course, sit-down dinner, with music performed by a live orchestra in the large ballroom. The evening continued with dancing, which lasted until after we left to return to Galveston. My wife and I were seated with Dr. Levin, the current president of the medical branch, and his wife, and Dr. and Mrs. Sternberg. Dr. Sternberg was doing research on childhood deafness for the foundation, which was an important interest of Mr. C's. Dr. Levin was puzzled about our being at the party, since we were the only other faculty members there. He did not understand our connections to Mr. C.

When I left the medical branch I was not on pleasant terms with the dean. He sent me a memo telling me that all of my research materials were to remain at the university because the university had purchased them. This would severely compromise my ability to continue my research at my new location, which I think was his intention. I called the medical director for Mr. C's foundation and discussed this with him. He believed in the research and thought that I should continue the research in my new location. He rationalized that the foundation had funded the research and purchased the equipment and materials for my use and therefore the foundation owned them and could determine their disposition. He insisted that I take the contact lens lathe and polisher, used to make the prosthesis, and all of my specimens with me. About ten minutes later, the dean called to say that he had reconsidered his memo and decided that I should take whatever I needed from the project.

Three years ago I received a Christmas card from Mr. C., telling me that he was still doing just fine and wished me well. He was well over ninety years old at that time.

As I cared for Mr. C., I learned that he started work as a copy boy for a small-town newspaper after he dropped out of school at the end of eighth grade. He rose through the ranks to become editor and owner of that newspaper, and he went on to own many newspapers. He told me on one visit that he was tired of his two sons fighting over money, so he gave them each several newspapers to run. He kept some for himself, and turned over several to his wife. I asked him about what he had done for his daughter. He told me he had put her in charge of his research foundation.

When Mr. C. was referred to me, I was cautioned that he was very rich and could be very demanding and might sue me if everything did not go well. I learned that this stereotype did not apply to Mr. C. He was kind and considerate and never demanded or threatened. He was actually a very giving and generous person who funded causes that were personal to him. He was very thankful for the care he received and showed his appreciation through the funding of my research. For a high-school drop out, he knew how to be wealthy in the best way.

Mr. C. proved to me what my father had told me many times. I developed a good rapport with Mr. C. as a patient, and he rewarded me with generous support and friendship. It probably did not hurt matters that he obtained an excellent result.

70

<o>

A Leading Lady of Galveston

ONE OF MY PATIENTS IN Galveston was a well-known person in both Galveston and Washington, DC. She was sent to me by Dr. Ferguson because she needed a contact lens. She had undergone cataract surgery in both eyes several years before. She had also suffered a central retinal vein closure in one eye and had very poor vision in that eye. Her good eye saw 20/20 with glasses or a contact lens. She had been using her bifocal cataract glasses, but she did not want to be seen in public with such thick, ugly glasses. She could read the paper over breakfast and would sometimes read at home in the evening with her cataract glasses. She was a socialite who gave and attended many parties, and she would not wear her glasses to a party.

I fit her with a contact lens for her good eye and taught her husband how to put it in the eye and how to remove it. I sent her back to Ed Ferguson to follow. I learned that her husband had contacted Ed, saying that he could get the lens into her eye very easily, but he had difficulty removing it in the evening. She could not manage the lens because she had only one eye, and both the patient and her husband had arthritis. The old thick, soft contact lenses were much harder to remove than to put into the eye. The thin, weekly-wear lenses were not available at that time, so soft lenses had to come out at night. Ed told me that he had solved that problem when he learned that one of the residents lived a few blocks from her and loved to jog in the evenings. He had the resident jog past at about 9:30 to 10:00 PM and stop in to take out her lens for her. The resident became very good friends with the patient and her husband.

I was invited to my first party at the Galveston Artillery Club when the patient gave a big dinner party for the society people of Galveston. She threw such big parties that she would split them to two nights. Ed was invited to one night, and I was invited to the other night. I figured out that she wanted an ophthalmologist at the party in case she had a problem with her contact lens. It was for this reason my wife and I were on the invitation list for her parties—a nice perk for fitting a contact lens. Later, I was the only lowly assistant professor at the big party given for her at the university library after she gave the university a big donation.

When I fit her contact lens, I talked to her about why she wanted the lens rather than her glasses. She told me that she wanted to see the faces of the people with whom she talked, especially at parties. She did not care very much what was going on across the room, but she wanted to see people's expressions so that she could tell if they were serious or being facetious. I ordered her lenses with one extra diopter of power so that she would be in focus at about three feet in front of her face.

This lady lived half of the year in Galveston and the other half in Washington, DC. Shortly after she left Galveston, the optical shop would get a call from her to order a new contact lens, with my prescription. We learned that whenever she would move back to Washington, she would go to see all of her doctors there for checkups. Her ophthalmologist there would take her contact lens and throw it in the waste basket, telling her that it was made wrong and that he would order her a new one that was correct. She told me later that she would never argue with him, that he was too intimidating. When she got the lens from him, she could see well at distance, but could not see the faces in front of her.

Her ophthalmologist in Washington, who shall remain nameless, had fit my wife with contact lenses when we lived there, so I knew who he was. I do not think he knew me very well, but I recognized him one winter, sitting with his wife on the outside terrace of the Red Lion Restaurant in Vail, Colorado. I introduced myself to him, and he said that he remembered my wife from George Washington

Medical School. I mentioned that we had a mutual patient, and I named her. As we talked about her, I wondered if he thought that I was the klutz who could not fit contacts, since he always tried to change them. I felt compelled to clear my name, so I suggested to him not to change the lenses, because she really liked having her contacts fit for near, rather than distance. I related to him how she always called Galveston to replace the contacts he threw away. He laughed, but I do not think he was amused.

She was a very proper lady who would probably have been embarrassed if she had known that I told her Washington ophthalmologist that she did not keep his lenses, but had them replaced with lenses from Galveston. She even announced at one of her parties that both surgeons who had done facelifts on her were present at the party. She was a typical down-to-earth, gracious, "Texas Lady."

When Ed sent this lady to me, he warned me that she was an important person, one of the wealthiest people in Galveston, and that I should treat her very carefully. I found that she was a very gracious lady who treated everyone with great respect and never condescended to me or my residents. I had nothing to fear from her because of her position or wealth. I saw how someone in her position could be unassuming and charming and interact without flaunting her wealth. She would be a good role model for other wealthy people.

71

<o>

The Man Who Survived Guadalcanal

ONE OF THE INTERESTING THINGS about practicing at a big medical center is the number of interesting cases you get to treat and the variety of fascinating people you meet. I was the eye infectious disease specialist in Galveston, so the residents asked me to see a patient who had been injured while he was clearing brush from a field in East Texas.

Bubba had been dragging a large iron ball at the end of a heavy chain around in circles with his tractor. The chain would snag the trunks of small trees and bushes and pull them out of the ground. The chain caught a small tree trunk and pulled tight before the tree trunk broke off. The tree snapped off, throwing the branch at a high speed, which had caught Bubba in the left eye. He sat around at home for three days waiting for the pain to subside, but it became worse. When it finally got too painful, he went to see his general doctor, who sent him on to us.

Bubba was a heavyset, red-faced, good-old-boy from East Texas. He loved to talk and soon told us how his injury had occurred. As soon as he had told us about his injury, he began telling us how he survived the invasion of Guadalcanal, including all of the bloody and gory details. Every time we went to his room, he was telling someone about his adventures on Guadalcanal. Sometimes we could get him to tell us how he won the plowing contests in East Texas. He could plow a mile-long furrow so that it looked perfectly straight and then double back and plow another one next to it just as straight.

Unfortunately, when we finally saw him, his eye was in a bad condition. It had a large laceration of the cornea and sclera. The lens was not in the right position, and there was hemorrhage in the front of the eye. There were also several large bubbles inside of the eye. He was developing a line of white blood cells along the bottom of the anterior chamber. All of these are bad signs.

The white blood cells and the bubbles probably meant infection. We cultured the eye, but because he could no longer see light with that eye, we knew that we could not save the eye. It was important to get rid of the infection before it could spread to the brain. We took him to the operating room and removed the eye.

After the surgery, we learned from the preoperative cultures that the bubbles in the eye were from Clostridium botulinum. If we had left the eye in place, he could have died from Clostridia in his bloodstream, or paralysis from the botulinum toxins.

He did well after surgery and continued to tell everyone he came in contact with all of his stories about Guadalcanal. For five days, to keep the swelling down, we kept a pressure dressing on the side where we had removed his eye. He did not develop any further infection from the injury. After the dressing was removed, we sent him home and told him to come back to see us in about six weeks. We would order the prosthesis then.

When he returned in six weeks, his wife was telling everyone in the waiting room what a wonderful man her husband was. When we called him back to the exam room, she had to tell us immediately why he was such a wonderful man. They had purchased an accidental death and accident insurance plan at Sears about a month before he had his accident. When they returned home from the hospital after his eye was removed, they checked the policy and learned that the loss of one eye was worth ten thousand dollars, so they filled out the forms and sent them into Sears. A man from Sears called them to remind them that they had paid the extra premium for triple indemnity, so the loss of one eye was actually worth thirty thousand dollars.

When they received the check for the insurance, she and her husband had a long discussion about what to buy with this windfall.

His wife was sure that he was the nicest man in the world because he decided to buy her a double-wide to live in. They had lived in mobile homes all of their married lives, but she had never had a double-wide. They almost seemed glad that he had lost his eye. I think he was as proud of buying the mobile home for his wife as he was of surviving Guadalcanal, even though he had to lose an eye to do it.

This patient was not well educated and lived off of the land, but he was smarter than the English he spoke would indicate. He was kind and sincere and very generous in deciding to spend his insurance money on a better home for himself and his wife. He was smart enough to know that when momma is happy, it is better for everyone.

72

<o>

A Nervous Resident

I HAD MANY RESIDENTS IN THE two programs in which I taught. One of the most dynamic residents was a little Cuban man, Juan, who had unbounded enthusiasm. Every cataract was the worst cataract he had ever seen, each edematous cornea was the thickest it could possibly be, and so on.

The day finally came when he was scheduled to do his first cataract surgery as first surgeon. I usually helped the residents when they did their first cataracts, so I scrubbed with Juan. As we were standing at the scrub sink at 7:30 AM, Juan turned to me and said, "Dr. Barber, I am as nervous as I was on my wedding night." He explained that he had never been alone with his bride before the wedding, because she had always been accompanied by her chaperone, in the Cuban fashion.

I assured him that every cataract surgeon did a first cataract surgery before she or he could do a second, and that he would do just fine. I also reminded him that he had assisted on many cataracts. I was there to be sure that everything was done properly, and I would lead him through the case. I assured him that the result would be good.

We entered the operating room where our scrub nurse, Blanca, had the patient properly positioned and prepped for surgery on his left eye. We put on our gowns and gloves and proceeded with the surgery. At that time, the surgeons used a jeweler's loupe for magnification during their first several cataract surgeries. After several cases they would graduate to using the surgical microscope, which added accuracy and complexity to the surgery.

He had turned down the conjunctival flap and was starting to make a groove along the edge of the cornea to start the incision. Juan, staring through his loupe, was holding the round-handled scalpel blade, making the round groove, when he stopped at the midpoint of the incision. I prompted him to continue to finish the groove. He did not move. When I told him again to finish the groove, I noticed that his eyes were rolling up behind his eyelids and realized that he had passed out while sitting on the operating stool. He then slowly leaned to his right, away from me, toward the scrub nurse. I told Blanca to catch him so that he would not hit the terrazzo floor with his head. She caught him as he started to fall off of the operating stool and eased him to the floor. She realized that she had contaminated her sterility in the process, so she checked his neck for a pulse. He had a thready pulse that was regular, so he had probably not had a heart attack; he had most likely passed out from the adrenalin rush caused by his nervousness.

The circulating nurse hit the panic button, which set off the alarm bells, and soon the room was full of anesthesiologists. They carried him to the anesthesia call room across the hall and put him on a bed. He soon woke up and talked with the resident from the medicine service who had been called to take care of him. The medicine resident learned that Juan had not eaten breakfast that morning and had very low blood sugar when he passed out.

Blanca changed her gown and gloves, I moved over to the surgeon's chair, and together we finished the cataract surgery. The patient did well throughout the procedure and had an excellent visual result.

Early that afternoon, a very despondent Juan came into my office and sat down. He was concerned that he would never be able to be an ophthalmologist because he had passed out during cataract surgery. For years he had wanted to be an ophthalmologist, but now his career was ruined. I assured him that we would have another cataract scheduled for him within the week and that he would do just fine. This time he would eat breakfast, which would keep him from passing out. I told him about a resident who had passed out several years before on his first cataract. That doctor was now a very successful cataract surgeon. He told me that he was so upset that he had not eaten anything since the surgery, and I told him to go to the cafeteria to get something to eat.

For some reason, I was still in my academic office at seven o'clock that evening when Juan walked into the office again and sat down. I asked him why he was still at the hospital instead of going home. He said that he had been told about the emergency bells being rung when he passed out. He reminded me that his wife was a resident in anesthesiology, so she would certainly know that he had passed out in the operating room. He said that he could not face her because she knew that he had passed out. He went on to explain that Cuban men had to be macho to their wives, and passing out in surgery was not very macho. I told him to emphasize the hypoglycemia part of the incident as the cause of his problem to his physician wife and to also emphasize his need to eat breakfast before he did his next surgery. She should be sure that he had a good breakfast. He never told me what he said when he got home.

Four days later, we scrubbed together on another cataract. Juan had eaten breakfast, and everything went smoothly. He told me after the surgery that he had not even felt light-headed. As far as I know, he has never fainted during surgery since then. He went on to become a very successful cataract surgeon, with etched glass partitions and leather doorknob covers in his office, and a Lincoln Continental in his garage. He told me that in the Cuban community you had to look prosperous or the Cubans would not come to you.

Juan taught me a lot about the Cuban personality. He was always excited about something, and his enthusiasm rubbed off on the people around him. His passing out in the operating room was a severe blow to his ego. I had to work with him to overcome his sense of failure and coach him about effective ways to work this out with his wife, who appeared to me to be far more forgiving than Juan anticipated.

I thought that it was very important for Juan to do another cataract under good conditions as soon as we could schedule it so that he did not ruminate over his fainting and build it into a psychological barrier. As they say, after the horse throws you, you have to get right back on before you become afraid of horses. Juan got back on his horse and has no fear of cataract surgery now.

73

A Shy Resident

DURING MY THIRTY YEARS OF teaching in residency programs, I participated in training over ninety physicians to become ophthalmologists. This was extremely satisfying and brought me in contact with many different personalities. One of the people I remember the most was a young man who was extremely bashful. Travis was married and already had one child, so he was not naive, just very shy.

One day the clinic received a consult request from psychiatry asking us to see a young girl, about fifteen, who was admitted for unusual behavior. She was a Girl Scout who had excellent grades and normal behavior. Recently she had become very promiscuous. They suspected Wilson's disease, a disturbance in copper metabolism that affects the liver and the brain and leaves a copper deposit ring in the cornea.

This shy resident escorted her back to his examination room and asked her to sit in the exam chair. As he turned to close the door, he heard a long zipping noise. When he turned around toward the patient he saw her standing in front of the chair, stark naked. She had unzipped her hospital jumpsuit and let it drop to her ankles.

I was walking down the corridor in the clinic as he came running out of the exam room, calling for Mrs. Pettaway, the practical nurse in the clinic. She went into the room and soon had the patient presentable and sitting in the chair. The patient did have the diagnostic brown copper ring in her cornea and was soon under treatment for Wilson's disease to restore her to her "normal self."

The other residents knew that this resident was very shy and lacked the usual amount of self-confidence of a second-year resident. The chief resident was in charge of assigning surgery to the various residents. He knew that this resident had a lot of self-doubt concerning his capabilities. The chief assigned an Alabama-Coushatta Indian to him for his first cataract extraction, where this resident was primary surgeon. He appealed to the chief resident for a different patient, but the chief was unrelenting.

Dr. Ferguson was instrumental in securing the contract for eye care for all Alabama-Coushatta Indians in Texas that was awarded to the University of Texas Eye Clinic. He wanted to keep the contract because it gave a lot of experience to the residents. To assure that the residents took special care of the Indians, he started a rumor that these Indians usually experienced vitreous loss during cataract surgery. This is a complication that is to be avoided if at all possible. The residents took every precaution possible against vitreous loss and usually had excellent results with the surgery.

Travis knew the standard lore that Alabama-Coushatta Indians were short, with bull necks, and had high blood pressure and diabetes. These are all warning signs of impending vitreous loss from cataract surgery. He was as nervous as a cat in a room full of rocking chairs when he scrubbed for his first cataract operation.

He had reviewed his lecture notes and had also read widely on preventing vitreous loss during cataract surgery. I was his surgical assistant and tried to reassure him that he could do the surgery. He did a marvelous job for his first cataract surgery, and he got through the surgery without breaking the vitreous face or losing a drop of vitreous. The patient had a perfect visual result. Travis became an excellent cataract surgeon and went into practice with his father-in-law, where he practiced for many years. He later had his own successful practice in the hill country of Texas, and has just retired to his ranch.

Travis started his residency as a very shy and retiring but smart young man. He remained shy and insecure until he was tested by difficult cases. Success with the difficult cases led to tremendous growth in self-confidence. By the end of the residency he was teaching the younger residents and taking on the most difficult cases. In this case, the trial by fire was excellent training.

Part IV
Prison Care
1971–2002

ONE OF MY DUTIES, IN both Texas and Pennsylvania, was taking care of the inmates at the state penitentiary. During the time I was in Texas, care for prisoners at the University of Texas evolved from a very loose surveillance system for hospitalized prisoners to a state-of-the-art maximum security prison hospital. Our clinic would see several prisoners from the Walls unit of the penitentiary in Huntsville, Texas, on any given day.

The people of Galveston were probably more upset by the presence of the prisoners than by anything else the medical branch did. Prisoners had simply walked away from the hospital in the early days. They were on the wards with only a red warning on their charts, indicating that they were not to leave the hospital floor without a guard escort. When they were placed in their own locked ward, one went through the ceiling of his hospital room and came down in an open hallway and walked out.

These escapes led to the building of an eight-floor maximum security prison hospital, considered to be state-of-the-art for security. No two consecutive steel gates, of which there were many, could be open at the same time. Guards rode on all of the elevators. Nurses used a set of corridors that were separate from the ones used by the prisoners. The prisoners had two-bed rooms with color TV and could have double portions of all food they were served. The prison patients joked about going to Acapulco when they went to the hospital. The prison hospital was connected to the main hospital by a windowless bridge, with many iron gates, that reminded me of the introduction of the TV show *Get Smart*.

My residents in Texas went to the Walls unit of the Texas State Penitentiary during their last year of residency. They drove to Huntsville on Tuesday morning, had lunch at the prison, saw patients all afternoon in the prison clinic, and stayed overnight in a motel and studied. On Wednesday morning they had breakfast at the prison, saw patients all morning, ate lunch at the prison, and then drove back to Galveston. Although I never ate at the prison, the residents told me that the food was excellent. To get to the prison clinic, they had to walk across the prison yard through the crowd of prisoners, but they never felt threatened. Patients were brought to Galveston if they needed surgery or faculty-level consultation.

When I arrived in Pittsburgh, the contract for all of the prison medical care was controlled by the St. Francis medical system. The prisoners with eye problems were being taken care of by a group of ophthalmologists who worked at one of the St. Francis medical system hospitals. The group decided to leave the system very suddenly and could no longer care for these patients. The man who had been in charge of the Texas Maximum Security Hospital had just moved to Pittsburgh to supervise the health care for the Pittsburgh penitentiary. We knew each other and had worked well together, so he asked me to take over the prison eye care.

74

Someone Must Care for the Prisoners

PRISONERS HAVE THE SAME EYE diseases as people who are not in jail, but they come with their own set of unique problems. Many prisoners have psychopathic personalities that complicate both their diseases and their care.

We had one patient who was being seen for a retinal detachment. When the retinal surgeon was examining him to map the detachment prior to a surgical repair, the prisoner was bothered by the bright light of the indirect ophthalmoscope and told the doctor to stop using it. The retinal surgeon explained that he had to map the retina so that he could repair it and restore his vision. The patient then told the doctor that if he shined the light into his eye one more time, he would take out a contract on the doctor's life. When the guards in the room heard the threat, they immediately took the prisoner back to the penitentiary, and we never saw him again. We do not know whether he had a miraculous spontaneous reattachment of his retina, or whether he went blind in that eye, as most people in his situation would without surgery. We had no influence with the warden to have him returned so that we could fix his retina.

One of the patients in Texas was a tall, heavyset man who was always very polite to the residents and staff. We were surprised to learn that he was the infamous "chain saw massacre" perpetrator. He may have been on massive amounts of medications, or maybe, we just did not make him upset.

There was another prisoner who was a pedophile, but we did not know why he was in prison when we did a corneal transplant on one eye. He was on the male ward in the days when prisoners were mixed with the other patients. About three days post surgery, the nurses discovered him molesting a young man with Down syndrome. The security guards from the hospital put him in bed, face down, and handcuffed him to the bed, spread eagle, by both ankles and both wrists until the guards from the prison could come to take him back to the penitentiary. This was not the position I prefer for my post corneal transplant patients, but I was not there at the time. It was Thanksgiving Day, so the prison had to call in two off-duty guards to drive from Huntsville to Galveston, about a hundred miles, and back to retrieve him on their holiday day off. We learned later that he was in solitary confinement for about two months after that. I did not see him for any postoperative care for about six months, and he eventually rejected his corneal transplant.

I had a prison patient who had been a prizefighter and had developed a cataract in the left eye, the one that caught all of the jabs during fights. He wanted the cataract out because he could not see to the left side. He considered that dangerous in his prison environment. He was very polite and appeared well educated. I never asked why he was in prison. Knowing why just gets in the way of dispassionate care.

I took out his cataract and put in an implant lens. Everything went as planned, and the patient got a very good result. When I saw him for his last visit after surgery, he thanked me for taking care of him and told me that he appreciated the great result he had obtained. He told me that even though he was in prison, he was still "very well connected." Then he said "If you ever need anything done, you know what I mean, just let me know. I can get it done." I wished that I had not heard what he said and hoped that the guards had not heard it either. I could not envision why I would need to know what he could do.

I did remember what he said about six months later when I was sued by another prisoner. That suit was a nuisance suit based on the Bill of Rights and deprivation of civil rights. I did not like being sued by prisoners after I had cared for them and helped them, when many other doctors would not care for them. I was slightly tempted to have my friendly prisoner lean on this one, but I decided to let the lawyers handle it instead. The lawyers got it thrown out, but it took three years until that prisoner had exhausted all of his rights of appeal.

I have been involved in four different lawsuits by prisoners. All were found to be baseless and were thrown out of court. The prisoners have a law library at their disposal and lots of free time to play lawyer. Usually the suits are linked legal clichés that are ludicrous to read. I am told that it costs the malpractice insurance company an average of twenty thousand dollars to go through the process of getting the lawsuit thrown out of court by both the regional and appeals courts. These suits count against a doctor's insurance record, even when they are thrown out as meritless.

When I left the St. Francis Hospital System (actually, the hospital went broke and went out of business), I had to obtain my own individual medical malpractice insurance. Because I had been sued so many times, I had to agree to not teach in a residency or medical school and promise not to see any prisoners, so that I could obtain medical liability insurance. It is illegal to practice without liability insurance.

An interesting aspect of caring for prisoners was the witness protection program. We operated on several adults with crossed eyes who had been admitted to the program. To change their appearance, we straightened their crossed eyes.

These cases were done after the end of the operating room schedule so the operating room would be almost empty and easier to control. We had to sign in and sign out every time we saw one of these people, and we rarely saw them after they left the hospital. We used an operating room that had only one door and was located at the back end of the surgical suite. This was to limit the possibility of someone assassinating our patient in the operating room. Sometimes we joked about who got to go through the operating room door first when the people our patient was being protected from rolled a bomb into the room. Nothing ever happened during these cases.

We also straightened the eyes of many of the prisoners who had crossed or wall eyes. They claimed that they had to turn to crime to support themselves since they couldn't hold jobs because of their eyes looking strange. We did not do this for the prostitutes because of the trouble the plastic surgeons experienced. The plastic surgeons got in trouble for doing face lifts and breast implants on the imprisoned prostitutes. The plastic surgery residents wanted the experience, but the press thought it was a free benefit and job enhancement paid for by the State of Texas. We were told that the legislature actually enacted laws prohibiting any appearance enhancing surgery on incarcerated prostitutes.

My friends sometimes asked me why I took care of dangerous patients who had such a propensity to sue me. Physicians are expected to give care to whoever needs it; in return, they are supposed to be treated decently by the patient receiving the care. Occasionally, I hear of a doctor taken hostage in a jail break, but that is very rare. We were told that the Texas Prison System had a no-hostage rule, which meant that they would not bargain for any hostage. If we got in that situation, we were on our own.

I was never threatened by any prisoner I treated. They understood that any misbehavior could jeopardize their medical care and the care of the other prisoners—the other prisoners might retaliate.

All people have the right of access to health care. I learned that I was better off not knowing why the person was in prison so that I could give unbiased health care to the inmates. Regardless of the conviction, it would be immoral to withhold care from a person because they have been convicted of a felony.

75

The Snake in the Alley

BEFORE THE PRISON HOSPITAL IN Galveston was built, the prisoners would be transported from Huntsville to Galveston by buses that looked like school buses. They would be taken off of the bus in front of the clinic building and locked to a chain by their handcuffs. It was too awkward for them to get off of the bus while locked to the chain, so they had to be chained after they left the bus. They would then be led through the hospital and clinics, where they would be taken off the chain, one or two at a time, and left with a guard to await their appointment.

One of the prisoners was to be seen in our clinic to check his glaucoma, which had been out of control. He had been seen in the prison clinic many times and had been followed by the resident physicians at the prison, where it was determined that the medications were not controlling his ocular pressure. He was to be presented to the faculty to consider whether he should have surgery for his glaucoma. However, when he was taken from the bus, before he could be locked to the chain, he made a run for freedom. The guards could not leave the other prisoners to chase him, and there were too many innocent people coming and going from the clinic to allow the officers to shoot their weapons, so he got away.

The newspaper reported that he had run several blocks to a residential neighborhood and hidden among some trash cans in an alley. As he was hiding there, several children came out of the surrounding houses to play in the alley. They saw the man hiding among the trash cans and asked him what he was doing there. He told them that he was trying to catch a big rattlesnake that was hiding in the trash cans. He told them to get away from the snake and out of the alley, trying to get rid of them.

One of the boys went home and told his mother that there was a big snake in the trash cans. She grabbed a shotgun and headed for the alley to kill the snake. She discovered the escaped prisoner in his orange jumpsuit, with TDC (Texas Department of Corrections) printed on the front and back, and she marched him back to the medical center at gunpoint and turned him over to the guards.

We did not see him that day, or ever again, in the clinic. When we asked the guards what happened to him, they told us that we would not see him for some time. He was presently in solitary confinement at Huntsville, awaiting trial for escape. It was unlikely that the warden would let him leave the prison for any reason except the trial. I do not know what happened with his glaucoma, as he was never operated on in Galveston. This prisoner had jeopardized his own medical care by trying to escape on a hospital trip.

By escaping, this prisoner took advantage of the prison's obligation to obtain medical treatment for him. Each time a patient came to our clinic, the warden had to grant him or her a temporary reprieve to leave the prison for medical care. To get this reprieve, the prisoner had to sign a promise that he or she would not try to escape. However, people who are in prison are known for not keeping their word. I occasionally intervened on behalf of a prisoner to obtain better care for him or her. I tried on several occasions to get prisoners back into the health care system after they misbehaved, but there is no intervention when escape is involved.

76

A Partially Blind Prisoner

ONE OF MY FIRST PRISON patients in Pittsburgh had glaucoma and had undergone a glaucoma filtering procedure. The surgery was followed immediately by a large retinal detachment in the operated eye. This was unsuccessfully treated surgically, resulting in a total retinal detachment and high intraocular pressure, which caused the patient considerable pain. The eye was blind and very painful. The best solution to this problem is removal of the blind, painful eye.

I was asked to take over the care of the prisoners at this point and to immediately treat this patient with the blind, painful eye. I discussed several options with the prisoner: we could remove the eye; leave the eye in place and administer an alcohol block to kill the pain (but the eye would be red and swollen); or do nothing surgical and treat the eye with eyedrops, hoping to bring down the pressure and relieve the pain. The patient chose to have the eye removed.

In Texas, the residents did the surgery on all of the prisoners, with assistance by one of the faculty. Since this would be the first procedure that I had done on a prisoner in Pittsburgh, I asked one of the residents to assist me. The patient was concerned about his ability to move his artificial eye so that it would look real. My father had an artificial eye, and he had stressed to me the importance of being able to move both eyes together so that the artificial eye was not apparent. I decided to do the removal using a hydroxyappetite sphere covered with sclera to replace the eye. This way the muscles could be sewn to the scleral covering of the sphere, creating movement of the prosthetic eyeball. The hydroxyappetite (synthetic

301

coral) sphere was porous and would allow vessels and fibrous tissue to invade the sphere. Once the sphere was totally invaded by vessels, a second procedure would be done to bore a hole in the sphere. This hole would receive a peg from the glass shell that looked like an eye. The movement of the sphere would translate to movement of the cosmetic prosthesis shell, moving it to follow the other eye.

We were finishing the procedure when the resident stuck his finger with a needle that had been passed through tissue. This was an immediate cause for concern because so many prisoners were HIV positive. The resident had to go to employee health to have blood drawn to determine if he was already HIV positive, as a basis for determining whether he converted later because of the needle stick. Fortunately, the patient gave permission for HIV testing and turned out to be negative, so there was no worry of HIV transmission.

The removal relieved the prisoner's pain, and I followed him for the glaucoma in the other eye, which was in an advanced state when I first saw him. We were able to control the pressure with eyedrops, but he had lost much of his visual field in the remaining eye and had lost all of the temporal field of vision he had on the removed side when the eye was removed. He was very worried about people in the prison sneaking up on him from his blind side.

After six weeks he was fitted with a cosmetic prosthesis, but it did not move very well. We could not drill the hydroxyappetite sphere until it had been incorporated by tissue, which would take about a year. He was very anxious to have the sphere drilled, so, at the one-year surgical anniversary, we did the bone scan to determine whether the sphere was incorporated into the tissue. The scan showed total incorporation, so I had our oculoplastic surgery specialist drill the sphere and insert the peg. After several weeks he was sent to the ocularist for a new prosthesis, which would accept the peg to move with the imbedded sphere and follow the other eye.

He was very pleased with the outcome after the peg was placed. I continued to follow his other eye for glaucoma, and the drops controlled the pressure. He was very worried about losing the vision in his remaining eye.

When the patient came for his pressure check one day, he asked if there was training he could take to be able to get around better with his limited vision. I told him that it was available on the outside, but might be hard to arrange while he was in prison. He told me he might be getting out soon and wanted to have the training. I always made it a habit not to ask why the prisoner was in prison or for how long, so this did not seem strange to me.

About three weeks later, six prisoners escaped from the penitentiary after they had dug a tunnel under the prison wall into a warehouse next to the prison. My patient was among the six. They apparently had cooperation from outside. Someone had left a car for them in the northern part of town. They stole a car at the warehouse and drove to the getaway car, abandoning the stolen car.

They made a clean getaway and disappeared for about a week. The first lead to their location came when my patient had a seizure in the bus station in Houston, Texas. He was taken to Ben Taub Hospital and admitted for observation. Apparently he had been on a number of psychiatric drugs before he escaped, but he forgot to take them with him when he escaped. The abrupt withdrawal of these medications may have caused his seizures.

Once in the hospital, he began bragging to the nurses that he had just escaped from the penitentiary in Pittsburgh. They called his sister in Pittsburgh, who he had listed as next of kin on the hospital forms, and she verified his story. The nurses called the police, who also eventually caught the others, when they caused a disturbance in a motel by having a loud party with beer and prostitutes.

All six were extradited back to Pennsylvania, but they were all assigned to other parts of the prison system, so I never saw my patient again. I hope he received care for his glaucoma. The guards who brought other patients to the clinic told me that when my patient was crawling through the tunnel, his glass eye fell out. He groped around in the darkness and found his prosthesis in the dirt and put the dirty prosthesis back in the socket before completing his escape.

It is amazing what the eye will tolerate.

I should have been more alert to the possibility that my patient might be planning an escape when he wanted mobility training because he was getting out soon, especially when the guards told me, after the escape, that he was in for life and wasn't supposed to be going anywhere very soon. He was obviously thinking about his impending "freedom" and wanted to prepare for it.

It was somewhat irresponsible for the ophthalmologists who had been treating this man to leave the case in the middle of it, while the prisoner was still in pain. I moved as quickly as possible to end his pain. He was always very respectful to me and thanked me for everything I did for him.

Part V

Pennsylvania Patients

1991–2004

WHEN I MOVED TO PITTSBURGH I had an abrupt change in the type of program I ran and the way I practiced medicine. My first task was to reorganize the residency and return it to full accreditation. When I left Galveston, I had seven full-time physicians on the faculty and three PhD research faculty members. Only a few things were taught by part-time people. I was the only full-time faculty member in Pittsburgh, however, and I relied on volunteer faculty to teach almost everything.

Pittsburgh was full of ophthalmologists who were in competition with the clinic. To create goodwill, I restricted by practice to corneal diseases and transplants and only removed cataracts if the patient also needed a corneal transplant. I saw patients one or two afternoons each week, and I did not use a nurse or technician in the office. If I had done any specialty surgery outside of my specialty, as I had done in Galveston, the lawyers would have been after me for not referring patients that I was not trained to treat. I found the referral patterns in Pittsburgh to be very political. I was treating about 15 percent of the number of private patients I saw in Galveston. There were six other cornea specialists in Pittsburgh and another ophthalmology residency at the University of Pittsburgh Medical Center (UPMC). Many of the people who worked in the hospital came to me for their eye care, especially the nuns who ran the hospital.

For a while I was the only full-time residency director at St. Francis, but that changed after three years, so there were many meetings with the other program directors and hospital administrators. I eventually became director of medical education over all seven residencies at St. Francis.

My administrative office was in the clinic, so I was called to see most of the complicated patients. I soon learned that I did not have time to do any research. To secure the residency financially and return it to full accreditation, I had to reorganize it. I formed a corporation to earn money to pay the part-time faculty so the accrediting board would count them in the faculty.

There were six residents in Pittsburgh, two each year, so I knew these residents better than I had known my Galveston residents. While I was not allowed to interview osteopathic (DO) residency applicants in Galveston, I was encouraged to take them in Pittsburgh. I found that they were on par with the allopathic (MD) residents.

77

The Lady from New Jersey

A MAN IN HIS FIFTIES BROUGHT his mother to the office to see if I thought her vision could be improved or, at least, that her pain could be alleviated. Alice was from New Jersey, but she was visiting her son in Pittsburgh for the holidays. I examined her and determined that she had Fuchs' dystrophy of the cornea in both eyes, which had caused corneal edema and clouding of the cornea. She had tiny blisters on the cornea that were painful when they broke several times each day.

I advised Alice that she should have corneal transplants to replace her damaged corneas. She related that she had been told the same thing by her ophthalmologist in Trenton, New Jersey. He had followed her eye problems for several years and treated her correctly with hypertonic eyedrops to dehydrate the blisters so they would not break. I told her that she should go home to New Jersey and have the surgery at home. She told me that she wanted the surgery done in Pittsburgh so that her son could look after her throughout the surgery and postoperative period. Her son was working in Pittsburgh and could not go to Trenton to look after her.

A situation arises when a patient who has been advised to have surgery wants to have it done by another surgeon in another city and return home for the recuperation period. Many older patients depend on their children to assist them when they have medical problems. They need someone to take them to the hospital and bring them home. They may have to take medication after the surgery and feel that they need assistance. They want someone to take care of them during the postoperative period.

Having surgery away from home could create a problem for the patient after she returned home and expected her ophthalmologist to follow her corneal transplant after I had done the surgery and been paid for it. Insurance pays the operating surgeon for the surgery and the entire follow-up period. If another surgeon sees the patient, they will not get paid for their time and effort. Medicare has developed a way to divide the fee, but it must be prearranged.

People show up in ophthalmologists' offices all the time wanting postoperative care for surgery done by someone else. This used to even out, with ophthalmologists taking care of each others patients, and not be a problem. Now that there are so many lawsuits suing doctors if the result is not perfect, there is a great deal of risk in taking on the management of a postoperative patient when someone else may have botched the surgery. If it does not turn out perfect, the second ophthalmologist will be sued, even though he or she is not the cause of the bad result. The unhappy patients, who are most likely to sue, are the ones who look for another doctor.

I asked the patient for the name and phone number of her ophthalmologist in New Jersey so I could call him and explain the situation. He was very gracious about the situation and suggested that I go ahead with the surgery and handle the immediate follow-up period. He agreed to care for her when she returned to New Jersey.

I did the surgery, which included a corneal transplant and cataract extraction, with the placement of an intraocular lens in her right eye. She stayed in Pittsburgh with her son for about two months. This was ample time for the transplant to settle in and begin to heal.

When she went home, I wrote a letter to her ophthalmologist, explaining the surgery and her postoperative course. She was to see him every two months and also if she had pain, blurred vision, or felt a loose suture. She did well and returned a year later to have the other eye done. This time she told me that she had moved to Pittsburgh to live with her son and would not be going back to New Jersey.

She continued to do well for several years. I saw her every three months and learned that her son had been laid off from his job and did not have a car. When she developed a red eye and sensitivity to light, she made and broke several appointments. By the time her son could borrow a car to bring her to the office, she had a full-blown rejection reaction in one eye. We poured on the steroids and stopped the reaction. Her cornea cleared to almost normal vision.

Over the next year, she had several other rejection reactions. Each time, she had more and more difficulty getting to the office for care; and each time, she lost some clarity in her graft. The other cornea stayed clear, and she did well with the limited vision in her good eye. I learned that the cause of her delayed treatment was that her son had become a drug addict and had no car or money for gas; further, no one would trust him with their car.

The last time I saw her, he was with her. He was in a rehabilitation program and was doing well. She had lost all of the clarity from one corneal transplant and was developing macular degeneration in her good eye. Her son had a job and was taking care of her. She was in her eighties, but did not show any signs of dementia. She was trying to keep him on the wagon so that he could look after her, and he was working hard trying to keep her happy.

This patient was a lesson in adult dependency on their children and the complications that arise from that situation. Alice was completely dependent on her son for office visits. Her care depended on her being able to come to the office within a day of rejection symptoms so that treatment could be started to save her corneal transplant. When her son lost his job, it became impossible for her to get to the office. She lost one transplant because she could not get to the office. After moving to Pittsburgh so that her son could take care of her, the son became unreliable to the extent that it jeopardized her care.

The other doctor in New Jersey acted very professionally, He could have refused to care for Alice when she returned to New Jersey, but he agreed to care for her even though he might not get paid. This may have been because I called him first and asked his permission, which was also the professional way to handle this situation. Alice had several years of good vision because of this cooperation.

78

<o>

A Hydrogen Fluoride Burn

A S I ARRIVED AT WORK one day, I learned that they wanted me in the emergency department immediately. I hurried across the street to the ER to find one of the eye residents irrigating the right eye of a barely cooperative man who was obviously in pain. I learned that he was a chemical manufacturing worker who had been mixing chemicals for a commercial car washing solution. When he opened a can of hydrofluoric acid to add it to the solution, the acid splashed into his right eye, causing sudden pain and spasm of his eyelids. His eye had been irrigated with water at the chemical factory before he was brought to the emergency room. We determined that he was not wearing his safety goggles that were furnished by the company.

We irrigated his eyes until pH testing using paper strips showed that his eye surface pH was more than 6.0. The normal surface pH is about 7.5, slightly alkaline. I once had a resident tell me he had irrigated an eye for three hours trying to get it back to neutral pH at 7.0 after an alkali burn, but he could not get it below 7.5. He did not realize that normal was 7.5 rather than a strictly neutral 7.0.

The hydrofluoric acid had coagulated all of his corneal epithelium (the outer layer) and damaged the conjunctiva for about three millimeters from the edge of the cornea. This made him very susceptible to bacterial infection and possible melting of his cornea. It would also cause a severe inflammatory response with redness and swelling.

As a rule, acid burns of the eye are less serious than alkali burns, but hydrofluoric acid is the exception to the rule. Where hydrofluoric acid burns are common, special solutions are kept on hand for ocular irrigation to neutralize the acid. These were not available in our emergency room, so saline, which we used, is the next best thing.

We treated his eye with antibiotics, steroids, and patching and sent him home with his wife. We saw him every day and were pleased to see that his epithelium began to grow back toward his cornea by the third day. He complained every time we saw him that his eyes burned and that he could not stand any light. He became theatrical in his protestations and would not let us shine any light in his eye to examine him until we had anesthetized his eyes with eyedrops.

By the end of the second week, he had completely healed his cornea with epithelium, which should have relieved his pain. His wife, who always accompanied him to the clinic, told us that he was spending most of his time in bed in the darkened bedroom. He would not come downstairs in the house unless she hung blankets over all of the windows, even when the curtains were pulled. This went on for several weeks, until she quit coming to the clinic with him. I learned that a driver from the chemical company brought him to the clinic for each visit and that they continued to pay the patient throughout his convalescence.

Six weeks after his burn, I noticed him sitting in the waiting area reading a magazine with no apparent discomfort. He did not see me. When he was called back to the examining room, he came in holding his hand over his eyes, peeking out from under his hand and asking that I turn out the lights. I dimmed the lights and checked his vision while he was looking through the phoroptor (the apparatus that holds the lenses for determining the power of glasses he would need.) This instrument allows each eye to be blocked off independently, and usually the patient does not know which eye they are using when they read the wall chart. He read 20/20 with each eye without any lenses in place. When I examined his eyes that day, they both looked completely normal. I congratulated him on his marvelous recovery and told him that he could return to work. He complained about his light sensitivity and how it would keep him from working, so I told him that I had seen him sitting in the brightly lighted waiting area with no sign of discomfort. He admitted that it had become much better recently.

He told me that his boss had been after him to return to work, but that he did not want to go back to work because he planned to sue the company. He asked me how much money I thought he could get for his injuries. I pointed out to him that 20/20 vision was normal, and better than many people have, so it would be hard to prove any lasting disability. He told me that before the injury he had seen much better. Some people do see 20/15 or even 20/10, so I asked him if he had seen an eye doctor of any kind where his vision had been recorded. He could not recall ever having his eyes examined before the injury. I also reminded him that he had not been wearing his safety goggles, which was a violation of OSHA safety rules, and that the company would bring that to the attention of the court. He told me that he already had an appointment with a lawyer, so he would see what the lawyer said.

He came back to see me about a week later, and he told me that he had gone to see his boss. He had tried to get the boss to give him money in compensation for his pain and suffering and threatened to sue the company if he was not paid. The meeting then degenerated into a shouting match, during which he had "royally cussed out" his boss. At that point the boss fired him. He now wanted me to speak with his boss to get him reinstated.

At this point, I decided to lecture him on his situation, including that: (1) he had sustained an injury through his own negligence by not wearing his goggles when he uncapped the hydrofluoric acid; (2) everyone, including his wife and I, thought he was malingering for the past several weeks; (3) he had experienced a miraculous recovery, considering the seriousness of his injury; and (4) he was very lucky to now have completely normal vision, with no residual effects from the injury. I advised him to use the knowledge he had from the former job to get a new job, while counting his blessings that the injury was not the disaster it could have been. I also told him that he should wear safety equipment when he worked around chemicals. He said that he saw my point and thanked me for the care I had given him. I never saw him again after that visit. Maybe he did not need any more care for his eyes.

From this patient I learned that many people are careless with their vision, and they tend to blame their employer when they do not wear safety equipment. Many see it as the lottery when they are

79

◄○►

The Blind Computer
Science Student

I HAD A REALLY REMARKABLE YOUNG man come to see me because he was having pain in his eyes. His mother knew my wife's family, who had told her that I could probably help him. One of my wife's distant cousins had brought him in that day.

Robert was born very prematurely and had been on oxygen for several weeks. When he was several weeks old he began having peripheral neovascularization of his retina from the retinopathy of prematurity. This progressed to the point that, by age two, he was completely blind in both eyes. He had seen many doctors, who had all told him that there was nothing to be done to bring his vision back. He had adapted to blindness as a child, learning mobility skills and how to read Braille.

He told me that he knew that he was completely blind most of the time, but that he had periods when he could see quite well; he gave examples of driving an all-terrain vehicle around his front yard without hitting any of the dozen trees there, and shooting nineteen out of twenty ducks on the Nintendo game that he played with his cousin. This seemed to me to be scientifically impossible.

Robert's complaint was that he had bouts of severe pain in one eye or the other from time to time. He wanted to know if I could make it go away. He said that he had seen several doctors about this, and that they all said that he was blind and there was nothing they could do about the pain of the blindness except take out the eyes.

317

Having not ever seen himself in the mirror, he had the concept that he was relatively good looking and did not want to lose his eyes for fear that it would make him look blind. He had good enough mobility that many people did not know that he was blind.

I examined him and found that, in addition to having severe traction detachments of both retinas caused by the retinopathy of prematurity, both corneas were deeply calcified. The corneas were vascularized and had large central calcium plaques about eight millimeters in diameter. These calcium plaques had several cracks running across the width of the calcium. When I pressed on the cornea with a cotton swab, he told me that it reproduced the pain he had been experiencing. I could hear the edges of the calcium grating together when I pressed on the cornea. At that time, I had never seen a case of calcific band keratopathy this thick and had never seen cracks in the calcium.

For cases of chronic corneal pain from exposure or chronic epithelial edema, the most effective treatment is to cover the cornea with a conjunctival flap. This covers the exposed raw nerves with a less sensitive tissue and prevents further deterioration of the cornea. In Robert's case, it would not keep his blinking eyelid from pressing on the calcium and grating the edges, so I decided that the best thing to do would be to remove the calcium plaques before advancing the flap to cover the cornea. This would also remove the nerve endings.

I took him to the operating room and performed the procedure on his right eye. This required taking off the anterior one-third of his entire cornea to remove all of the calcium plaque. The conjunctiva was easily mobilized, pulled over the remaining cornea, and sewn in place to cover the cornea completely.

The next day, Robert said that he was very happy because he had not had any pain in the operated eye since surgery. His other eye was still having pain, so he wanted to know how soon I could operate that eye. We operated that eye about two weeks later. I saw him about once a week for several weeks after the second eye was operated. The flaps healed into place covering both corneas, and he remained pain free.

Every time I saw him after the surgery, he was accompanied by two or three beautiful coeds. They looked after him very nicely and made sure that he got to his follow-up appointments. He said that they were all very nice to him and helped him get around when he needed to travel by car. He told me that his grades had dropped during the time that he was having so much pain, but that since the surgery he was able to concentrate again and had gotten nothing but As.

Robert asked me why none of the other doctors had been able to fix his painful eyes, while it had seemed so simple for me to do just what he needed. It is always hard to explain why someone did not do something. My best guess is that they did not listen to him, but assumed that he wanted someone to repair his eyes to restore his vision—something that no one could do at that time or since. It may be that they did not recognize that the cracked calcium plaques were the cause of the pain, but thought he had the pain that occurs internally in a blind eye.

I felt that he knew that he was permanently blind, in spite of his stories of seeing, and that his problem was one of recurring pain. The pain was related to his blindness, but his blindness was not the cause. Getting rid of the pain was not going to restore his vision, and he knew that also. Robert's condition is a rare condition. I have seen only one other case, during my career, of calcific band keratopathy that contained cracks, which I encountered after I treated Robert. That other person did not have pain.

Removal of the plaque by itself, without the conjunctival flap, would have been only a temporary solution. Calcium will recur and continue to deposit in the cornea after it has been removed. The flap stops the pain in the operated cornea immediately and keeps the calcium from being deposited again.

Several months after doing the surgery, I had occasion to attend church with my mother-in-law in a town outside Pittsburgh. I was pleasantly surprised to see Robert there that morning with his family. I learned that he was a regular member of the congregation and an active participant. That morning he read the scripture lessons for the service from his Braille Bible. His parents saw me at the church before the service and told Robert that I was there that day. While he was at the lectern, after reading the scripture, he took the occasion to tell the congregation about his problem and to thank me for treating him when all of the other doctors had told him that nothing could be done. My mother-in-law seemed to be very impressed.

I saw him about a year later for a routine follow-up of the surgery. The flap was healed in place, and he no longer had any pain. He told me that he was about to graduate from a local college with a degree in computer science. He could program computers and was proficient in several standard programs. He was interviewing for a job with one of the power companies.

When I asked him how he was able to work with computers with no vision, he told me about a computer card that a computer company had donated for him to use in his computer. The card would read what was written on the screen to him verbally on a voice synthesizer so he could proofread his work. The professors at the school had also written programs to help him. He used a Braille keyboard that could read to him from the screen and that he could use to enter programming and text to the computer.

In mid-June I received a phone call from him asking for a letter of intercession from me. He was still interviewing for a job and had been under consideration by several companies, but he still did not have a job offer. He had just received a letter from the computer company that had given him a computer card to use, telling him that unless he got a computer-related job within thirty days after his graduation, he would have to return the special computer card. He was afraid that the job offer would not be made before the thirty days expired. Without the card, he did not think he could do the job for which he applied.

I wrote a letter to the computer company reminding them that Robert had graduated with honors from college and was being interviewed by at least two companies, and, to date, he had not been accepted or rejected by them. I explained to them that if he kept his card and went on to become gainfully employed, that he was a tremendous success story of which the company could be proud. But, if they reclaimed the card prematurely, then all they would have was an expensive failure, with a wasted education to show for their generosity in providing the card.

I received a reply from the company saying that they would give Robert several months to find a job before requesting the return of the card for someone else to use. About three weeks later I received a postcard from Robert telling me that he had been hired by one of the local power companies and was doing well on the job. I did not hear from him after that and assumed that he was still pain free and continued to be employed working with computers.

I am always impressed when I see a person like Robert who overcomes blindness to become a useful and independent citizen. I see them almost everyday. They learn Braille and mobility skills and adapt their work stations so that they can be independent and productive. So many people have much less to conquer, but give up and look for someone to provide care and support. I was glad that I could help him return to his studies pain free so that he could graduate and become the productive citizen he is.

I learned that Robert's original doctors had assumed that they could not relieve his pain, rather than searching for the cause of the pain and finding that it could be treated without removing his eyes. Perhaps they did not listen to him say that he wished to get rid of the pain, and thought he expected them to restore his vision, which no one can do.

I also learned what "a chick magnet" blindness can be. Robert, who was not the most handsome guy on the block, had the best looking, nicest girls looking after him.

I learned that a company that had the right idea in furnishing the special card for Robert's use while in school apparently did not realize that by taking back the card that made education and work possible for Robert, they were undermining his skills learned through the card. They were short-sighted in realizing the dependency the card created by its use in the education process.

80

<o>

The Irish Lady with Pemphigoid

ONE OF THE MOST PLEASANT patients who came to me was an elderly Irish lady who complained of "scratchy eyes." Coleen wore normal amounts of make-up and had coal black hair, which was done in a stylish manner. She always had a broad smile, even when she was telling me how much her eyes bothered her.

When I examined Coleen, her eyes were very red. I found that she had several eyelashes in both eyes that came out of the top edge, rather than the front edge, of her eyelids and turned toward the cornea, rubbing and scratching the cornea in places. This is known as trichiasis, which has many causes. Upon further exam I found that there were thick bands of tissue that bridged the pocket between the back of her eyelids and the front of her eyeballs, holding the eyelids against the eyes, which indicated an advanced stage of benign mucous membrane pemphigoid, a disease caused by an autoimmune reaction (allergy to oneself).

This reaction causes the conjunctiva to shrink and may progress to the extent that it causes the eyelids to adhere to the eyeball, freezing the movement of the eye and stopping the blinking of the eyelids. This becomes very painful. She had been treated with steroids, but it did not prevent this shrinkage. Coleen's eyelids were so tightly bound to the eyes that she had limited movement of the eyes, and had pain when she tried to look to the right or left without turning her head.

When I was a fellow in Boston, I learned a surgical procedure used to free the eyelids from the eyes and prevent their immediate reattachment. This procedure has become known as a "rubber glove graft" operation. The eyelids are dissected free from the eyeball, and all of the loose tissue is removed from the surface of the eyeball where the conjunctiva should be. It is also removed from the back side of the eyelids. If these bare surfaces were allowed to be in contact for more than a few hours, they would stick together. To prevent this, pieces of a plastic sheet that are part of a plastic drape (or a rubber glove) are fashioned to separate the tissues. These pieces are usually the size and shape of a large lima bean. To hold the lower eyelid away from the eyeball, the plastic is sewn to the back of the lower eyelid because it moves very little with respect to the eyeball. Since the upper eyelid constantly moves over the eye with every blink, the upper plastic membrane is sewn to the upper eyeball above the cornea.

During the postoperative period, fluorescein is used to stain the denuded tissue. It will not stain epithelium as it grows beneath the plastic membrane. Once the entire surface under the clear membrane does not stain, the surface of the eye and eyelids have been covered by new epithelium and will not stick together so the membranes can be removed. The cul-de-sac that is formed around the membranes will shrink about one-third to one-half in size, but the eyelids and the eyeballs will move independently.

I have done this procedure on several patients who had this rare disease and had some success. I explained the procedure to Coleen and her daughter, who was a nurse. They both thought we should do the surgery to try to stop the progression of the disease. Coleen tolerated the surgery very well, and the plastic membranes were removed at about three weeks. I knew that we had not removed the underlying cause of the disease and that it would probably recur, so I needed to treat the cause.

One drug that does have some effect in slowing the shrinkage is dapsone, a drug used in the treatment of malaria. I looked up the dosage of dapsone for this disease and started Coleen on this medication by mouth. After the eyes had recovered from the surgery, they continued to remain white and quiet, with no recurrence of the bands or shrinkage. The lashes still grew and rubbed the cornea, so

I had to pluck them about every three weeks. I offered to send her to an oculoplastic surgeon to have the lashes excised or epilated, but she refused.

She continued on the medication for about six months, until I received a call from her medical doctor who asked me why I had her on this antimalarial medication when she did not have malaria. He wanted to stop the medicine because she had turned blue and was short of breath. One of the unusual side effects of the drug was methhemoglobinemia, in which the hemoglobin in the red blood cells is bound by the medicine and will not pick up oxygen. The red blood cells turn dark red (blue) like they are when they return to the heart, but they stay blue after they go through the lungs. This makes the patient look blue and become short of breath. This was a life–threatening, situation so we discontinued the drug, and her doctor treated the complication.

If her eye disease was left untreated, it would lead to pain and possible blindness. Another drug that was used to treat pemphigoid was methyltrexate, an immunosuppressive, chemotherapy agent that was widely used in early chemotherapy, but had been replaced by better agents. I started her on a low dose of methyltrexate. This drug may lower the number of white blood cells produced in the body, so she had monthly monitoring of her white blood count and her liver function.

I continued to pluck the lashes every three to four weeks, and her pemphigoid stayed under moderate control, with very slow progression. After she had been on the medication for about four months, her internist called to tell me that her white blood count had fallen to dangerous levels, so we had to stop the drug.

At about that time there was a report that cyclosporine A, a drug that was used for immune suppression after kidney transplants, was being used as an anti-inflammatory drug and was used for treatment of corneal transplants to prevent rejection. It was not commercially manufactured in eyedrop form, but I learned that a compounding pharmacy in California was making it for ocular use in a 0.2 percent solution. I contacted them and learned that the solution could be ordered from them with a prescription, so I gave the patient a prescription, and she was soon taking the drops three times a day, which stopped all progression of the disease. Except for some stinging, when the eyedrops were instilled, there did not appear to be any complications or side effects.

After the patient had used these drops for two years, Restassis was brought onto the market to treat dry eyes. This was a 0.05 percent solution of cyclosporine A. We decided to try this in place of the 0.2 percent solution, which had caused significant stinging whenever it was placed in the eye. This new strength proved successful in stopping the progression of the disease without the stinging, but the lashes still grew and had to be plucked periodically.

Somewhere along the course of all of these changes in medication, she came in one day with beautiful snow white hair, which was very nicely styled and made her look years younger. She was always a spirited lady who was willing to go along with my suggestions and try new medications. For the ten years I followed this lady, she maintained her vision, and the progress of the disease was kept in check.

This lady had a miserable disease, but always managed to remain cheerful. When offered a permanent solution to her chronic irritation, she refused. It seemed to me that she enjoyed her visits to the office and wanted to come in every three or four weeks as a social event and to have her eyelashes plucked. The surgery for her conjunctiva was successful, but it took constant changes in her medication to keep her disease under control. Her disease moved faster than the research, so she had to use experimental drugs and off-label usage drugs that were not approved for her disease, to keep ahead of it.

I had to go back to the books and journals to find new ways to treat her disease. I finally had to use a drug that had not been used in this disease. I used it because the theory of why the drug worked for immune suppression of transplant rejections fit the need we had for a treatment to suppress the autoimmunity of the pemphigoid disease. I eventually used this medication on three patients with this disease, and it worked well in each case. However, I never assembled enough patients to prove that cyclosporine A worked in this disease, so I couldn't publish the results.

81

One in a Million

ONE OF THE MOST UNUSUAL cases I have had was that of a doctor in his sixties, who came to me with failing vision. Bob was still very busy in administrative medicine and needed to read doctor's handwriting and printed regulations every day. He had posterior subcapsular cataracts, the young person's cataracts, and they were interfering with his vision.

I removed Bob's right cataract and placed an intraocular lens in the eye. Everything went very smoothly. The day after surgery he was very pleased with the improvement in his vision. The eye looked good in both the front and the back. He improved to 20/40, without glasses, over the first two weeks, but he then became more sensitive to light and began having inflammation in the eye. This change was worrisome, since this would be about the time that a micrococcus infection within the eye might show itself. I put him on ten days of clindamycin by mouth and the inflammation decreased.

About two weeks after stopping the clindamycin, the inflammation started again. I decided that the micrococcus must have been somewhat resistant to the clindamycin, so, with his consent, I started Bob on chloromycetin eyedrops. Chloromycetin is very good for eye infections because it penetrates the eye very well and has a good spectrum against both gram positive and gram negative bacteria. Unfortunately, it has been known to cause aplastic anemia, a fatal blood disease, so it has not been used much since that was discovered.

During the chloromycetin therapy, Bob noticed a sudden decrease in vision. Examination of the retina showed a line of hemorrhages surrounding the optic nerve and inflammation in the overlying vitreous. I immediately sent him to a retina specialist for advice. The specialist called me to ask if I might have put the needle for the surgical anesthetic into his optic nerve before the surgery, by error. I explained that he had good vision after surgery, without any hemorrhages in the retina on the day after surgery. Both of these would have been affected immediately after the surgery if a needle had been placed into the optic nerve.

The appearance of the retina became worse over the next week, giving the appearance of intraocular herpes simplex in an AIDS patient. He also began having severe headaches. The headaches made us think of a type of brain tumor that occasionally presents as inflammation within the eye. The test for this is an MRI of the brain to look for a tumor. The MRI did not show any abnormality. There is another test in which either aqueous humor or vitreous humor is withdrawn from the eye for an antibody test for tumor cells. This test was not available in Pittsburgh, so Bob was referred to the Wills Eye Institute in Philadelphia for this test. The test at Wills was positive for tumor cells, so he was sent back to Pittsburgh for further workup. The MRI of the brain done three weeks later was again negative for a brain tumor.

About two weeks after that, he passed out at home and was brought into the hospital, with a possible stroke. Another MRI done this time showed three areas of tumor density near the ventricles of the brain. These had not been visible there at the time of the prior MRI. His condition rapidly deteriorated, and he died two weeks later.

I rarely went to the funerals of my patients, but I had known Bob very well and worked on committees with him. I went to the funeral home to pay my respects. When I arrived, there were only a few people there, so I talked for some time with his widow, who I also knew fairly well.

She told me that the doctors at Wills Eye Hospital had told her that the tumor he had was extremely rare, that it occurred only once in a million people. She told me that she would always remember that because she had always thought that Bob was a "One in a Million" husband. Sometimes a word or phrase like "One in a Million" will stick with a grieving person and be a great comfort.

Bob was a difficult case to manage because his disease mimicked so many other diseases and the actual disease is so rare. When things did not go right, it always looked like something other than what it was: herpes, needle in the nerve, or nonvirulent infection. When the treatment did not work, I had to stay flexible and look for something else to treat. Even when he started having neurological symptoms, the MRIs were negative. Once we thought of the correct diagnosis, it had to be confirmed at another eye center because the disease was so rare.

82

The Stevens-Johnson
Syndrome Lady

I RECEIVED A CONSULT TO SEE an eighty-plus-year-old black woman from Donora, Pennsylvania, who was in the medical center for the treatment of Stevens-Johnson syndrome. She had been taking ciprofloxacin by mouth for an infection, when she developed a skin rash and became very ill. In this disease, the mucous membranes in the body form blisters that break and weep. This creates a problem that is much like a severe thermal burn of the skin. The mucous membranes break down and form scars. If the conjunctiva is involved, the eyelids stick to the eyeball with adhesions, and the denuded areas are subject to infection. This involves the eyes, the lining of the nose and pharynx, the mouth and esophagus, and other mucous membranes throughout the body. Years ago the fatality rate was over 50 percent. Now with steroids and better antibiotics, many of the patients survive, with severe scarring of the mucous membranes. In the eye, there is often severe vision loss.

When I saw Velma, she had red, watery eyes, with ulceration of the conjunctival surface and beginning formation of adhesions of the eyelids to the eyeballs. I immediately started antibiotic ointments and steroid drops. In the past, we used glass thermometers with mercury in them to sweep between the eyelids and the eyeball to break these adhesions. These have disappeared from the hospital floors, with the advent of the new electronic thermometers. These new thermometers have a thin metal probe, which is covered with a plastic sleeve, and are not suitable to sweep the conjunctiva to break adhesions. Instead, we used cotton swabs covered with ointment. The swabs are more traumatic to the tissues, but they do the job.

She was on high doses of systemic steroids and soon recovered from the acute phase of this disease. However, her conjunctiva continued to scar. The scarring closes the tear glands in the conjunctiva and the tear ducts from the main tear gland, causing a very dry eye. This drying creates scarring of the cornea, which turns white. The roughness and whitening scatter the light entering the eye, causing corneal blindness. The retina is not affected by this disease. She also had significant cataracts in both eyes, further reducing her vision to seeing a hand moving a few inches in front of her eyes.

Her corneas continued to break down into ulcerations. I treated her with topical antibiotics, lubricating antibiotic ointments, and steroids, until she finally healed. This entailed seeing her twice a week to be sure that she did not have enzymatic degradation or infection of the cornea where it was exposed.

Velma was always accompanied by her daughter, but she would always go to the waiting room to call in her "driver" to see when he could bring her for the next visit. She introduced this man as the pastor of her church. He was a short, very well groomed, black man, wearing a clerical collar, who appeared to be about fifty years old. It was not until about her forth or fifth outpatient visit that I learned that he was also her son.

Although she was near ninety years old and weighed about ninety pounds, she was always very stylishly dressed and carried very nice purses that coordinated with her clothes. In spite of her very poor vision and constant discomfort or pain in her eyes, she maintained a pleasant personality and had a devout religious belief.

Velma developed trichiasis, a condition in which the shrinking of the underside of the eyelids causes the eyelashes to be pulled in so far that they rub against the front of the eye. This rubbing leads to breakdown of the corneal surface, with epithelial defects. This, in turn, causes more irritation and leads to infection in the form of corneal ulcers. Every two or three weeks I would pluck these eyelashes so they would not rub the cornea. She would obtain temporary relief for about three weeks, until they grew back. I offered her permanent ablation of these lashes, but she refused.

One day Velma called to say that she was having much more pain than usual, so I had her come in immediately. She had a deep ulcer of the right cornea that had almost perforated the cornea. I treated that eye with very frequent antibiotics and collagenase inhibitors, but the cornea perforated, and aqueous humor leaked from the eye. The condition of her cornea prohibited closing this leak with tissue adhesive and forced me to do an emergency corneal transplant to close the leak and get rid of the ulcerated cornea. I knew that the chance of keeping a corneal transplant clear and visually useful in the aftermath of Stevens-Johnson syndrome was very slim.

When the scarred cornea was removed, her dense cataract filled the pupil, so I knew that she would not be able to see after the surgery unless we also removed the cataract. I had anticipated this and obtained permission to remove the cataract as part of the informed consent. I performed an extracapsular cataract extraction through the open cornea before placing an intraocular lens in the capsule bag. The donor cornea button was placed on the cornea and sewn in place. Because of the S-J syndrome, I transplanted the donor corneal epithelium with the button and babied the epithelium throughout the procedure, hoping that it would not break down and scar and cause her to lose her vision again.

After I took the patch off of Velma's eye the next day, she looked around the room and cried out, "I can see again. Thank you Jesus." I checked her vision in the operated eye and found it to be 20/50 using a pinhole occluder instead of glasses. She was so happy that I had difficulty getting myself to caution her that the vision might not last. It did last for about three weeks, until the epithelium sloughed from the graft and left her with the optically rough corneal stroma. Using soft lenses, steroids, and carbachol, I nursed the epithelium until it grew back onto the cornea, but by this time she had rejected the endothelial layer of the new transplant, and her transplant had become cloudy, decreasing her vision to about 20/400.

The cornea slowly vascularized, and her vision further declined to counting fingers held about six inches before her eyes. When the cornea vascularized, it was stable again, with very little likelihood that it would ulcerate again. Velma wanted me to repeat the corneal transplant, but I explained to her that this time we had been successful in stopping the leak in her eye without it becoming

83

The Eye and Sex

S HORTLY AFTER I ARRIVED IN Pittsburgh, I received a panic call from a man with an accent I did not recognize. He told me that he was a patient of Dr. Weisser's, the doctor who started the program I was running at St. Francis Medical Center. Dr. Weisser was about eighty years old and was winding down his practice. He had referred the patient to me because the patient needed to be seen immediately and would need long-term follow-up. William was excited because Dr. Weisser had told him that if he ever saw flashes or floaters, he should be seen immediately. He had just experienced some new floaters and wanted to be seen.

I was supervising the eye clinic that day and not seeing private patients, but I told him to come in as soon as possible, so I could take a look at him. Flashes and floaters are considered an ophthalmic emergency because they are the first signs of retinal detachment. Immediate detection and repair of retinal detachment is key to saving vision in these patients.

When William came in, I took one look at his glasses and knew that he was highly myopic (-10 diopters). Myopic people are at high risk of developing retinal detachments. Since flashes and floaters are a sign of retinal detachments and he was highly myopic, I knew that I would have to dilate his eyes and check him for a retinal tear or detachment.

He introduced me to Mable, his woman companion, as a close friend of his who had driven him to the office. While we were waiting for the dilating drops to work, he told me that he and Mable had both lost their mates several years ago and that they were dating each other. Both were over seventy.

When I examined his eyes, I did not find a retinal detachment, but I did determine that the vitreous gel, which fills the back of the eye, was shrinking and that it had started to separate from the retina. This mechanism also produces flashes and floaters. There is no treatment for vitreous separation except to recheck the retina in six weeks to make sure that no new hole has been created.

Several months later, Mable came to see me because of decreasing vision in both eyes. I found that she had cataracts in both eyes, with one worse than the other. She was also highly myopic and had a partial vitreous separation. The worse of her two cataracts had progressed to the point where changes of glasses did not help her vision. The cataract would have to be removed to restore useful vision to her. She decided that she wanted cataract surgery, so we proceeded to do the preoperative tests and set up the surgery.

In the process of setting up the surgery, my bookkeeper discovered that Mable's insurance did not cover cataract surgery. William then checked with his insurance and determined that his insurance covered cataract surgery and would also cover it for a spouse. One week later, William called to say that he had married Mable and that she now had insurance coverage, so we could proceed with the surgery. The surgery went well, and about one year later I removed the other cataract.

I continued to follow both of them for a long time. About once or twice each year, one or the other would call me because of new flashes and floaters, so I would see them immediately. They were very nice people and seemed to be very devoted to each other. They were very religious and worked through their church to take infirm people, several days each week, to see the doctor, shop, or attend church.

One day William called and wanted to speak to me immediately. He told me that he had the sudden onset of a visual problem that looked like smoke curling around in his vision. This was a pretty good description of an intraocular hemorrhage, possibly associated with a tear in the retina, which could lead to a retinal detachment. I told him to come right in so I could examine him.

I dilated his pupils and examined his retinas and vitreous bodies and found a light haze of blood in the vitreous in one eye. I did not find a retina hole or a clot, which would tell me the source of the bleeding, and by this time he had stopped bleeding into the eye. I warned him that this could recur and that I should examine him if it did. At this point, his wife spoke up and reminded William that he had promised to "tell me everything."

I looked at William, who was blushing and looked somewhat sheepish. He told me that the visual disturbance had happened at noon that day while he and his wife were enjoying sexual relations. What they really wanted to know was whether it was likely to recur the next time they had intercourse.

Fortunately, I had attended the Pittsburgh Ophthalmology Society meeting several weeks before. One of the presentations was a report on retinal hemorrhages during sexual activity—what serendipity, again. Dr. Friberg had reported ten or twelve cases of hemorrhage during sex. He had followed these patients and determined that most did not have recurrence of the hemorrhage with later sexual activity.

I did caution William that retinal hemorrhages are often associated with trauma and active sports activity, so they should avoid strenuous physical activity. This emboldened William to ask if I knew of any positions that should be avoided. I told him that the presentation did not go into that aspect of the problem and cautioned him to moderation. I followed him for several years after that incident, and he reported that the ocular bleeding had not recurred.

William and Mable had verified for me that there can be good sex after seventy, although it may be risky. They were among my favorite patients because they were so helpful to other people and such support for each other. They were both role models for the people around them. William loved Mable so much that he married her so that she could have her cataract removed under his insurance, even though it created a tax disadvantage for them.

84

<o>

A Corneal Melting Problem

SISTER MARY JUDITH WAS REFERRED to me by a colleague because she had a corneal ulcer that was not responding to conventional antibiotics. She also had severe rheumatoid arthritis, which may enhance corneal ulcers. People with rheumatoid disease tend to have decreased tearing and dry eyes that complicate healing of corneal ulcers and epithelial defects.

Sister Judith had noticed corneal irritation about two weeks before and had sought care from a very good local ophthalmologist. He found an epithelial defect on the cornea, with a shallow ulcer within the defect. There was no infiltrate and no anterior chamber reaction, which should be present for a bacterial ulcer. She had suffered from rheumatoid arthritis for many years, which was now under moderate control with medications. During her severe bouts with arthritis, she had sustained crippling contractures of the hands and had some difficulty walking and turning doorknobs.

My examination revealed mild redness of the conjunctiva in her left eye. She had a shallow ulcer in the mid-periphery of her right cornea, with an epithelial defect over that area. The absence of inflammatory infiltrate was striking. My opinion was that she was having a sterile corneal ulcer caused by rheumatoid disease. I started her on Mucomyst eyedrops to stop the ulceration, and covered the possibility of secondary infection with quinolone antibiotics. Mucomyst is a smelly sulphydril compound that inhibits the enzymatic activity of the collagenase, which is released from the edges of corneal epithelial defects.

When I saw Sister Judith several days later, she had developed a second, smaller ulcer about three millimeters from the first. One of the theories of corneal ulcers associated with rheumatoid disease is that there is inflammation at the edge of the cornea, which causes enzymatic degradation of the avascular cornea. To quiet this inflammation, I began treatment with steroid eyedrops. This treatment is risky since steroids have been shown to enhance the enzymatic activity, which ulcerates the cornea, while stopping the inflammation, which is the cause.

She had a protracted course, with slow healing followed by slow progression that lasted several months. A soft contact "bandage" lens probably slowed the progression but did not lead to complete healing. During this time, I got to know Sister Judith. She was an emancipated nun who lived outside of the convent and who wore blue jeans and sweat shirts rather than a habit. She served as manager of a local mission and soup kitchen. Her politics were naturally liberal. This was diametrically opposite to my political leanings, but we had many interesting political discussions.

One day I was wearing a Library of Congress necktie that my wife had given me. It has rows of books on shelves, giving it an academic appearance. Sister Judith complimented my tie, so I told her it was my Newt Gingrich tie. I had seen Newt Gingrich on TV wearing the same tie. She feigned great offense that I was wearing a tie worn by a conservative republican, and we joked about it. When she came to see me about one week later, she handed me a long flat box and asked me to open it. It contained a beautiful, maroon necktie with Frank Lloyd Wright designs in grey and blue. She said that it was to replace the obnoxious Gingrich tie.

Over the next several weeks she continued to ulcerate the cornea, and the remaining cornea beneath the ulcer became thin. I knew that the best way to stop this thinning of the cornea was to cover the tissue with special ophthalmic superglue to keep the enzymes away from the surface of the corneal stroma.

I did not have any "Blue Glue," N-haptyl-cyanoacryllate, which is the best glue to use on the cornea. This glue is made by Firma Braun in Melsingun, Germany, and is not approved by the Food and Drug Administration (FDA) for sale in the United States. It is usually purchased by mail, directly from Germany or from colleagues in Canada, where it is legal.

My friend, and colleague, at the university had developed a variation of this glue and was in the process of obtaining FDA approval, and I knew that he had a supply of his glue. Wanting to do the best for my patient, I referred Sister Judith to this colleague for him to put glue over the ulcer to stop the ulceration.

Sister Judith returned a week later with an even larger ulcer and no glue. I called my colleague to determine why he had not used the glue. He told me that he did not like to glue ulcers as large as hers and that he was having trouble about the glue with the FDA. He had started her on Provera eyedrops, another collagenase inhibitor, and told her that he could do a corneal transplant if her cornea perforated.

While both my colleague and I were out or town at a meeting, she did perforate the cornea and went to the university for care. Another corneal surgeon performed an emergency corneal transplant. This stopped the melting and stabilized the situation temporarily.

About a month after the surgery, Sister Judith came in to see me, saying that she had noticed increased tearing in that eye. When I looked at her eye, I saw that she had begun to melt at the edge of the transplant in the superior nasal quadrant and that aqueous humor was leaking from the eye. I had obtained some superglue by this time, so I glued this area to stop the melting. When she returned about two weeks later, she had developed another area of melting adjacent to the previous area. I extended the glue area to include this area.

Sister Judith had discomfort in that eye several weeks later and returned to the ophthalmologist who had done her transplant. He discovered that the glue had worked loose and that the cornea was leaking along the incision. Rather than glue the cornea again, he did a repeat corneal transplant, larger than the first one.

She did well for several weeks with the new transplant, but developed epithelial defects over the graft. I tested the defects with Rose Bengal dye. Rose Bengal stains damaged tissue, particularly cells damaged by herpes simplex infection. The edges of the defect stained heavily with Rose Bengal, in the pattern typical of Herpes.

I immediately started her on trifluorothimadine (F3T) eyedrops to treat her herpes infection.

In retrospect, her original disease was probably herpes simplex, which triggered the rheumatoid ulceration. Herpes simplex usually does not cause melting and deep ulceration unless it is long-standing. The ulceration probably got better when the herpes went away and got worse when it recurred. It was now recurring in her transplant.

Sister Judith went through a prolonged series of epithelial defects that stained for Herpes and then healed, only to recur within days. This series of defects, some with ulcers, caused the corneal graft to become opaque, hindering her vision. Finally the cornea became quiet and healed, but with poor vision.

Several weeks after the eye settled down, she began to ask if the cornea could be transplanted again to give her binocular vision. I told her that she should wait until the eye had been quiet for one year or longer before attempting another transplant.

Apparently she did not like my answer. I talked with her transplant surgeon at a local meeting about two weeks later. Sister Judith had just been to see him wanting another transplant. We were both in agreement that she had just been through about two years of constant eye problems, weekly or more frequent eye appointments, two surgeries, and a lot of discomfort. We also agreed that repeat surgery would have very little chance for success and only prolong the problems.

When she returned to see me in about two weeks, I went over all of this with her and told her that it was time for her to use the good vision in her uninvolved eye and get on with her life. She thought about it for about a week and came to agree with us.

I see her from time to time around town. She is still very much involved with running a very successful mission and soup kitchen. The last time I saw her she was with her close friend, the republican congresswoman from this area. I kidded her that her politics had changed, but she told me that her companion was a friend and that they enjoyed arguing politics just as we had.

In this case, I had been lulled, by an obvious diagnosis of a rheumatoid corneal melt, into missing a case of recurrent herpes simplex corneal disease. It was not until late in the game, when I recognized the typical appearance of this disease and stained for herpes, that I finally discovered the root cause of her problems. Her rheumatoid disease complicated her underlying problems and led to the surgeries and subsequent problems. My previous experience with rheumatoid patients had caused me to avoid surgery on her, but the other surgeons she consulted performed the surgery that I was trying to avoid. Fortunately we were able to overcome the complications and save the eye.

She was such a game patient that we had to talk her out of further surgery. I think that her complications were an eye opener for the other surgeons, who also eventually advised her against more surgery. We finally all agreed upon that.

This patient demonstrates what happens when more than one doctor is involved in the care of a complicated patient. The other doctors did things that I was trying to avoid, and I am sure that they wondered why I did or did not give her certain treatments for her problem. The transplant that I tried to avoid developed the melting in the incision that I was trying to avoid. I think the glue that I asked for would have obviated the need for a transplant. The other surgeons obviously disagreed. We do not know what would have happened if the treatment had been different than it was.

85

Missions to Montserrat

ONE OF THE INTERESTING ASPECTS of the St. Francis program was the mission work that we did. Dr. Dorothy Scott's father had retired to the island of Montserrat in the Caribbean. Dorothy was a Pittsburgh ophthalmologist who traveled there frequently to visit him and got to know the Minister of Health for the island. The minister asked her to help with the eye care of Montserratian children. Dorothy asked me to help Dr. Al Biglan organize a trip to Montserrat to examine all of the children on the island.

We received many donations from ophthalmic supply and pharmaceutical companies to use on the mission. Dr. Biglan paid for several of his technicians and his wife to go, and St. Francis Eye Association paid for several residents and a technician. The practicing physicians all paid their own way. My wife went as a general physician and pediatrician. We managed to examine fourteen hundred children in two weeks.

We returned two years later to examine six hundred fifty people who had been identified as glaucoma suspects. Four hundred and fifty actually had glaucoma and were started on medications.

On our third trip to the island of Montserrat, we were prepared to do as many cataract extractions as we could in two weeks. There were two residents on the trip who were in their second year of training and did not have sufficient experience with cataract surgery to do this operation. They were hoping that we would find patients who needed other surgery that they were qualified to perform. They worked the pre- and postoperative clinics and saw some of the glaucoma patients we had identified on the previous trip. Three senior residents were present to perform most of the cataract operations.

The native nurses were accustomed to performing one or two surgical cases per week and spent the remaining time cleaning the surgical suite and preparing the linens and equipment. We knew it would be difficult to get them to do the six to eight operations per day that we needed to do to care for the people who needed surgery.

We arrived on Montserrat on Saturday night and learned that the capital city of Plymouth had been evacuated for several weeks because of the possibility of an eruption of the long dormant Soufriere Hills volcano. The all-clear announcement had just been made a few days prior to our arrival. Typical of our prior experience on the island, the local authorities waited for our arrival to begin moving back into the new Glyndon Hospital. On the following Monday, the nurses spent most of the day moving all of the equipment that had been evacuated to the North end of the island back into the new hospital in Plymouth. The head nurse for the clinic/hospital sent a message to us on Monday evening that they would be ready to assist us with surgery on Tuesday morning.

We had spent Monday in the newly constructed clinic building, next to the new hospital in the town of Plymouth, seeing patients who had been screened for surgery. We scheduled eight patients for surgery on Tuesday. In the afternoon on Monday, several surgeons went to the hospital to set up a progressive presurgical area where the patients would put on a hospital gown, give a complete medical history, receive antibiotic and pupil-dilating eyedrops, and a local anesthetic injection prior to surgery. The hospital was so new that the regular operating rooms were not functional, but the trauma room and another adjacent room were available for eye operating rooms. The trauma room had an anesthetic machine, x-ray boxes, and operating room lights. There were both 110 AC and 220 AC electric current available in the walls. There was a surgical operating microscope from South America that was almost identical to the German one that we used at home.

All eight patients had been told to arrive at 8:00 AM, and they were all very prompt. Four were sent to get breakfast and were to return at 11:00 AM. We began preparing the four remaining patients for surgery. At about 8:30 an elderly woman appeared, saying that Dr. Scott had sent her over to talk to us about doing surgery on her that day. At first we told her that we were fully booked for surgery and could not do her until another day. She was quite dismayed and said that she could not come back another day. She had walked all the way from the village of Coujoe Head that day and had to walk home that night. She would be much too tired to come back again that week. From Plymouth, Coujoe Head is about eight miles by road and over several mountain ridges.

It was obvious from looking at her that she had a large mass on her left upper eyelid. The mass was about as big as the end of my thumb and was so heavy that she could not open her left eye. It was so large that we could not evert the eyelid to look at the underside of the eyelid, so one of us held it up while the other looked under the upper eyelid from near her chin. It was smooth underneath, so we decided it must be a chalazion, or cyst. I had never seen one this large in thirty years of practice and considered it a challenge to remove it without damaging the underlying eyelid. We told her to have a seat and that we would work her surgery in sometime during the day.

As soon as we had dealt with this problem, a young black girl, about fifteen years old, arrived at the surgical area, saying that Dr. Scott had sent her for us to see and treat surgically. This girl had very crossed eyes. When she looked at me with one eye, the other looked at the side of her nose. We sent a nurse assistant to the clinic to retrieve the prisms for measuring crossed eyes. Dr. Sterrer helped me measure her, and we determined that she had about ninety prism diopters of crossing. She would need the maximum amount of surgical correction that we could do. Fortunately, she lived in Plymouth, so she could come back another day. We made arrangements to operate on her on Thursday morning.

When we had completed the first cataract operation and determined that we had all of the supplies and equipment that we needed, we immediately set up the next cataract surgery and started the second cataract extraction. Once this was under way, we began setting up a small minor surgery room across the hall from the trauma room. Since chalazion surgery does not need a surgical microscope, we could do the lady from Coujoe Head in this second room.

I gave her several local blocks by injection to numb the upper eyelid. Dr. Sterrer made a skin-only incision in the upper eyelid over the mass and proceeded to shell out the cyst without breaking the cyst. The skin was stretched so far over the mass that we had to excise some of the extra skin before closing the remaining skin of the upper eyelid. She was very happy because she could open her eye again and see with both eyes. She told us that it had been closed for several months and that she had almost fallen several times because she could not judge distances. As soon as we were finished with her surgery, she wanted to set off for her walk to Coujoe Head. We made arrangements for her to get a ride home and for her trip back to see us in several days.

The young black girl returned on Thursday, as scheduled, to have her eyes straightened. She told us that she had a major role in the school play that was to be given in about one month and wanted to have her eyes straightened so that she could become an actress in the movies. Dr. Sterrer and I used the minor surgery room, without the microscope, for her surgery. We needed to lengthen or shorten each of her four horizontal rectus muscles (the right and left muscles in each eye) to get enough correction to possibly straighten the eyes. We sent her home after surgery to return the next day and again in one week. When we measured her one week after surgery, she was perfectly straight. The following year I received a letter from her saying that she was still straight and that she had performed leading roles in several plays on Montserrat.

We treated many patients on the island of Montserrat including more than one hundred operations. The people there are very polite and very religious. They told us over and over again how much they appreciated our group coming to the island to care for them. We were rewarded by comments like, "Thank the Lord, I can see again. How soon can I ride my donkey?" and "I sat on the rock wall all day, just looking. I had not seen a thing for years."

The group from St. Francis Medical Center has now been to Montserrat six times, and plans are being made for another trip, though the St. Francis medical center itself no longer exists, having gone bankrupt in 2002. When the eye unit and residency program were functioning, the airfare of the residents and most of their meals were paid for by St. Francis Eye Associates, the private corporation that helped finance the eye residency program. The teaching staff all paid their own way. Thousands of dollars worth of supplies and medications were donated by pharmaceutical companies, and a rotary club from Kerrville, Texas, loaned us a surgical microscope and other equipment.

When we first went to Montserrat, there were over fifteen thousand people on the island. After the volcano erupted violently a few weeks after out third trip, many of the Montserratians left the island. About three thousand people stayed on the island. Those who stayed were relocated to the north end of the island. The capital city of Plymouth, including the new hospital and clinic, was totally destroyed by the volcano. Other towns on the southern rim of the island, like St. Patrick's, were completely covered by volcanic ash. The airport was also destroyed so recent trips have had to use the ferry or helicopter service to reach the island. The next trip will have the benefit of a new airport with a five hundred meter airstrip.

The residents and faculty all received more in satisfaction from these trips than they paid in expenses. Everyone who has made one or more of these trips has told me that they want to go back to Montserrat or some place similar.

We all felt very blessed that we could use our talents to help these wonderful people who were without any provider of eye care and surgery. The British system of government health care provided a fixed allotment of funds for medical care. By the time they purchased the basic medicines for heart disease, infections, diabetes, and other major diseases, they had no money for glaucoma drops, so we left several hundred bottles of the latest glaucoma drops for the people of the island. We learned that the British health care system does not work well on the island for the peripheral diseases.

86

◄○►

The Blast Injury

I RECEIVED A CALL ONE DAY from an ophthalmologist who wanted me to see a patient of his who had suffered a severe injury to both eyes from a blast. Jerry was a temporary worker who was hired to work on a remodeling project, turning an old factory into lofts. He was cutting a pipe with a cutting torch when it exploded. No one had told the workers that the factory was once a munitions factory and that the pipes might still contain explosive material.

His face and the front surface of both eyes were peppered with black specks of the exploded material. Hundreds of the black specks were imbedded in the corneal and conjunctival tissue of both eyes, where the eyelids did not cover them. The blast actually blew his eyes open wider than normal. A piece of metal had lacerated his right cornea and was lodged within the lens of his eye, making it a cataract. Another small piece of metal had penetrated his left cornea near the edge of the cornea and had passed through his iris, leaving a small hole. This piece of metal came to rest on his retina. The hole in the cornea was so small and clean that it did not leak aqueous from the eye and did not need to be sutured. The piece of metal had apparently missed the lens as it went through the eye.

The original ophthalmologist had repaired the corneal laceration and removed the ruptured lens and the metal fragment from the right eye. That eye was doing well and was regaining good vision. A retina specialist had examined the left eye and could see the metal fragment, but did not have a clear enough view be able to remove it surgically. He wanted me to do something to improve the visibility through Jerry's cornea, which was covered with little black specks. He suggested a temporary keratoplasty.

I saw the patient and found that the cornea was speckled with little black dots that were embedded superficially. There were too many to dig out without scarring the cornea and making it worse. The lens in the eye appeared clear, but the view through the cornea was very poor.

I went to the literature and researched temporary corneal prostheses. I discovered that two ophthalmologists, Dr. Landers and Dr. Foulks, had designed a round plastic plug with an optical center that had threads on the sides that could be screwed into a trephine opening in the cornea. Dr. Landers was a retina specialist and Dr. Foulks was a cornea specialist. The prosthesis had a flange with holes so that it could be sutured to the eye to hold it in place during surgery. The retinal surgeon could see very well through the temporary cornea to be able to remove the metal foreign body. At the end of the surgery, the prosthesis would be replaced by a live corneal transplant.

I ordered one of these temporary corneas, which arrived in about one week. We coordinated the surgery at Mercy Hospital, where the retinal surgeon usually worked. This meant that I had to get temporary privileges at Mercy Hospital. Since my residents rotated through the hospital on a regular basis, it was a matter of filling out all of the papers so that privileges could be granted.

On the day of surgery, I removed the central cornea with a round trephine and screwed the temporary cornea into position. I placed several sutures through the holes to stabilize the plastic cornea and turned the case over to the retina surgeon. He started the vitrectomy in preparation for removal of the metal piece, but he noticed that his visibility was not as good as it should have been. He focused the microscope up to the lens and discovered that there was a thin posterior subcapsular cataract.

We knew that this would get worse immediately after the surgery, because of the vitrectomy, so he removed the cataract using an aspiration technique. Once the cataract was out of the way, he completed the vitrectomy and removed the piece of metal.

The retinal surgeon returned the case to me to remove the temporary cornea and sew in a round button of donor corneal tissue to restore long-term visual function. Since the lens in the right eye had been removed during the initial repair, we did not put an implant lens in his left eye. In this way he could use cataract glasses to see with both eyes and possibly regain depth perception.

The patient returned home after the surgery and came to see me the next day. His transplant was in good position and looked healthy. I started him on frequent steroid and antibiotic eyedrops and checked him every few days. His vision cleared, but it was too early to fit him with glasses. About three weeks after the surgery he had a violent rejection episode, with a heavy response of white blood cells in the eye. In about three weeks he had completely rejected the transplant, in spite of the heavy steroid therapy to stop the rejection.

He could see about 20/25 with his right eye. The left eye was stable, although his vision in that eye was poor. I convinced him that we should wait about one year for the eye to quiet down from all of the surgery and the trauma and give the body a chance to "forget" the rejection.

He told me that he did not have any workmen's compensation coverage because he was a temporary worker. He was on welfare and had Medicaid coverage, which in Pennsylvania is worthless. They almost always deny claims for the strangest of reasons, and then deny appeals on other strange reasons, so that many doctors do not even try to bill Medicaid. Since most of my career was spent running indigent clinics, I was used to not being paid for surgery.

His good vision in the right eye qualified him for a driver's license, but he told me that he could not trust himself to drive. He had damaged his car trying to put it in the garage, and the few times he tried to drive he had run off the road, because he drove to the right if he was not careful.

After about a year, Jerry talked me into operating again with another corneal transplant. This one lasted about six weeks, until he had another overwhelming rejection episode. Even coupling systemic and injected periocular steroids with the steroid eyedrops would not stop this rejection. This graft became cloudy like the first one. I told him that we had not waited long enough and suggested that he wait for five years before trying again. He would be a good candidate for a permanent corneal prosthesis, if there were one that could be retained. The prostheses available at the time did not have good records for long-term retention.

Jerry waited patiently for five years, and then we tried again. This one stayed relatively clear under high dosages of topical steroids, but his vision was not as good as he had with his right eye, so it did not help him very much. He was, however, very proud of having given it a good try and said he was lucky to have any vision at all after the blast injury to both eyes.

I learned a new technique, using a temporary prosthesis, in the course of treating Jerry. The practice of medicine requires constant learning to keep up with the advances of technology and knowledge.

I also learned that Jerry had more patience than I expected and was willing to try repeatedly to restore his vision. When I finally fixed his cornea, it did not add much to his vision, other than some vision to his left side. He was appreciative of the time and effort put forth to restore his vision by all of his doctors, even when it did not add much to the vision from his other eye.

87

Complication of Contact Lens Wear

I HAVE FOUND IT DIFFICULT TO take care of friends, especially when they do not respond to the standard treatment. My wife was talking with a neighbor, who told her that the neighbor's sister had a serious eye problem. Norma had developed discomfort in both eyes and had seen her local ophthalmologist. He treated her with antibiotics and steroids, but she was not getting better. She usually wore contact lenses for a high degree of myopia. Since she had this difficulty, she could not wear her contract lenses and could not see very well. When this problem persisted for several weeks, I offered to see her in consultation.

When I examined her, Norma had large epithelial defects on both corneas. The epithelial surface layer was missing over part of the cornea, and what remained had rolled edges that stained with Rose Bengal dye in a pattern that was typical for herpes simplex infection. I started her on antiviral eyedrops, and she showed immediate improvement. The defects did not heal completely, and some became large again. After a week, she did not stain with Rose Bengal, but she began having a low-grade inflammatory reaction within the eye. I had her continue the antiviral eyedrops and asked her to put her sterilized contact lenses back in her eyes and leave them there. This would prolong the effect of the drops and support the epithelium as it tried to grow back across the cornea. It would also keep the eyelids from pushing the epithelium back from the bare areas.

This change helped, and one cornea healed completely, although the defect in the other cornea remained small. As I followed her, the healed cornea broke down again and the other cornea became worse. She continued to have a mild reaction within the eye, and new blood vessels began growing onto the cornea. Norma continued to complain of pain in her eyes. This indicated that there was still an active disease process. I was worried about a corneal disease caused by amoeba, which usually occurs in contact lens wearers who use tap water on their lenses or lick the lenses to clean them. I quizzed her about this, and she assured me that she used only recommended cleaning solutions and never put her lenses in her mouth.

In thirty-plus years as a corneal specialist, treating hundreds of cases of corneal herpes simplex, I had seen only two other cases of herpes simplex in both eyes. For some reason, this is very rare. This fact made me suspicious that this problem was not simple herpes simplex. I had seen several cases of amoebic corneal infections, and I had also attended many presentations on amoebic eye disease at meetings. These cases usually start with some nondescript corneal irritations and progress to a corneal epithelial defect, with a ring infiltrate in the cornea. Norma had clear corneas without a ring infiltrate.

I was seeing this woman about once each week to follow her progress. She was having more pain than usual one day and came in when I was not in the office. She was seen by one of my colleagues, who noted the appearance of a white infiltrate on one side of her worst cornea. She noted this on the chart with question marks and one word: "?amoeba?" When I saw her later that week, the infiltrate had become a partial ring. Not the typical ring, but enough for me to send Norma to the university for cultures.

The amoebas that infect the cornea do not grow on normal culture media in colonies, like bacteria. They wander around on the surface looking for food. To find the amoeba, the culture sample was placed on a culture plate that had a confluent growth of E. coli bacteria on the surface. Once the amoebas are on the plates, they devour the bacteria like Pac Man eating dots on a TV screen. This leaves little clear trails on the surface of the culture plate. The microbiologist looks at the plate surface through a microscope and follows the little trails until he finds the amoeba and identifies it. Most laboratories do not keep these plates available, so it was necessary to send her to the university where these plates can be prepared. The microbiologist at the university found numerous amoebas on the surface of the culture plate.

Now that we had the diagnosis, we needed a treatment. There is a medicine called Brolene that is available in England, but not in the United States. It is a relative of Neosporin, but Neosporin is not very effective against these amoebas. There is an anti-amoebic that is usually in tablet form, but the powder form is available. Eyedrops had to be made from the powder, from scratch, in a sterile manner, and placed in sterile eyedrop bottles. These eyedrops do not have the usual preservatives used in commercial eyedrops, so each bottle was good for only one week. Then the bottle had to be discarded to avoid excessive contamination. The university had a supply of this medication. Experience with this medication has shown that it does not work very well by itself, so I looked for another medication to use with it. Through Internet searches, I learned of a chemical that is used to keep algae and amoeba from growing in swimming pools. It comes as a powder in quart containers. Fortunately, the compounding pharmacy we use had some on hand and was licensed to make up eyedrops with the chemical.

This all developed as I was planning to retire. I realized, once we had this diagnosis, that the patient would need long-term treatment to kill the amoeba and would probably need corneal transplants and long-term follow-up. I decided that the university was the correct place for her treatment and referred her there. The corneal specialists there had treated amoebic keratitis before, and they would know how to manage this disease.

One year after I retired, an epidemic of amoebic keratitis broke out in the United States and Europe. Almost all of the cases were in patients who had worn contact lenses and used one particular brand of contact lens cleaning solution. I checked with this patient and determined that she had used the same brand. She had been sure that she had caught the disease while walking in the park with her sister on a rainy day. Water had dripped from the trees and landed on her face.

Norma endured over two years of near blindness that severely interfered with her profession as a painter of children's furniture and decorative items. The inflammation caused her to develop cataracts in both eyes. She has now undergone corneal transplants and cataract extractions, and her vision has returned to a point that her ophthalmologist has told her she could drive her car again. In Pennsylvania, that would be 20/40 vision, with a good field of vision from right to left. Norma thinks that her vision is still too fuzzy to allow her to drive.

I have seen many presentations about this disease, emphasizing that the ophthalmologist was fooled at first and usually treated the eye for several weeks as if it had herpes. I was sure that I would recognize this disease when I saw it, but I too was deceived and missed the diagnosis, and treated this patient for herpes for several weeks. If we had made the diagnosis at an earlier stage, it is possible we could have avoided the need for a corneal transplant. That was the road not taken.

I learned that I was not able to avoid the trap that most other cornea specialists had fallen into, by treating this amoebic infection as though it was herpes simplex. Once the diagnosis was made, I knew that the books said to treat amoebas with Brolene, which was not available. I had to go to the literature to find medications that would treat amoebas. This resulted in finding a pharmacy to make eyedrops from swimming pool chemicals. Medical practice requires an open mind and willingness to be creative.

88

<o>

A Lady with a Recurrent Cornea Problem

IT IS ALWAYS SATISFYING WHEN you can make a difficult diagnosis and help a patient, especially when someone else missed the diagnosis. I received an e-mail from the husband of a woman who wanted to be seen about the recurrence of an eye problem. It was bothering her local ophthalmologist, who had never before seen what she had. The e-mailer had found my name through the American Academy of Ophthalmology "Find a Doctor" service on the American Academy of Ophthalmology Web site. My resume had also been posted on the Web site.

This was the first time that I had received a patient inquiry by e-mail. I responded by e-mail with the phone numbers of my office and the name of my receptionist. Several days later I received another e-mail telling me that they had made an appointment to see me but needed directions to the office, so I replied by e-mail with the directions to the office.

When I saw Liz in the office, she told me that she had been to a famous eye hospital about ten years before, because her vision had become poor in one eye. Her local ophthalmologist had not known why her corneal epithelium was rough, so he had sent her to the famous eye hospital. They had examined her and told her that she should have this roughness removed from the cornea to allow normal epithelium to grow back. They told her that they would examine the tissue to learn what it was. Liz told me that she never learned the results of the pathology examination of the tissue.

Her eye had healed with good vision. At the advice of the eye hospital, Liz saw her ophthalmologist every year and was declared normal for about eight years. About two years before I saw her, her ophthalmologist told her that the surface was becoming irregular again. She slowly lost some visual acuity and eventually decided to seek another opinion. She lived about seventy miles from Pittsburgh and considered going to the University of Pittsburgh Medical Center Eye Department, but she was put off by the lack of follow-up by the distant famous eye hospital. Her husband had searched the Internet and found my page on the American Academy of Ophthalmology Web site.

When I looked at Liz's cornea, I saw three ridges of heaped up epithelium running horizontally from a vertical ridge along the limbus temporally. The abnormal tissue looked like a three-fingered glove lying on the cornea, or a backward "E." The ridge at the limbus was pink and highly vascularized. My first thought was that it was cancer, but I did not know if it was superficial or invasive. I explained to her that this growth should be removed along with some of the underlying tissue to determine whether it was invasive or localized. She agreed to the surgery.

At surgery, an incision was made in the conjunctiva surrounding the limbal ridge of involved tissue. The ridge was removed with about one-fifth of the thickness of the underlying sclera. The tissue was pinned to a piece of cardboard, which was marked for the pathologist. The ridges on the cornea were easily scraped from the corneal surface and placed in a test tube to be prepared and examined by the pathologist. The surrounding conjunctiva was pulled forward and sutured, but did not cover the area of possible invasion of the cancer, so that any remnants would not be buried under the conjunctiva and hidden from observation.

It took about two weeks for the epithelium to completely cover the area where it had been removed. By then the pathology report had arrived with the information that the tissue was cancer, but that there were no signs of invasion into the underlying tissue. The epithelial cancer was growing on a thick basement membrane, which is a hallmark for carcinoma in situ, or localized cancer. This is probably the same as the tissue that had been removed at the famous eye hospital ten years before. It is possible that they had incompletely removed benign hyperplasia, which had later mutated to carcinoma.

I have followed this patient for several years, and she has not shown any signs of recurrence of the cancer. With her history of an eight-year silent period before the recurrence was detected, she will have to be followed for the rest of her life. I recently received another e-mail from Liz's husband, asking for the name of another ophthalmologist who could check his wife's eyes for recurrence, since I had retired; so I e-mailed the contact information to him.

I never looked for patients through advertising or listings on doctor referral pages, but this lady found me through my membership in the American Academy of Ophthalmology. She and her husband were intelligent in looking for a doctor who could deal with her problem. Through the academy Web site they were able to learn my training background and subspecialty area. They knew that they were looking for a specialist in corneal diseases.

This was the first patient who found me and corresponded with me by e-mail. Her husband made all of her appointments and corresponded with me about her medications and follow-up visits by e-mail. She lived about seventy miles from Pittsburgh and did not know the city, so I e-mailed her directions to my office. She could have used MapQuest or a similar service to get the directions to my office. This relatively new technology is changing the practice of medicine.

I enjoyed being able to diagnose the disease in this patient who had been seen years before at a leading eye center, where the diagnosis was not told to the patient. By knowing the diagnosis from my biopsy, I was able to tell her what to expect and to emphasize the need for future examinations for possible recurrences.

89

A Nun with Glaucoma and a Red Eye

During my tenure at St. Francis Medical Center, I cared for many of the nuns. I was on call one weekend and received a call at about five o'clock on a Sunday afternoon. One of the medicine resident physicians had a patient she was admitting to the hospital, and the patient had high blood pressure and a very red eye.

The patient was a Sister of the Order of St. Francis that ran the hospital. The resident knew that she had been treated for glaucoma for many years at the University of Pittsburgh Medical Center. Sister Agnes had come to the emergency room that morning because her eye was red and very painful. She had been given some gentamycin antibiotic drops to take four times daily and told to call her ophthalmologist on Monday morning. She had returned to the convent to attend mass, but she had to leave the chapel because her eye had become too painful to sit still in mass.

By mid-afternoon the pain was so bad that she had some of the sisters bring her back to the emergency room. The emergency room doctors discovered that Sister Agnes had developed high blood pressure in response to the pain, and her medical doctor decided to admit her to the hospital to treat her high blood pressure. The resident told me that Sister Agnes had a red eye and wanted to know if she should be doing anything else to treat it. I asked the resident to describe the eye to me. She said that it was red all over, except for one area that was snow white. The cornea was clear and the iris looked all right.

I decided that her description did not fit with the simple conjunctivitis for which she was being treated with the gentamycin drops. I needed to get a better look at the eye myself, so I drove to the hospital to see her. When I examined Sister Agnes I discovered that the eye was very red over the entire visible sclera, except for a round area about six millimeters in diameter above the cornea. She had obviously had a glaucoma filtering procedure, and the white area we were seeing was the avascular bleb that forms after that procedure. It was not red, because it had no blood vessels within it to dilate to make it look red. There probably was pus within the bleb that would make it white. A close look at her eye revealed that she had a haze in the fluid that fills the front of the eye. The haze, combined with her pain, told me that she had an infection inside of her eye, which was probably caused by bacteria entering the eye through the bleb.

I needed to withdraw some fluid from the eye for culture and give her an injection of antibiotics into the eye at the same time. I called another ophthalmologist who was a retina disease specialist and who had treated many of these infections to ask him what the latest thinking was on antibiotic treatment for these intraocular infections. He told me the antibiotic mixture to use, and I ordered it made up in the appropriate syringe by the hospital pharmacy. It was ready in about twenty minutes. I used the same type of syringe to withdraw fluid from the eye, and then changed syringes on the needle in the eye and injected the antibiotics.

The sister was very stoic during the entire procedure and told me that her eye was feeling much better. I ordered her some pain medication and turned her over to the medicine resident who was admitting her to the hospital. On Monday morning, I called her to the eye unit to check her eye. If the antibiotics are correct for the infection, the patient usually experiences dramatic relief from pain within eight to twelve hours from the onset of antibiotic treatment. I asked Sister Agnes if she was still having the pain, and she replied that she was feeling much better. I then learned that she had received a pain shot about one hour before she came to the eye unit. On further questioning she told me that she had been feeling much better before the pain shot. I was relieved to know that the antibiotics were working.

Her internist was concerned about the infection in her eye, so he called in the infectious disease specialist. The expert added intravenous antibiotics to her treatment. I knew that studies had shown that intravenous antibiotics do not add much to the treatment, because the direct injection achieves such high levels of antibiotic within the eye compared to the amount that reaches the eye from the intravenous route. I did not object, because they were sure that they were helping the patient, and they might help prevent spread of the infection from the eye. Her high blood pressure was being controlled by medications.

I continued to ask the patient every time I saw her, which was usually twice each day, if the pain was gone. On about the fifth day, when the eye was showing neither improvement nor deterioration, she finally admitted that the pain was still severe during the time when the pain shot was wearing off. I gave her another injection of antibiotics into the eye at that time. She did experience relief from pain after that injection, but the eye did not clear, and the vision had decreased to no perception of light or color. The infectious disease expert insisted that she receive the full ten days of antibiotic treatment. At the end of the ten days, she had shown no improvement and the eye was full of pus.

The internist and the infectious disease specialist were willing to continue treatment until she got over the infection and reaction, but I knew that it could take six weeks or longer and that vision would not return, even if the infection was sterilized. I suggested to Sister Agnes that we perform an evisceration of the eye. This procedure is done to remove all of the infected contents of the eye and pack it with antiseptic gauze to sterilize the sclera and surrounding tissue. The empty eye will fill with granulation tissue until it is almost normal in size. The muscles are still attached to the sclera and will continue to move the eyeball. Once healing is complete, a glass shell with a normal looking eye painted on the front is fitted over the eye to make it look normal. Because the muscles are attached to the sclera, the eye moves naturally and many people cannot tell that it is not a normal eye.

We did the procedure, and on the next day the sister told me that she was pain free for the first time since the start of her infection. She filled her sclera with granulation tissue very quickly, and after six weeks she was ready to be fitted for the glass-shell prosthesis. Although she was in her eighties, she returned to work in her job at the convent.

About one year later, one of the other nuns told me that she thought I did a marvelous job in saving Sister Agnes's eye. She thought it looked even better than before she had the infection. I did not tell the second nun that the sister was wearing a glass eye. If the patient wanted people around her to think that she had two good eyes, I would not ruin that illusion for her.

My problem treating this patient was relying too much on the nun's truthfulness. I should have been more suspicious and checked her use of pain medications more closely. In retrospect, she was never relieved of the pain and should have had repeated antibiotic injections on days two and three. The continued pain, although denied, was hidden evidence that the infection was not under control. The Sister's desire to please the doctor hid the truth about the condition of her eye.

I was also glad that I did not rely on the opinion of the resident that the nun's problem was only conjunctivitis. Had I relied on the resident, I might have stayed at home and missed the diagnosis of the ocular infection. That would have delayed the treatment by twelve or more hours. Since the eye was lost, it may not have made a difference. This reinforced my opinion that doctors who are not ophthalmologists do not understand eye diseases. It takes a person who is really experienced to give reliable information about the eye over the phone.

90

An Unusual Shingles
Treatment

ABOUT A YEAR BEFORE I retired, I was referred a problem patient who had stumped several other ophthalmologists. Clare was suffering from an epithelial defect that would not heal. She gave a history of having herpes zoster (shingles), which extended from the corner of her eye onto her forehead on the left side of her face. She was bothered by severe photophobia (sensitivity to light) and decreased vision in her left eye. Her eye started feeling dry and scratchy after the shingles had disappeared. She had been treated with antibiotic ointments, steroid eyedrops, and artificial tears.

When I saw her, Clare had a central defect in her corneal epithelium, which was about seven millimeters in diameter. The edges of the epithelium around the defect were raised and slightly whitened. Her cornea was clear and her pupil was dilated. The eye was quiet because she was taking steroids four times each day.

I started her on oral gancyclovir to control her herpes. She did not stain with Rose Bengal at the time I first saw her, so I did not feel that she had active corneal herpes zoster. She had probably had a herpetic vesicle or dendrite on her cornea that was no longer active but had not healed. The gancyclovir was used to prevent recurrences.

Over the next several weeks, Clare showed some slight healing. I stopped her steroids to help her heal, but she developed more inflammation. I restarted the steroids, but only twice each day. I needed to suppress the inflammation without delaying the healing process. The advancing edge of the epithelium stalled and did not heal.

I fit her with a soft contact lens in that eye to support the healing epithelium and to create a microenvironment to encourage healing. She started developing some blood vessels in the cornea, which was a good thing. These would nourish the epithelium to help it grow across the denuded area. We had to carefully determine the amount of steroids to suppress the inflammation, while allowing enough inflammation to cause the new vessels to invade the cornea to prevent future enzymatic melting of the cornea. If I cut back too much, her eye would get red and have inflammatory cells in the aqueous humor in the eye. If I gave her too much, the drops would inhibit the vessels that were growing into the cornea to stabilize it. She was a nurse and understood the value of regular dosages, and she wanted the eye to heal. I believe that she did everything we asked her to do, but the edge of the epithelium would not budge.

I followed Clare for six months, and she never healed the defect. Fortunately, she did not melt her cornea either. Dr. Steve Rogers and I saw her many times. Whenever I was not in the office when she came in, they would call Dr. Rogers to see her. Dr. Rogers and I discussed possible tricks to get the epithelium to heal, including the ancient treatment of putting the patient's own blood serum in the eye to enhance the environment for healing. Because of the AIDS scare, there was a reluctance to use any blood-related products, but in this case we would be putting the patient's own serum into her eye. It was unlikely that she could catch something from herself. We presented the idea to Clare, who was willing to try anything to get her eye to heal. Dr. Rogers looked up a report of using the patients own serum for epithelial defects and found the formula for making up the serum drops. The serum was to be separated from the blood cells and diluted in an equal volume of artificial tears.

The hospital was not equipped to make the serum eyedrops, so we had to find an outside compounding pharmacy. Fortunately I found one with a very understanding pharmacist who agreed to make up the artificial tears from her serum, using sterile technique, and then place them in sterile dropper bottles. Dr. Rogers found a sympathetic phlebotomist who agreed to draw the blood at no charge and give it to Clare in Vacutainer vials to take to the compounding pharmacy. She was to take the serum eyedrops four times a day with the soft contact lens in place.

Within a week, her epithelial defect had closed to half the size it had been before she started the serum. These drops were not preserved, so they had to be kept cold. The pharmacy would make up five or six bottles from one blood specimen. Clare would freeze all but one of the bottles and use one thawed bottle until it ran out or was a week old. Then she would thaw another bottle to use.

By the end of the second week, the defect was entirely closed and the soft contact lens was riding well. I left the soft contact lens in the eye to protect the new epithelium. Actually I was afraid to remove it for fear of losing the new epithelium, which had just covered the defect.

After six weeks, I finally got up the nerve to remove the bandage from the eye to see if the epithelium would stay. It held beautifully, and no new epithelial defects developed. I left the soft contact bandage lens out and watched her closely to be sure that the epithelium stayed on the cornea.

When I retired and turned her over to Dr. Rogers, the defect had been healed for four months with no breakdown. The eye was quiet on two drops of steroids per day and four drops of the patient's own serum diluted one to one. We were all afraid to stop anything for fear that the magic would go away and the defect would return on her cornea.

Because of all of the inflammation in the eye from zoster iritis, she developed a cataract in that eye. It is possible that the steroid drops that she used also contributed to the cataract, which they are known to do. To rehabilitate the eye, she would need a corneal transplant and a cataract extraction. The prolonged defect has left a scar and an irregular surface that is optically unsatisfactory.

Corneal transplants do not do well in corneas without sensation of touch. The zoster attacks the nerves and leaves the cornea numb. The epithelium must cover the transplanted cornea. It might have covered the new cornea if we had given it serum eyedrops, but that was a big risk. We tried to convince the patient that not having pain and not having a cornea at risk of perforation was good reason to postpone surgery indefinitely and to rely on the good vision in her other eye. Sometimes it is hard to accept victory over disease when it does not leave an optimum result. A return to normal life without one or two visits to the doctor every week is good enough.

I see Dr. Rogers every few months, and he is always anxious to tell me that this patient is continuing to do well without epithelial defects or discomfort. She still hopes to have a corneal transplant and cataract extraction some day, but has adapted to having only one eye that sees well. I wish her all the best.

She had one of the most difficult cases of herpes zoster of the cornea that I have ever treated. I had to resort to the old-fashioned treatments used before medications were developed for this disease. I was glad that I trained at MEEI where Dr. Dohlman taught me the use of serum eyedrops. I learned that when the usual treatment does not work, it is good to have other means of therapy to use, even old fashioned ones.

Epilogue

THESE ARE BUT A FEW of the many patients I cared for in my forty years of medical experience, from medical school through retirement. I hope that the reader enjoyed reading these stories and learned something about the practice of medicine. My greatest joy in my practice was the many interesting people I met and the pleasure I received being able to solve their problems and to help them in some way. I also enjoyed the training of ninety future ophthalmologists. The interaction with these young physicians kept me young and on my toes.

I can sum up the many lessons I learned from my patients into a set of rules or concepts:

1. Always respect and believe the patient, but reserve a spot for skepticism.
2. Keep an open mind until the diagnosis is secure, and do not jump to conclusions.
3. Consider the feelings of the patient, and always obtain permission for treatments.
4. When the usual treatments fail, do not be afraid to use other treatments that have been successful or are theoretically sound.

5. Read, study, and attend conferences to keep current with technology and pharmacology in your field.
6. Look for the underlying causes of diseases and treat those causes for effective and lasting cures.
7. Remember that the patient is a whole being, with interactions throughout the body, and psychological and historical barriers to deal with and sometimes overcome.
8. Successfully treating patients is a great source of satisfaction and self-worth.
9. Knowing your patient is invaluable in applying the correct treatment.
10. Reserve moral judgment of the patient unless it becomes important in the treatment, and never let it interfere with the appropriate treatment for the patient.
11. Serendipity plays a major role in the proper diagnosis and treatment of disease.

As this book goes to press, I have just returned from my sixth trip to the island of Montserrat since 1993. I joined two other ophthalmologists to provide eye care for the people of that tiny nation. In one week we performed over one hundred and forty examinations and fourteen surgical procedures on native Montserratians.

The lower half of the island remains closed because the volcano, which has been erupting since 1995, remains active. Business is returning to normal and the three thousand people remaining on the island continue to develop cataracts as they age. The Montserratians demonstrate a warm appreciation for the care we provide. I look forward keeping active in medical practice by continuing to provide ophthalmic care for the wonderful people of this island.

I have turned over the organization of these trips to Dr. Matthew Sharpe, one of the former residents in the St. Francis Ophthalmology Residency, with the promise to continue to help him to organize that effort.

John C. Barber, MD.

Acknowledgements

I WOULD LIKE TO THANK MY wife, Dolores Smith Barber, for her constant support and encouragement. She heard these stories and helped me select the ones that appear in this book. A thank you is also due to my many friends who have heard many of these stories and insisted that I publish them so that they can enjoy them and recommend them to their friends. I would also like to thank the editors at iUniverse for their encouragement and for their many suggestions and corrections and the very professional manner in which they convey them.